God Save Uls

Steve Bruce is Reader in Sociology at The Queen's University of Belfast. His books include *No Pope of Rome: Militant Protestantism in Modern Scotland* (1985) and *The Rise and Fall of the New Christian Right: Conservative Protestant Politics in America 1978–1988* (1988).

GOD SAVE ULSTER

The Religion and Politics of Paisleyism

STEVE BRUCE

Oh God, save Ulster from popery!
Oh God, save Ulster from apostasy!
Oh God, save Ulster from going into an Irish Republic!
Save Ulster from being sold down the river!
Oh God, give us a great deliverance!

(Ian R. K. Paisley, Bannside 1969)

Oxford   New York
OXFORD UNIVERSITY PRESS
1989

Oxford University Press, Walton Street, Oxford OX2 6DP

Oxford New York Toronto
Delhi Bombay Calcutta Madras Karachi
Petaling Jaya Singapore Hong Kong Tokyo
Nairobi Dar es Salaam Cape Town
Melbourne Auckland

and associated companies in
Berlin Ibadan

Oxford is a trade mark of Oxford University Press

First published 1986 by Oxford University Press
First issued as an Oxford University Press Paperback 1989

British Library Cataloguing in Publication Data
Bruce, Steve
God save Ulster!: the religion and politics of Paisleyism.
1. Paisley Ian   2. Presbyterians—
Northern Ireland—Biography   3. Clergy
—Northern Ireland—Biography
4. Politicians—Northern Ireland—Biography
I. Title
941.6082'4'0924   BX9225.P24
ISBN 0-19-285217-5

Library of Congress Cataloging in Publication Data
Bruce, Steve 1954-
God save Ulster!
Includes index.
1. Paisley, Ian R. K.   2. Free Presbyterian Church
of Ulster—History.   3. Northern Ireland—Church
history.   4. Northern Ireland—Politics and government—
1969-   I. Title.
BX9225.P24B78 1989 285'.23[B] 86-17961
ISBN 0-19-285217-5

Processed by the Oxford Text System
Printed in Great Britain by
Biddles Ltd
Guildford and King's Lynn

For Deirdre, 'who was lovelier than
I knew and whose worth I could
hardly acknowledge'

Preface

In the spring of 1984, Ernest Rea, then a producer with the BBC Northern Ireland religion department, asked me to research a film about Ian Paisley.[1] I imagined that it would be largely a matter of reading the official histories of the Free Presbyterian Church and the Democratic Unionist Party, and then finding a few people who could be interviewed as representatives of those who were actively involved in either of the two elements of 'Paisleyism': Church and Party. Instead I discovered that there was almost nothing by way of official history and even less by way of serious scholarly writing about Ian Paisley. The only published book was Patrick Marrinan's *Paisley: man of wrath*, which, although it contained some useful material drawn from media sources, had the interesting characteristic, for a biography, of showing no sign that the author had ever interviewed Ian Paisley or any of his close associates.[2]

So I was forced to collect my own primary material. Arranging filming also brought me into contact with Dr Paisley and his colleagues, whom I discovered to be quite happy to talk about their movement. Having had to undertake this amount of original research for the film, it seemed sensible to continue the research in order to fill a significant gap in our knowledge of the conflict in Northern Ireland, and of religion and politics in general.

I was fortunate to be able to consult two Queen's University doctoral theses, and, although I came to disagree with a number of the points in both, I am grateful to Clifford Smyth and David Taylor for the stimulation their work provided. For different reasons in each case, neither work contained much that was derived from close contact with Ian Paisley or those people near to him. Although Smyth was actively involved in the DUP for a number

[1] The film was shown on BBC 1, 25 April 1985 as 'Paisley: Child of Wrath . . . Man of God?'.

[2] Patrick Marrinan, *Paisley: man of wrath* (Tralee: Anvil Books, 1973).

of years, he left the Party in 1976 and his thesis relies heavily on defectors' accounts of the DUP.[3] In themselves, these are valuable sources, but they are primarily sources for information on what defectors thought about the Party. They tell us little about the beliefs and attitudes of those people who did not leave the Party. Taylor's work is primarily ethnographic.[4] He was concerned to understand what the 'ordinary' Free Presbyterian thought about the world and, like Smyth, has done an excellent job within the limits which his interests set. Those interests meant that he tells us little about the history of the movement or the intentions of its leader, and he does not explore the wider sociological and political questions that arise from comparisons of Free Presbyterianism and Democratic Unionism with other similar movements.

This book is intended to fill a major gap in the literature on conservative Protestantism and to continue the series started with studies of militant Protestantism in Scotland and other parts of the English-speaking world.[5] To give the reader a chance to judge the data on which I base my arguments, it is worth saying a few words about my sources. The primary source was interviews with twenty-seven ministers of the Free Presbyterian Church (including Dr Paisley), five leading activists in the DUP, and twelve others who had at one time been active in either Church or Party. A large number of others were briefly interviewed by telephone. I attended a large number of Free Presbyterian services and frequently engaged in long conversations with elders and ordinary members of the Church.

Dr Paisley and his associates have produced a considerable amount of documentary material. The *Revivalist* has appeared as the official organ of the Church fairly regularly since 1951. Since the mid-sixties, the *Protestant Telegraph* (later replaced by

[3] Clifford Smyth, 'The Ulster Democratic Unionist Party: a case study in religious and political convergence', Ph.D. thesis (The Queen's University of Belfast, 1984).

[4] David Taylor, 'The Lord's Battle: an ethnographic and social study of Paisleyism in Northern Ireland', Ph.D. thesis (The Queen's University of Belfast, 1983).

[5] For a number of years I have been interested in trying to illuminate the relationship between religious beliefs and political philosophies and strategies by comparing conservative Protestant politics in a variety of different social, economic and political settings. See my *No Pope of Rome: militant Protestantism in modern Scotland* (Edinburgh: Mainstream, 1985) and the chapters in the third part of Roy Wallis and Steve Bruce, *Sociological Theory, Religion and Collective Action* (Belfast: The Queen's University of Belfast, 1986).

the *Voice of Ulster*) has acted as a record of the political campaigning arm of Paisleyism. Almost complete sets of these publications were made available to me by Free Presbyterians and by the Linenhall Library, whose staff were extremely helpful. Although interviews are always preferable to questionnaires when one wishes to explore complex issues, questionnaires can be useful for collecting basic data from a large number of people and I was able to collect some simple information about the ministers and their congregations from almost all of the Free Presbyterian ministers whom I did not personally interview. I am indebted to all of those people who took the time to answer my questions but I am especially in the debt of John Douglas, the Clerk of the Presbytery of the Free Presbyterian Church, who gave me considerable assistance with contacts and with historical information about the Church. In view of the slightly awesome public reputation that the supporters of Ian Paisley (and Dr Paisley himself) have, it is worth noting that only three people (all of them ministers) declined to be interviewed and that everyone else I contacted went out of their way to be helpful.

Had they not been, I would not have written this book. I owe a considerable debt to Professor Roy Wallis of the Queen's University who taught me when I was an undergraduate at Stirling University, supervised my doctoral research, and has since been closely associated with my work. Although I learned a great deal from him, the most important lesson was that if you want to know what people are doing and why they are doing it, you go and ask them. They might not always know, or they might know and not tell you. But all other sources are inferior. This is a simple point but one sadly often neglected by social scientists.

It is also worth noting that the considerable co-operation I received from Free Presbyterians and Democratic Unionists is not explained by my sharing their beliefs. I have never disguised the fact that I am agnostic and have no personal commitment to the beliefs and values discussed in this book. Equally well, I am not committed to criticizing their beliefs. My primary concern has been to understand and explain. The reader must be left to do the judging.

This book has not been written for sociologists, although I make no apology for being a committed social scientist. I am concerned to popularize my discipline. In the heady days of the early sixties, sociologists sought to mimic economists and advance their discipline by claiming that it was an essential tool for policy planners. For a while there was even a sub-discipline called 'socio-technics' which arrogantly regarded itself as the basis for a new science which would permit the design of efficient and good societies. Fortunately such optimism about the impact of sociology—and about the willingness of governments to listen to non-partisan opinion—has faded and a more realistic, some would say pessimistic, view of the discipline now prevails. My own view is that sociology will only survive, will only deserve to survive, if it can show that its methods and ideas can illuminate important and interesting parts of people's worlds. To do this, we must write for people outside the charmed circle of fellow sociologists and this I have tried to do.

To make the book accessible to the reader with a general interest in Northern Ireland, conservative Protestantism, or the links between religion and politics, I have tried to confine the narrowly sociological to the footnotes. Those readers who are interested in pursuing more technical sociological issues will find references in the footnotes to other publications in sociology journals. Despite this parallel construction, however, the book is thoroughly pervaded by the intellectual tools of the sociologist. I can only hope that those who have previously been hostile to, or dismissive of, sociology will conclude that the discipline can enhance our understanding of important parts of our world.

Finally in this preface, I would like to acknowledge those people and organizations whose contribution has not already been mentioned. The British Academy and the Queen's University of Belfast both gave me considerable financial assistance with my research. The staff of the Northern Ireland Census Office were kind enough to produce detailed breakdowns of statistics relating to Free Presbyterians. Ann Brown and Evelyn Hunter of the Social Studies Department were involved in the production of the typescript as were Margaret Drumm and Margaret Mullany of the Queen's University Secretarial Centre. In addition to Roy Wallis, whose contribution can hardly be exaggerated, Professor David Martin of the London School of Economics and Dr Bryan Wilson of All Souls College, Oxford, have, by their example and their comments on my work, been of considerable assistance. But my greatest debt, as always in this sort of research, is to all the people, too numerous to mention, who were prepared to talk to me about their involvement in the Free Presbyterian Church and DUP.

Contents

List of Tables

Map

Introduction

On 23 November 1985, almost 200,000 people crowded into the centre of Belfast to hear unionist politicians denounce the recently signed accord between the British and Eire governments over the future running of Northern Ireland. Fourteen of the fifteen unionist MPs stood on the platform erected outside the City Hall, the grand Victorian building which had housed the Northern Ireland Parliament while Stormont was being built. Spontaneous applause greeted the sight of Dr Ian R. K. Paisley and the Rt. Hon. James Molyneaux, the leaders of the two main unionist parties, raising their clasped hands in a gesture of solidarity.

Later that week, a BBC news reporter referred to 'Dr Paisley and other unionist leaders', a piece of shorthand which neatly, if unconsciously, illustrated the position which Paisley now holds in public perceptions of Ulster unionism.

Three days earlier, Paisley had officiated at the ordination service of Stephen Hamilton, a young man who had been called to pastor the Mount Merrion, South Belfast, congregation of the Free Presbyterian Church of Ulster. Hamilton had not even been born when the Free Church was founded in 1951. He was probably the first minister never to have attended another denomination.

The mass rally and the ordination represent the two related careers which have occupied Ian Paisley since the start of his ministry in 1946. They also illustrate the success he has achieved in both. It is rare in modern industrial societies for the same individual to occupy senior positions in a church and a party. Apart from Paisley, the only one who comes to mind is Abraham Kuyper, who was a leading figure in the Dutch Reformed Church, leader of the Calvinist Anti-Revolutionary Party, and Prime Minister of Holland from 1901 to 1905. But although he was influential in both, Kuyper founded neither church nor party. Ian Paisley was instrumental in the creation of a schismatic Presbyterian church in 1951 and has seen that organization grow to the point where it has more than ten thousand members in forty-eight congregations in Ulster and has outposts in England, Australia, Canada, America, and the Republic of Ireland. The political party which he formed in 1972 has grown in popularity to the point where it gains almost as many votes as the 'Official' Unionist Party,[1] and his own personal popularity was amply demonstrated in 1979 when he won more first preference votes in the first direct election to the Parliament of the European Community than any other candidate in the whole of Europe.

This book is an attempt to describe and explain the religious and political careers of Ian Paisley. However, it is more than biography. That Paisley so stands out from other religious and political leaders in Europe in his synthesis of religion and politics suggests what is well known from other sources: that Northern Ireland is an exception among modern democracies. Hence the main focus of this study is not so much Ian Paisley as his followers. The book is not concerned with why Ian Paisley wanted to lead but with why people wanted to follow.

[1] The 'other' unionist party is actually called the 'Ulster Unionist Party'. The 'official' tag dates from the early 1970s when the party was divided between liberal and conservative wings. The conservatives gradually regained control of the party organization and acquired the 'Official Unionist Party' label. With a large number of smaller parties having names which began with 'U', it made sense to call the conservative Unionists the 'OUP'. Although the name really only applies to one short period, I have followed custom in using 'Official Unionist Party' or 'OUP' to refer to the party led by O'Neill, West, and Molyneaux.

I

Religious Conflict, Presbyterians and Schism

The Presbyterians in Ireland

The continuing conflict between two populations who identify themselves by religious labels—'Protestant' and 'Catholic'—has fascinated historians and social scientists and produced a catalogue of excellent histories of this small island on the western fringe of Europe.[1] I do not mean to add to that catalogue but some historical background is required to understand the twin movements of church and party led by Ian Paisley.

The Protestants in Ireland come from two sources: England and Scotland. While most of the English and many of the Scots were deliberately 'settled' in Ireland in a planned process of plantation, the majority of the Scots settled in the north east of the island before the plantation of James VI and I or in the period after the Williamite revolution of 1689. What makes the religious history complex is the fact that the clear threefold division of Roman Catholic, Church of Ireland, and Presbyterian is a relatively late development. The British government and its agents in Dublin were generally concerned to make the Church of Ireland a national state-supported Protestant church but they largely failed to recruit the Irish natives to such an organization: they remained Roman Catholic. The Presbyterians had a shifting relationship with this national organization because the doctrines and practices of the church were in flux. The first Presbyterian ministers in Ulster actually held parishes of the national church and were for some years tolerated, even though their rejection of government by bishops—episcopacy—brought them into conflict with their local bishops. The first Presbyterian clergy came to Ulster between

---

[1] L. M. Cullen, *The Emergence of Modern Ireland, 1600-1920* (Dublin: Gill and Macmillan, 1983); J. C. Beckett, *The Making of Modern Ireland, 1603-1923* (London: Faber and Faber, 1969).

1620 and 1630 from Scotland because they could not accept James VI and I's attempts to reimpose Bishops on the Scottish Church. As they came to establish themselves and to hold meetings of like-minded dissenting clergy, the Irish Bishops increased their persecution, and Archbishop Laud in London instructed his agents to have them suppressed. Driven out of the province, the Presbyterians tried first to sail for America and were driven back by the seas. Instead they retreated to Scotland. The collapse of the monarchy of Charles I saw Charles, Laud, and his agent in Ireland, Wentworth, executed, but this gave little immediate advantage to the Presbyterians. The native Irish rose in rebellion in 1641, and many Protestants, both Episcopalian and Presbyterian, were killed. A large Scots army was raised and sent to Ireland to suppress the rebellion where it gave a considerable boost to the Presbyterians by bringing its own chaplains who created the framework for the revival of a Presbyterian ministry.

However, the Presbyterians continued to be caught between the Irish Roman Catholic natives and the English. Although they had been persecuted by the Stewarts, they remained committed to the idea of a legitimate monarchy and so were seen by Cromwell as a threat. Only towards the end of the Protectorate were they accepted and given government financial support. The Restoration of the Stewarts after the death of Cromwell brought a restoration of persecution. Sixty-one Presbyterian ministers were expelled from their parishes and the arrival on the throne of James VII and II in 1685 only increased their problems. With James fleeing from London to Ireland as William of Orange was invited to take the throne, the battle lines were drawn. James led a largely Catholic army which quickly took most of Ireland. The gates of Derry City were only closed, against the advice of the local bishop and civil leaders, by a group of apprentice boys whose action immortalized them in Protestant mythology. Then came William and the battles of Aughrim, the Boyne, and Enniskillen and the establishment of a Protestant monarchy.

If the Presbyterians thought that the expulsion of the Stewarts and the defeat of the Romanists had finally stabilized their position in Ireland, they were mistaken. As happened so many times in a period when religion was regarded as a tool of foreign policy or a device for ensuring loyalty, they soon found that princes, even Protestant princes, were more interested in stable government than they were in religious orthodoxy. William gave his support to the Episcopal national Church of Ireland and left the Presbyterians in the awkward position in which they had been caught since their migration from Scotland: sandwiched between the native Irish and the Episcopalian 'Protestant Ascendancy'.

The isolation of the Scots Presbyterians from the Ascendancy made it possible for the more liberal and affluent Presbyterians to consider alliance with the Irish. Thus one finds a number of liberal Belfast Presbyterians active in the United Irishmen movement and the 1798 rebellion. But although there were strong democratic elements in Presbyterianism, it would be a mistake to suppose that the liberal element represented the majority of Presbyterians. Modern historians seeking to transcend the present-day divisions of Orange and Green have exaggerated the popularity of the liberal position and, in noting the number of Presbyterians in the United Irishmen, have overlooked the anti-rebellion motions passed by the General Assembly of the Presbyterians.[2]

The rising failed and the majority of the Presbyterians threw their lot in with the British government. For all that they had been excluded from political power and suffered periodic insults to their religious culture, such as the refusal to recognize Presbyterian marriages as binding on a non-Presbyterian partner, they were persuaded that their best interests lay with their fellow Protestants rather than with the Catholic Irish. The increasing politicization of the Irish produced a strong conservative movement within Presbyterianism. The combination of an increasingly confident nationalism and a strengthening of the power and claims of the Catholic Church were enough to fuel the development of a shared 'Protestant' identity. In the 1830s one finds Henry Cooke, the leader of the conservatives in the Irish Presbyterian Church, taking the side of the Episcopal Church when there was pressure to disestablish it by removing its legal superiority and its claims to income from rents. Cooke argued that state support for a Protestant church, even if it was the wrong Protestant church, was better than a free market system in which Roman Catholicism would come to be dominant by virtue of numbers.

Furthermore, rank-and-file Presbyterians began to join the Orange Order, the fraternal Protestant society which had developed

---

[2] R. F. G. Holmes, 'Eighteenth Century Irish Presbyterian Radicalism and its Eclipse', *Bulletin of the Presbyterian Historical Society of Ireland*, 3 (1973), pp. 7–14.

from early agricultural 'vigilante' groupings and which had previously been predominantly Episcopalian.[3] By the time of the home rule crisis at the start of this century, the Anglo-Irish were returning the compliment and borrowing symbols from Presbyterian culture. To display their implacable hostility to a united and independent Ireland, the Protestants modelled their protest on the old Scots 'covenants': petitions couched in the form of a legal contract between the people and the state with God as the third party.

It is easy for modern people, raised in largely secular societies in which religion plays little part in public life, being largely relegated to Sundays and the family home, to fail to appreciate the importance of religious beliefs in social identity. One way to grasp the significance of religion in Ireland is to try to imagine recent Irish history and development if the Scots and English settlers had also been Roman Catholics. Differences of power, status, and wealth between settler and native would have remained, of course, but a common religious culture would have encouraged intermarriage and eroded the ethnic boundaries. It is the fact that the settlers were of a different religion to the natives, and that the settlement took place in an era when religion played a major part in politics and foreign policy, that explains the maintenance of the divisions between the three ethnic groups.[4] We should also recall, for it is crucial to the rest of this book, that Protestantism and Roman Catholicism were not *any two* different religions. They stood in opposition to each other. The former began as a 'protest' against features of the latter and, after they separated, each developed those elements which most clearly distinguished it from the other. They were thus fundamentally irreconcilable. This point has to be made forcefully here because a failure to grasp it will make the course of the religious and political developments described in the rest of this text incomprehensible.

There is now a considerable liberal movement within the major

[3] Hereward Senior, *Orangeism in Ireland and Britain, 1775–1835* (London: Routledge and Kegan Paul, 1966); Tony Gray, *The Orange Order* (London: The Bodley Head, 1972); David A. Roberts, 'The Orange Movement in Ireland, 1816–1916; a study in the sociology of religion and politics', Ph.D. thesis (London, 1974).

[4] A more technical discussion of the relationship between religion and ethnic identity in settler societies can be found in Roy Wallis and Steve Bruce, *Sociological Theory, Religion and Collective Action* (Belfast: The Queen's University of Belfast, 1986), Ch. 10.

Protestant churches, and to a lesser degree in the Catholic Church, which seeks to play down the differences between Protestant and Catholic, and which promotes those things which unite, rather than separate, the two traditions. I do not dispute the rights of those who promote such ideas to do so but these movements should be seen for what they are: radical departures from the Protestant and Catholic traditions. The liberals are innovating. They are giving up beliefs and practices that previous generations held dear. It is not my intention to offer any judgement on the morality or theological validity of such movements. The job of the social scientist is to describe and explain; the reader may make his or her own judgements. All that needs to be established is that the Scots settlers belonged to an earlier Presbyterian culture which held distinctive beliefs which were crucially opposed to many of the cardinal beliefs of the Roman Catholic Church.

The points of dispute were many and it is no easy task to present a very brief summary of them without simplifying to the point of caricature but I will attempt to outline enough of the difference for the gravity of the disagreements to be appreciated. All religions are concerned with salvation. What must we do to be saved? The Protestant Reformation can be seen as a simplification of the previous dominant tradition. Man is sinful. God gave his only Son so that his death would wipe away our sins. Believe that and you will be saved. We know this to be the case because the Bible says so and the Bible is the word of God; everything that we need to know is presented in the Bible, most of it in terms plain enough for ordinary people to appreciate. Hence there is no need for professional priests to act as mediators between man and God. In contrast, the Roman Catholic doctrine of the mass, as it was understood in the seventeenth century, almost argued that Christ's sacrifice had to be repeated and that, by taking the consecrated bread and water, the believer was, in some mystical sense, replaying Christ's sacrifice. In addition, the Roman Catholic tradition has added a variety of events and activities which are held to be, if not absolutely essential to salvation, at least extremely useful aids. In particular, the Protestants object to the addition of confirmation, penance, extreme unction, holy orders, and matrimony to the two sacraments of baptism and the Eucharist (or communion).

The major disagreement about necessary beliefs and actions has its counterpart in a fundamental disagreement about organization and authority. The Protestant Reformation was profoundly democratizing in that its assertion of the sole authority of the Bible removed the need for properly ordained priests and reduced considerably their role. The Protestants argued that the Holy Spirit working in us to allow us to understand the words of the Bible was enough: professionals might have been useful as preachers of the word of God but they were not essential. The Roman Catholic Church (and, among others, the Orthodox churches) accepts the Bible as central but argues that it must be understood within the historical traditions of the organized church. Although most genuinely Protestant traditions have evolved some sort of structure which can settle disputes about doctrine and preserve the faith, such structures are essentially matters of convenience and gain little support from central beliefs. Most of them take the form of what has become debased as a result of its association with Stalinist forms of communism: democratic centralism. The authority of the organization comes from the bottom upwards. The people choose their ministers who choose their representatives. The Roman Catholic Church maintains a hierarchical form of authority in which power comes downwards from the Pope and his cardinals to lesser functionaries. Bishops impose priests on the people: the people do not choose their priests.

A third general principle of the Reformation was the rejection of the idea that religious merit was transferable. In many religious traditions, there is a division of labour in which the majority of the people do very little religion but financially support an élite which acquires religious merit and transfers it to members of the secular mass of the population. Varieties of Buddhism allow a transfer of credit from those who feel assured of their salvational status to others who are in need of some bonus points. Roman Catholicism, in permitting the living to act on behalf of the dead by, for example, saying masses or offering prayers which hasten the dead's move from purgatory to heaven, operates a transfer system. The Protestant Reformers found any such system to be profoundly abhorrent because it reduced the necessity for each and every individual to recognize his or her religious and moral responsibilities.

One could continue to list other differences. The above points are made, not because they encompass what separated Protestants and Catholics, but because they are enough to show the fundamental nature of what separated them.   The fact of conflicting religious allegiances added to and cemented other differences of language, status, and wealth between the populations. It is clear that being Presbyterian was important in the explanation of the behaviour of the Scots in Ireland. It is also likely that being Calvinist was important.

John Calvin made a number of contributions to Protestant theology, but the doctrine most associated with him is that of predestination. Although he defended the doctrine by reference to Bible texts, I will explain it in terms of much more general notions about God. Let us suppose that God is all-powerful. If that is so, he is hardly likely to be impressed by anything that we do, especially given the state of utter sinfulness we have been in since Adam turned his back on God in the Garden of Eden. As Paisley put it:

If God gave me the due reward for my deeds, he would send me to hell. I am a sinner. There is nothing good about me. From the sole of the foot to the crown of the head there is no soundness in man, but wounds and bruises and putrifying sores.[5]

We are thus incapable of winning God's favour through our own efforts. If we are to be spared eternal damnation, it can only be as a result of a *gift* from God; we can have done nothing to earn or deserve it. So whether we are to be saved or damned is in God's hands, not ours. So far, so good. But God is not only all-powerful, he is also all-knowing. And if he knows everything (which seems like a sensible attribute for a divinity) then he knows the future as well as he knows the past and present. He thus knows whether we are damned or saved in advance of our being born and becoming moral actors in the world. These ideas should make it possible to see how Calvin could argue that we are *predestined* to salvation or damnation by God.

Although there are innumerable problems in the working out of the implications of this line of thinking, one consequence is to suppose that some of us have been chosen for salvation, are part of the elect, and others are not. Calvin himself and Calvinist theologians have always argued that only God knows who is part of the elect and that, for all practical purposes, one must suppose that all

[5] I. R. K. Paisley, *Paisley: the man and his message* (Belfast: Martyrs Memorial Publications, 1976), p. 158.

humans living at any particular time might be part of the elect. Hence the evangelist preaches the gospel to all people, even though it will only be accepted by the elect. After all, he has no sure way of knowing who is a member of the band of saints. But the social scientist is usually more interested in *common* theology, in what ordinary believers make of a set of doctrines, rather than with the refined clerical version, and there has always been a strong tendency for popular Calvinism to slide into a form of racism. Calvinists have tended to suppose that their children have a higher than even chance of being part of the elect and conversely they have tended to suppose that people of other races, especially those which have rejected the gospel, are unlikely to be part of the elect.

It should be easy to see how a group of Calvinist Presbyterians can turn inwards, suppose that the hostile outsiders are not part of the elect, and then concentrate on preserving their own religion rather than taking the evangelical position of trying to convert as many of the heathen as possible. As one Presbyterian historian puts it: 'Congregations could easily identify with Israel, taking possession of the promised land, threatened by the hostility of its fierce inhabitants.'[6] Such a tendency becomes especially strong when the non-Calvinists, instead of being disorganized followers of a variety of folk religions, are organized into membership of a disciplined anti-Presbyterian organization. When the heathen act badly towards the Calvinists, as some native Irish did in the rebellion of 1641 or the Scullabogue Massacre of 1798, it is tempting for the Calvinists to see such acts as confirmation that the natives are not part of God's chosen people.

All religious traditions predispose believers to think of themselves and their descendants as being privileged in the eyes of their God. The point about Calvinism is that, in contrast to other variants of Protestantism, it offers a ready justification for the believers to refrain from even *trying* to convert the heathen, and hence for the shared religion to create a further barrier between one ethnic group and another. It is likely that the Scots Presbyterian settlers would have failed, even if they had tried hard to convert the native Irish to their religion, but they hardly tried. It is noticeable that when the Presbyterians divided into two competing camps, with followers of the Seceder Church in Scotland starting

[6] R. F. G. Holmes, *Our Irish Presbyterian Heritage* (Belfast: Publications Committee of the Presbyterian Church in Ireland, 1985), p. 9.

to recruit in Ireland, the recruitment was directed almost entirely to the Scots settlers. The competition was confined to the ethnic Scots and there was little attempt by the Seceders to expand by taking in the native Irish.[7]

People who find this argument unconvincing will point out that Paisley and others who call themselves Calvinists now make considerable efforts to convert Roman Catholics. Although more historical research would have to be done to confirm this thesis, it is my feeling that the Presbyterian settlers only became committed to evangelizing the natives once their own ethnic identity had become secured and once other differences between the competing populations had become firmly established. Let us suppose that all people have an interest in belonging to some social group with a shared history, shared traditions, and a world-view that makes sense of their lives and of who they are. Such identities require that some other people be excluded. Nationalism, for example, is not only about who we are as a nation but it is also, by definition, about who we are not. Our superiority depends on some other group's inferiority. When one has two or more social groups inhabiting the same geographical boundaries, every shared identity is precarious unless the boundaries between the groups can be established and maintained. The initial dimensions of ethnic conflict in Ireland were laid out in an era when world-views were still heavily informed by religious beliefs. For the Scots settlers to have succeeded in sharing their religion with the natives (either by converting them or by changing their own religion) would have been to remove a crucial dimension of difference, and for the obvious reason of wishing to maintain their own cultural and social identity and to explain and justify their economic superiority, this is not something which the settlers would have welcomed. Hence it was only relatively late in their sojourn in Ireland, once it was clear that for a Catholic to become a Protestant would also mean giving up his Irishness and his national identity, that Protestants engaged seriously in missionary activity. The Methodists began an Irish mission in 1799. Magee threw the Episcopal Church into the 'Protestant crusade' when he became Archbishop of Dublin in

---

[7] David W. Miller, 'Presbyterianism and "Modernization" in Ulster', *Past and Present*, 80 (1978), p. 74. For a general history of the Seceders, see David Stewart, *The Seceders in Ireland with Annals of their Congregations* (Belfast: Presbyterian Historical Society, 1950).

1822. But 'the Presbyterians were not in the vanguard of the crusade',[8] and they were not heavily involved in evangelism until the 1840s; almost 200 years after their arrival in Ireland.

A similar pattern can be found in another Presbyterian settler country: South Africa. There the Dutch settlers, united by, among other things, their reformed Protestantism, did not initially seek to convert the natives. It was only when social boundaries were firmly established that the Dutch undertook missionary activity, and the extent to which the boundaries were fixed can be seen in the fact that, when the natives did begin to convert in large numbers, they were segregated in black churches and not brought into the main structure of the Dutch Reformed churches.

A final preliminary point can be made about the consequences of the Scots' Presbyterianism. Presbyterian church government is a compromise between congregational independence and centralized government. Although Presbyterians share the cardinal Protestant principle that all men can know the will of God, they have always tempered this democratic principle with a healthy suspicion of the anarchy that might ensue if every group of believers was allowed to make its own decision about what God was telling them. So Presbyterianism groups congregations together in presbyteries, collects presbyteries in synods, and then brings all synods under the control of a General Assembly composed of representatives from all the congregations. The pyramid of democratic centralism prevents anarchy. But the centralization is not strong because there is no doctrinal support for an authoritarian hierarchy. Unlike the Catholic, Orthodox, and Episcopalian systems, there is no notion that Christ's authority had been delegated to any one office, the holders of which have the power and authority to instruct the lower levels. In practice, Presbyterianism permits local autonomy. Individual congregations do go their own way and there are no sanctions equivalent to the Catholic Church's power to excommunicate deviants.

This has a very important consequence for Presbyterians who leave their mother country to settle some foreign part. The clergymen who were sent as missionaries to southern Africa by the Anglican Church were controlled by the Anglican hierarchy in England. Their values and interests remained those of England and, if they began to change to suit local conditions, they could be

<hr />

[8] Holmes, op. cit., n. 6 above, p. 111.

recalled and either disciplined or replaced. But when Presbyterians left northern Europe to settle in other countries, they quickly developed local interests. Apart from anything else, they were paid by the local settlers and not by the sending church. The Seceder Presbyterians in Scotland were in fierce competition with the national Kirk, but when their missionaries went to America and Canada they developed co-operative relations with the representatives of other Protestant churches and simply ignored the instructions from the Seceder Synod in Scotland to break such contacts. The centre could not control the outposts. The fact that the Scots who settled Ulster were Presbyterians is thus important because it explains how they could develop and operate their religion in a way which suited the social and political conditions in which they found themselves. In particular it explains why in both South Africa and Ulster it was the Episcopalian and Methodist churches which began, and were most active in, efforts to convert the heathen.

These points have been made to establish the combination of religious and social factors which led to the religious element of the ethnic identity of the Scots settlers in Ireland remaining central. The Scots arrived with a set of religious beliefs which gave them good reason for feeling superior to the Irish natives and which separated them from the native population. Their very presence caused social conflict as the natives resented and attacked the status advantages of the Scots settlers. Those settlers in turn interpreted the conflict as proof of the superiority of their religion and the godlessness of the natives. That interaction of religious ideology and social conflict established the foundations for the later development of political ideologies. The native Irish adopted a nationalist ideology and, in reaction, the Presbyterians became fully committed to union with the country which not only guaranteed their political position but which also, in rhetoric at least, was Protestant. This last point, like so many things in this introductory history, has to be reinforced because it has become buried by the subsequent changes in British culture. British civil society of the eighteenth and early nineteenth centuries was deliberately and self-consciously anti-Catholic. The rising bourgeoisie which had invited back the Stewart monarchy to re-establish order after the chaos of the later Cromwellian period had concluded that papist monarchs could not be trusted to rule in the manner in which the new élites wanted; hence the invitation to William of Orange and the development of the idea that basic civil liberties and good government could only be preserved by a Protestant monarch. Until the Catholic Emancipation Act of 1829, Catholics were excluded from most parts of civil society and, under that Act, Catholics continued to be excluded from many senior and influential political offices.

Thus, although the Irish setting raised the conflict between Protestants and Catholics to a level not known in the rest of Britain, the mainland shared a similar commitment to anti-Catholicism. Although such rhetorical devices as the Coronation Oath, which requires the monarch to promote the Protestant faith and reasserts the perils of Catholic rule, created much deeper resonances in Ireland where they could be translated into judgements on the political conflict between unionists and nationalists, such devices were fabricated in London and had a similar, albeit attenuated, resonance in the rest of the realm. If this point seems to have been laboured, it is only because it is very easy for modern commentators to suppose that Irish evangelical Protestants such as Ian Paisley have somehow invented a new set of religious beliefs to legitimate their political struggles. The embarrassment of modern British liberals at their forefathers' anti-Catholicism should not be allowed to justify the neglect of history.

The Orange State and Religious Revival

The popular agitation in Ireland for 'home rule' persuaded the Liberals under Gladstone to attempt to free themselves from the disputes of the Irish. The Protestants organized their resistance to any breaking of the Union and in the first decade of this century demonstrated their opposition to a united and independent Ireland by joining Sir Edward Carson's Ulster Volunteer Force. The onset of the First World War prevented the 1912 Home Rule Bill from completing its passage. The Ulster Volunteer Force was recruited into the British Army and almost completely destroyed in the Battle of the Somme. However, Protestant opposition to 'Rome rule' was not eradicated. If anything, it had been reinforced by the republican 'Easter Rising' in Dublin in 1916 and the violent struggles which followed it. For the Protestants, the rising was proof positive of the treachery of the Catholics who had waited until Britain was occupied in a bloody struggle for democracy and freedom, and then attacked from the rear.

Ireland was partitioned. The Protestants of the north-east were given six of the nine counties of the province of Ulster, the demand for the other three having been dropped once it became clear that the inclusion of all nine would have threatened a unionist majority, and the state of Northern Ireland was born.[9]

Partition had the effect of increasing the importance of Presbyterianism in Irish Protestantism. Although a large number of Presbyterians were left stranded on the wrong side of the border, especially in Monaghan, the majority were in the new state of Northern Ireland and a large part of the Church of Ireland Protestants were in the Free State. And the Church of Ireland people in the new state were well organized into a working alliance with the Presbyterians through the Orange Order and the Unionist Party.

The period after the foundation of Northern Ireland as a political unit was a time of considerable Protestant unity. The Catholics had been given the Free State so Ulster would be a Protestant country for a Protestant people.

Although not all religious revivals are reactions to periods of social or political unrest, it is generally speaking the case that popular movements of increased religious commitment follow times of social dislocation. Collective recommitment to the shared religious tradition is one way in which people who have felt under some sort of threat can rebuild their sense of community and reaffirm those values which they hold to be central to their identity. The great shifts of population in the Scottish highlands, caused by the landlords' desire to clear the peasants off the land to make way for sheep farms, were followed by the conversion of most of the highlands to evangelical Protestantism. In a similar way one can see the first Nicholson crusades in Ulster as a reaction to the unrest of the early 1920s. The author of one account of the Nicholson revival saw a link between civil strife and enthusiastic religion:

Ulster has undergone many changes during the past four years. Its boundaries have been modified, and its Government recast . . . Four years ago, the North of Ireland was in a state of chaos. Fear and uncertainty filled the minds of the people. Politicians were at their wits' end. Murder and

---

[9] For a good history of the foundation of the Northern Ireland state, see David Harkness, *Northern Ireland Since 1920* (Dublin: Helicon Books, 1983).

destruction, for the time being, seemed to be on the throne. No one could possibly describe the hopelessness of the situation, as things continued to travel from bad to worse . . . (but) man's extremity is always God's opportunity and in the day of trouble He never fails those who call upon Him. [10]

What God provided was William P. Nicholson, an Ulster-born evangelist who was at home in Bangor recuperating from an illness contracted while working in America. He was asked to address a local meeting of Christian workers. The crowds attending the meetings grew and many were converted. Nicholson's fame soon spread and he was invited to preach at meetings in Portadown, Lisburn, Newtownards, and Dromore. The services held in the Albert Hall in the Shankill Road in Belfast were conducted to the background accompaniment of rifle and machine-gun fire. In his blunt and sometimes vulgar manner, Nicholson preached the message of eternal damnation, repentance, faith, and salvation, and thousands responded.

What is significant about these revival meetings is that they were sponsored by clergymen of all the major Protestant denominations and attended by sizeable numbers of working-class people. Ship-yard workers marched from the yards to the services in the Presbyterian church on the Ravenhill Road in East Belfast:

It was in one of these services that about 200 men openly came out for Christ, many of them publicly destroying their betting books, cards, etc. Salvation became epidemic and on the street and the car, the topic was either Nicholson or the work he was accomplishing. Tramwaymen, railwaymen, postmen and policemen were all roped in.[11]

It is this unusual appeal to the working classes which makes these meetings interesting for the sociologist. It is well documented that the major Protestant denominations had little contact with the urban working classes in the British cities. Although the Irish immigrants to Liverpool and Glasgow retained a strong tie with the Catholic Church, the urban working class was by and large

---

[10] J. A. Gamble, *From Civil War to Revival Victory: a souvenir of the remarkable evangelistic campaigns in Ulster from 1921 to December 1925 conducted by Rev. W. P. Nicholson* (Belfast: Emerald Isle Books, 1976), pp. 1-2. See also S. W. Murray, *W. P. Nicholson: flame for God in Ulster* (Belfast: The Presbyterian Fellowship, 1973) and John Barkley, *St Enoch's Congregation, 1872-1972* (Belfast: St Enoch's, 1972).

[11] Gamble, op. cit., p. 6.

unchurched and indifferent to Christianity. Of course, what made the Belfast situation so markedly different was the importance of Protestantism in establishing the social identity of Protestants in relation to the Irish nationalists. To make sense of their opposition to the home rule movement, and of the crisis from which Ulster was just emerging, they had to retain at least a nominal attachment to Protestantism. Nicholson was then able to use the sense of crisis to call large numbers of these people from their nominal Protestantism to a serious personal commitment.

The strong sense of Protestant denominational co-operation was short-lived. Nicholson's first campaigns between 1920 and 1923 had been integrating; his second series of meetings three years later tended to be divisive. There were two general reasons for this shift. From the point of view of the audience, the strong sense of crisis had evaporated. The civil war in the Free State had taken the pressure off Ulster and the world appeared to be settling down. With the grave outside threat removed, the overwhelming pull to dramatic commitment to a shared religious ideology was attenuated and people could return to their own denominational attachments. The second general reason concerns a shift in the religious climate most easily described as the rise of 'fundamentalism'.

Modernism and Fundamentalism

The end of the Victorian era had seen some significant developments in Protestant religious thought. Perhaps the most important was the popularity of what was rather arrogantly called 'the higher criticism'.[12] German scholars had begun to search for the historical Christ, the real figure who had been buried under the various myths of the early gospel writers and the early Christian church. If one may simplify their intellectual approach, it can be expressed like this. Every civilization has its own world-view; its own set of background beliefs expressed through its language. The early Christians were no different in this respect. Thus while Christ was a real historical figure, what we know about him has been heavily overlaid with the world-view of the people of his time. In

[12] For brief accounts of the 'higher critical' method, see Robert Grant and David Tracy, *A Short History of the Interpretation of the Bible* (Philadelphia, PA: Fortress Press, 1984) and Edgar Kretz, *The Historical-Critical Method* (London: SPCK, 1975).

order to discover what God really intends for us we must strip away the Hebrew and Aramaic myths and get to the real heart of the Christian message.

The same scholars were drawing on recent historical and archaeological discovery to dismantle the Bible. It was no longer to be regarded as the revealed word of God but as a collection of writings put together by a variety of authors, borrowing from and embellishing various ancient texts as they tried to make sense of what they saw and experienced by drawing on their own mythologies. The 'higher criticism' was coupled with a desire to remove the miraculous and supernatural elements from Christianity in order to produce a rational version of the faith which would be acceptable to a culture which knew about science and technology and which, so the higher critics reasoned, could no longer believe that the Red Sea really parted or that Jonah lived inside a big fish.

The rationalism of the higher criticism gradually permeated all the major Protestant denominations, but it was not only a theological movement. The higher critics tended also to be socially liberal and progressive. To simplify the difference between them and their opponents, they believed that the gospel entailed Christians being socially reformist because the improvement of people's material conditions would make them more receptive to the preaching of the Word. The conservatives tended to the view that man was beyond redemption and that only religious conversion could improve anything. Hence they thought that one should preach the gospel, get men saved, and then social and economic reform and prosperity would follow naturally from a saved population acting righteously.

Fundamentalism as an organized movement had its origins in America, although the controversy which produced it was to be found in all the Protestant churches. The title of the movement came from a series of pamphlets called 'The Fundamentals: a testimony to the truth' published in America between 1910 and 1912.[13] The higher criticism and the 'social gospel' produced a conservative reaction. The fundamentalists argued that the Bible was the divinely inspired and revealed word of God. It was infallible. If there was a conflict between science and religion, then

---

[13] George M. Marsden, *Fundamentalism and American Culture: the shaping of twentieth century evangelicalism, 1870–1925* (Oxford: Oxford University Press, 1980).

science was wrong. There was a Trinity of God the Father, the Son, and the Holy Ghost; it was not just a case of Jesus being a particularly inspiring and holy man. And he was born to a virgin, as the Bible said.

W. P. Nicholson was a fundamentalist and he brought to Northern Ireland an aggressive approach to the liberals in the Protestant churches. By 1925, he was being seen, not as a unifying force who increased Protestant solidarity, but as a divider whose preaching against the evils of modernism and liberalism would split the denominations.

The anti-modernist Nicholson struck a chord with some Irish Presbyterians. An initial skirmish in the inevitable war between the liberals and conservatives came with a split in the Scottish Free Church. Although the Free Church had been formed in 1843 by conservatives who left the national Kirk because it was unable to divorce itself from the civil state enough to purify itself, the Free Churchmen had quickly become advocates of liberalism and modernism. In 1900 the majority of them united with another organization of Presbyterians which had grown from earlier splits from the national Kirk. A rump refused to accept the merger and claimed that, as they were continuing in the beliefs of the original Free Church, they were entitled to all the property of the Free Church. At the end of a bruising legal battle, the House of Lords found in favour of the small conservative remnant.[14]

Given that the Irish Presbyterian Church was not only a sister reformed Church but had in its early difficult years been supported by the Scots, there was considerable interest among the Irish in the Free Church's battles. The leading spokesmen of the Irish Presbyterian Church supported the main body of the Free Church in its desire to unite with the United Presbyterians. James Hunter, a leading conservative in the Belfast Presbytery, proposed a motion supporting the conservative rump. He was heavily defeated.

With the legal disputes in Scotland and the fundamentalist movement in America, it was inevitable that the Irish Presbyterians would eventually turn from taking sides in other people's controversies to staging their own version of the dispute and it was

[14] The best modern Scottish church history is Andrew L. Drummond and James Bulloch, *The Scottish Church, 1688–1843*; *The Church in Victorian Scotland, 1843–1874*; and *The Church in Late Victorian Scotland, 1874–1900* (Edinburgh: The St Andrew Press, 1973, 1975, 1978).

in this context that Nicholson was influential. Although he did not openly argue that the conservatives should abandon the Presbyterian Church, he was increasingly aggressive in his preaching against the liberals in the Irish Presbyterian theological colleges. One consequence of his preaching was the formation of the Bible Standards League to maintain 'the Infallible Truth and Divine Authority'[15] of the whole Bible against liberals such as Professor J. Ernest Davey, who wished to argue that one could select from the Bible certain general principles which were 'infallible' and dismiss other sections as wrong or mythical.

Although the Bible Standards League never attracted the support of more than a handful of Presbyterian ministers it did draw a lot of grass-roots Presbyterian support and under James Hunter's leadership it organized a major campaign of publicity for the notion that true Protestantism was under attack from within. Hunter 'regarded it as his supreme task to stem the tide of theological liberalism, and he now became confirmed in his opinion that the Church was less than loyal to her creedal statements'.[16]

The creeds were a major rhetorical obstacle for liberal Presbyterians. Although Presbyterians, as Protestants, accepted the Bible as the only standard of authoritative knowledge, they accepted the Westminster Confession of Faith and the Longer and Shorter Catechisms as 'subordinate' standards. These were documents drawn up by a group of 'divines' in the 1640s and accepted by the Church of Scotland in 1647. They had long been an embarrassment to liberal Presbyterians and in 1829 a group led by Henry Montgomery was driven out of the Irish Presbyterian Church when Henry Cooke persuaded the majority of the church that all ministers and elders should subscribe their name to the Confession. In the last quarter of the nineteenth century, liberals in the various Scottish Presbyterian churches had modified their churches' commitment to the Confession by a delightful sleight of hand. They did not have the support actually to drop the Confession, so instead they passed 'Declaratory Acts' which supposedly expressed modern principles which were to be used to 'interpret' the Confession but which actually undermined its basic

[15] J. Austin Fulton, *J. Ernest Davey* (Belfast: The Presbyterian Church in Ireland, 1970), p. 172.

[16] Robert Allen, *The Presbyterian College, Belfast, 1853–1953* (Belfast: William Mullen and Son, 1954), p. 256.

principles. By the 1920s, there was pressure in the Irish Presbyterian Church for a similar relaxation of commitment to the
Westminster Confession. Conservatives such as James Hunter and
other members of the Bible Standards League were naturally
firmly opposed to any such move.

The simmering dispute in the church was brought to a head by
liberals. In 1924, thirteen college students petitioned the Belfast
Presbytery to know exactly what obligations would be imposed on
them by their subscribing to the ordination formula, which included the Westminster Confession. The General Assembly established a commission to consider whether the questions asked of
ministerial candidates, and the ordination formula, needed
revision. Although this was almost certainly an example of an
organization avoiding controversy by side-tracking the issue into
the dead end of a 'working party', the Bible Standards League
stepped up its anti-modernist campaign and Hunter issued a series
of pamphlets criticizing the theological teachers. The Belfast Presbytery replied by censuring Hunter for pursuing his campaign
outside the church instead of using the formal procedures for such
disputes. He appealed against the censure and was defeated in the
Assembly by 499 votes to 115: a fair reflection of the balance of
power in the church.

In one of his pamphlets, Hunter had accused Professor Haire of
modernist deviations. The Assemblies College set up a committee
to investigate Haire's teaching and decided that he had no case to
answer. 'Having put his hand to the plough, however, Mr Hunter
had no intention of turning back; and, towards the close of 1926,
he, with several other ministers and a number of elders formulated
a charge of heresy against Professor J. Ernest Davey.'[17]

Davey's teaching was subject to detailed scrutiny by the Belfast
Presbytery and, after fourteen sittings, it was decided that he
should be acquitted on all charges. Hunter and the other accusers
then appealed to the General Assembly and had their appeal dismissed by 707 votes to 82. Although the vote might seem like
an overwhelming endorsement of Davey, the politics were more
complicated. In the first place, Hunter and his colleagues had made
themselves unpopular with many conservatives who shared their
dislike for modernism by their public campaign against Davey.
As in most large organizations, there were many who felt that,

[17] Ibid., p. 258.

whatever the provocation, it was important for the Presbyterian Church to present a united front to outsiders. Washing dirty linen in public was not a popular strategy.

While Hunter lost the support of many who shared his views, Davey conducted himself in such a way as to win over many of his opponents. While Hunter disregarded an order from the Belfast Presbytery to make no further comment on the case until the General Assembly, Davey kept his silence and refrained from preaching until the case was settled. Furthermore, Davey diverted attention from the central issue by concentrating, not on the substance of his teaching, but on his own spirituality and conversion experience. Thus when the issue came to a vote, people found themselves voting for either Davey or Hunter on the grounds of which seemed like a nicer person or a better Christian, and not on the issue of whether or not Davey's beliefs had moved so far from the tradition of reformed Presbyterianism as to be unacceptable.

A further point that is of some importance concerns the structure of the Presbyterian Church. Although all congregations are theoretically bound together in presbyteries, synods and the General Assembly, in practice many Presbyterians relate to their own congregation and have little sense of a denomination beyond. It was thus easy for them to know that some other clerics, or the professors at the College, held views with which they did not agree, and yet feel unmoved to act against perceived error. For a congregation in Tyrone, what did it matter what Belfast thought or did? The organizational structure made it easy for a desire for a quiet life to outweigh a desire for doctrinal rectitude.

What was the heresy trial really about? I have already given some idea of the doctrinal issues at stake. Davey was a good representative of the liberal tradition in theology and the 'higher critical' tradition in biblical criticism. He wanted to modify the traditional Protestantism of the seventeenth and eighteenth centuries to something which could encompass the new ideas of science and Freudian psychology. Davey was a believer in 'new light': the idea that God's revelation was not fixed but was always changing (or improving). We knew more about the world than the Westminster Divines, and we certainly knew more about the way in which the Bible texts had been constructed, so why should we be constrained by the categories of thought they used?

A subsidiary element in the controversy concerned professionalism. The liberals, although they were hardly aware of it, were snobs. They slid very easily from arguing that new forms of scholarship were useful tools for understanding the Christian message, to suggesting that they were, in some sense, essential, and that only skilled professional theologians who understood the new German rational philosophy or Freudian psychology could speak with authority on matters of doctrine. The conservatives were extremely bitter at this shift from the basic tenet of reformed Protestantism that all that was necessary for salvation was in the Bible and available there for any normal person to comprehend. One of the conservative protagonists said of the liberals' view of the Bible that it was now 'a discredited scrap-book that requires a Professor at your elbow to tell you how much or how little it is worth, either for reading or believing'.[18]

While such a judgement was a little harsh on the liberals, it was not unfounded. A biography of Ernest Davey, written forty years after his trial for heresy, begins by denigrating the conservatives for a lack of scholarship: 'The people whose antipathy to Professor Davey was aroused had, for the most part, little qualification, if any, for forming theological opinions and less for pronouncing theological judgements.' [19]

This tension between the professionals and the 'democrats' was to be found in the fundamentalist controversies in Scotland, England, and America, as well as Ulster. The conservatives saw the theologians as advocating a new priestcraft. The liberals saw the fundamentalists as promoters of ignorance and anti-intellectualism; hiding from the modern world with their heads in the sands of seventeenth-century knowledge.

The Failure of the Schism

Twenty-seven years after he had first protested against the lack of doctrinal orthodoxy in the Irish Presbyterian Church, James Hunter felt driven to leave it. In July 1927 he resigned from the Belfast Presbytery. Very few others resigned with him. Most of the supporters of the Bible Standards League remained in the church, arguing that they could best defend orthodoxy from

[18] James Edgar, *Presbyterianism on Trial: an answer to the 'Record'* (Belfast: James Edgar, 1929), p. 8.
[19] Fulton, op. cit., p. 33.

within. Over that summer small groups met in the Belfast area and in the autumn the Irish Evangelical Church was formed. If success is to be measured in numbers, the schism was a dismal failure. William J. Grier, the student who had approached Hunter to complain about Davey's teaching, came out but many others who had been vocal in their support for Hunter's campaign preferred to stay within the Presbyterian Church and the great public interest in the controversy evaporated. Slowly congregations were established but by the 1930s there were only nine; six in the Belfast area, two in County Antrim, and one in County Tyrone. Although these congregations became well established, the Irish Evangelical Church made no further inroads into Irish Presbyterianism and there was no further church extension.

The failure of the 1927 schism will not be explained in detail here, but it forms the baseline of some of the comparisons in the rest of this book. The classic issues had been starkly raised and debated. What was at stake was clear to all participants: liberalism versus orthodoxy. The formation of Ian Paisley's Free Presbyterian Church in 1951 was a replay of the 1927 split and raised the same issues. That second schism was successful. By 1980, the Free Presbyterian Church had over ten thousand members in some fifty congregations and was well represented across Northern Ireland. Much of the rest of this book is concerned to explain why the later split achieved what the first attempted and failed to do. However, we can make a few brief comments at this point. The first is that Hunter and Grier were working in a barren environment. Although there were many conservatives in the Irish Presbyterian Church who were unhappy at the direction in which the church was moving, there was a distinct absence of *networks* of disaffected Presbyterians. By the time Ian Paisley created his church, there had developed a considerable infrastructure of mission halls, evangelistic organizations, and so on, which had been created by small groups of people gradually distancing themselves from what they saw as increasing apostasy within the Presbyterian Church. In this sense, Hunter and Grier were trying to do too much at once and while their action laid a marker for future disaffection, it was too abrupt. It forced people to make a radical choice at a time when they had not yet readied themselves.

A second problem was the new church's lack of a clear identity. Although it was a Presbyterian schism, the title used by the church for over twenty years was the 'Irish Evangelical Church'. The word 'Presbyterian' was omitted and, in a culture with such a strong Presbyterian heritage, that was a tactical mistake. The confusion of name reflected a confusion of identity. Within five years of its foundation, there was a serious doctrinal controversy with some leading men being pushed out for deviation on beliefs about the 'second coming' of the Lord. Only then did the IEC clarify its doctrinal basis and signal its commitment to a Presbyterian sort of orthodoxy rather than to conservativism generally.[20]

Although it is difficult from this distance to assess the effort that Hunter and Grier put into recruiting, it does seem that the schismatics did not engage in a serious province-wide campaign of agitation on behalf of their new church. In retrospect it looks as if, having made their position crystal clear and well known through the heresy trial, and taken their separatist stand, they would wait for others to join them.

Finally, there is a small point with profound implications. Hunter and Grier decided to have their students for the ministry trained by the Free Church of Scotland in Edinburgh. In many ways this was sensible as the two churches were extremely close in doctrine and practice and the Free Church College was well staffed with extremely able teachers. But this decision made it very difficult for a clear 'Irish Evangelical Church' identity to develop among the ministers, who instead saw themselves as being simply 'evangelical' Presbyterians. A dynamic movement needs a strong sense of identity and purpose and while the decision to work with the Free Church of Scotland was superficially rational it was sociologically unsound.

But by far the most important difference between 1927 and 1951 was the general social climate of the times. I have already mentioned the tenor of the early Nicholson crusades with their appeal to social cohesion and the way in which that harmonized with a very general desire of Ulster Protestants to pull together after the crises which accompanied the formation of the Ulster state. The 1920s were a period of consolidation. The Unionist Party was firmly established as the political voice of the Ulster Protestants and there was little desire to create other divisions in a society which felt that it had just survived a major crisis. Putting

[20] W. J. Grier, *The Origin and Witness of the Irish Evangelical Church* (Belfast: Evangelical Bookshop, 1945).

it simply and bluntly, what was missing in the twenties was a major threat to Protestant identity in the political sphere. In a later chapter we will deal in detail with the ways in which Paisley's fledgeling Free Presbyterian Church benefited from political instability. Here we would just make the point that Hunter and Grier, by having their critique of liberalism confined to *religious* liberalism, were denied an important aid in the promotion of their conservative views.

2

The Early Years

The Paisley Family

James Kyle Paisley was born to 'staunch Protestant parents' in Co. Tyrone in 1891. Apprenticed to the drapery trade in Omagh, he was converted at a YMCA meeting and he began to take an active part in preaching. Parlour meetings were still common in the 1950s, but at the start of the century in the country areas of Ulster many pious families held prayer meetings in their kitchens. People who had been converted were encouraged to talk about their experience at such meetings and those who showed a gift for 'witnessing' to what the Lord had done for them would be encouraged to speak at more formal, larger meetings such as open-air rallies. Kyle Paisley followed such a career in evangelism:

As I look back upon those days I can see the guiding hand of the Lord upon my life. He led me to conduct monthly meetings at Grangemore a short distance from Armagh and this meeting continued with great blessing for approximately four years . . . the third Armagh Presbyterian Church Hall was opened for me for the preaching of the gospel . . . for young men thirsty for the Water of Life . . . This was really the foundation of a great work of God in the city of Armagh and led finally to the commencement of the first Baptist church in the Mall.[1]

The Baptist assembly in Armagh asked James Kyle Paisley to become their pastor, and he trained at the Baptist College in Dublin. While pastoring in Armagh, Paisley met and married a Scots girl from a Covenanter background. The Reformed Presbyterians, to give the Covenanters their formal title, were the most orthodox of the various Scottish Presbyterian churches. Unlike

[1] R. J. Beggs, *Great is thy Faithfulness: an account of the ministry of Pastor James Kyle Paisley and a history of the separatist testimony in Ballymena* (Ballymena: Ballymena Free Presbyterian Church, n.d.), p. 12.

other conservative denominations, such as the Free Church of Scotland, which were the results of schisms from the national Church of Scotland, the Covenanters had always been outside the main church. They believed that the legally established position of the Church of Scotland as the 'state church' had been gained on unfair terms which gave too much influence over religion to the monarchy, without the monarchy making a reciprocal commitment to impose religious orthodoxy on the population. Although almost extinct in Scotland, the Reformed Presbyterians have to this day maintained a conservative theology and an old-fashioned style of worship. They refuse to permit musical instruments into worship and they will sing only the metrical psalms of David. All other songs are inappropriate for worship because they are human inventions and not the word of God. In addition, the Covenanters have remained distanced from the secular state, refusing to vote in elections or to hold public offices. Although such a position has never looked like influencing modern governments, they insist that they will only fulfil their side of the 'covenant' by supporting the state, when the state accepts its responsibilities to maintain and promote the true religion.[2]

It was to these parents—an evangelical Baptist and a Covenanter—that Ian Richard Kyle Paisley was born in 1926. Shortly after his birth, the family moved to Ballymena in County Antrim, where Kyle Paisley became pastor of the Hill St Baptist Church.

The desire to maintain religious purity, so strong in the younger Paisley's ministry, was inherited from his father. Shortly after going to Ballymena, Kyle Paisley came to the decision that he could no longer be associated with the Baptist Union of Great Britain and Ireland. Although most of the Irish Baptists were very conservative in their theology, many English Baptist assemblies were adopting 'modernist' ideas and Baptist pastors were, albeit tentatively, becoming involved in the various interdenominational meetings and associations which were later collectively dubbed the 'ecumenical movement'. Kyle Paisley resigned from the Baptist Union and, with a few of his flock, began to hold services in a carpet warehouse. With almost no funds and few supporters, Kyle Paisley trusted in the Lord to provide and acquired a building site by the railway lines. A plain single-storey building—the Waveney

[2] J. G. Vos, *The Scottish Covenanters: their origins, history and distinctive doctrines* (Pittsburgh, PA: Crown and Covenant Publications, 1980).

Road Tabernacle—was erected and the small congregation set out in its Covenant its firm opposition to 'the anti-super-naturalism of modernism, and the deceptions of fanaticism, and the formality of a dead and defunct orthodoxy'. In a 'day of apostasy, declension and compromise', the remnant would maintain a faithful witness to the belief that the Bible was 'the whole Word of God . . . verbally inspired by God the Holy Ghost . . . the final authority on all matters of Doctrine, Faith, Practice'.[3]

Although James Kyle Paisley was a Baptist, his small church drew people from other denominations, many of them disaffected Irish Presbyterians. The parents of William Beattie, who was later to become one of Paisley's early ministers and political supporters, were Antrim farmers, the descendants of the old Scots settlers, Presbyterians since their arrival in Ireland. But they were opposed to the modernism of Ernest Davey and other leading figures in the church and they wanted to hear orthodox preaching. The Irish Evangelical Church formed by Hunter and Grier had no congregations in the Ballymena area (they had only three outside Belfast). There was no nearby Reformed Presbyterian Church and so they found themselves drawn to the Baptist congregation led by Kyle Paisley.

Although the foundation of a small independent Baptist work in Ballymena was a matter of little significance in Ulster, it was part of the wider fundamentalist controversy which was dividing denominations across the English-speaking Protestant world. Although its later importance could hardly have been anticipated, it is interesting to note that the foundation stone for the Waveney Road building was laid by Dr T. T. Shields, one of the leading lights in the fundamentalist movement on the American continent.

It is commonplace that people who emerge as great public leaders have banal childhoods and Ian Paisley was no exception. His schooling was perfectly normal. Early on, he accepted his parents' religious beliefs and, after a brief period working on the farm of a family friend near Sixmilecross in County Tyrone, Ian began to preach at small meetings. He was sent for a year to Barry School of Evangelism in South Wales, a non-denominational college which offered practical training in the skills of open-air preaching and door-to-door visitation, and rigorous Bible study. In 1943, he returned to Ulster and was permitted to enrol as a student with the

[3] Beggs, op. cit. p. 17.

Reformed Presbyterian Church in Belfast, although he had no intention of becoming a minister in that denomination. Here he acquired a thorough grounding in Calvinist theology and biblical scholarship and acquitted himself well enough to win a prize in each of his three years of study.[4] He also began to make contacts in the evangelical milieu. In addition to the Reformed Presbyterians who taught him, he became acquainted with W. J. Grier, who, since the death of James Hunter in 1942, had become the leading figure in the Irish Evangelical Church. He acted as a 'supply' preacher for Grier.

On Christmas Sunday, 1945, Ian Paisley preached an invitation sermon to a small congregation in working-class East Belfast which called itself the Ravenhill Evangelical Mission Church. His performance was acceptable and he was invited to become its pastor.

The Ravenhill Church

The history of the small Ravenhill congregation is worth detailing because it shows all the fine threads of influence which linked the world of evangelical Protestantism in Ulster. It had been formed as a result of a schism in the Ravenhill Presbyterian Church, the building which had been packed in 1922 by the shipyard workers coming to hear W. P. Nicholson preach against modernism. The minister of that church and his elders had been signatories to the heresy charges laid against Davey, and the congregation was generally very conservative; many of its members supported Hunter's Bible Standards League. Like so many splits in religious organizations, the occasion for the division in the Ravenhill Church was almost trivial and involved a large amount of personal friction in addition to the basic tension between theological positions. Some members took strong exception to modern dress and hairstyles, and in particular they wanted the Kirk Session to censure some girls in the congregation for having their hair 'bobbed' in the fashion of the day. One of the girls was the daughter of the minister, John Ross. Despite the fact that Ross was himself deeply conservative and had been a signatory to the charges against Davey, the issue divided the Kirk Session against him. The Belfast Presbytery tried to find a solution to the dispute but the more conservative

---

[4] I would like to thank Professor Adam Loughridge, a former Principal of the Reformed Presbyterian Theological Hall, for making these details available to me.

members were not satisfied and in March 1935 they left to form
the Ravenhill Evangelical Mission Church which met in its own
building three hundred yards down the Ravenhill Road from the
church in which Nicholson had made such an impression.[5]

Most schisms involve arguments about which side best represents the tradition and hence are accompanied by bitter arguments about the right to make use of the tradition. In some
disputes, it is ownership of actual property which is at issue (as in
the legal wrangles which followed the formation of the Free
Church of Scotland in 1900 when twenty-six ministers managed
to convince the House of Lords that they had the right to the
property of the Free Church despite the fact that the other 200
ministers had voted to merge with the United Presbyterian
Church). In others, it is not so much 'real estate' as *symbolic* estate
which is at issue, and the formation of Ian Paisley's Free Presbyterian Church in 1951 began an argument, which still runs, as
to whether or not it has any right to call itself a 'Presbyterian'
church. Such arguments are not trivial. They have major implications for the public images of the contending parties and their
ability to recruit others with the claim that they represent the
continuation of the true tradition.

The people who walked out and down the road to form their
own congregation were Presbyterians and the leaders of the newly
formed church were ordained elders of the Irish Presbyterian
Church. They had taken the Hunter side in the Davey heresy trial
and so, although they were in a minority within the church, they
could, and did, claim to be the true heirs to the Presbyterian
tradition. In this sense, when Ian Paisley accepted their call, he
was stepping into that tradition, albeit into what was rapidly becoming a despised minority and a marginal part of that tradition.
However, eleven years had elapsed since the Ravenhill split and
by the time Paisley had been called, some of the original Presbyterians had left and been replaced by evangelical Protestants
drawn from across the denominational spectrum. There were
Methodists, Baptists, and Brethren and, for eighteen months prior
to Paisley's call, the congregation had been led by Tom Rea, a
Brethren evangelist. None the less, Paisley was consolidating the
foundations of the Presbyterianism he had acquired from both his

[5] Joseph Thompson, *Your Church is on Fire: the story of Ravenhill Presbyterian Church* (Belfast: Ravenhill Presbyterian Church, n.d.).

mother's influence, his own training with the Reformed Presbyterians, and his connection with Grier's schismatic Presbyterians, by accepting the call of a secession Presbyterian church.

Ordination

Different denominations have different notions about how someone is 'called' to the ministry. The Catholic, Orthodox, and Anglican churches have a 'high' theory of ordination. They believe that the ability to interpret God's will correctly and to perform certain religious rituals was passed from Christ to the apostles, and from them to a succession of office holders. Only people in the correct succession have a valid calling to the ministry. Reformed denominations have no such 'magical' conception of the ministry—there is no mystical quality which is passed from one generation of priests to the next—but most still have some sort of ceremony in which representatives of the church test and then accept into their membership aspiring ministers. At the extremely 'low' end of the spectrum, denominations such as the Baptists and the Brethren have no theory of ordination. Whether or not someone has been genuinely called to lead a community of Christians is known only by the fruits of his ministry. It is a *laissez-faire* free market economy. Almost anyone can claim to have been called by God and may start a congregation or take the lead in one which already exists. The test of the validity of the call is in its consequences.

Ian Paisley himself tends to the 'low' position while the traditional Presbyterian view has usually been somewhere between the high apostolic succession notion of the Catholics or the Anglicans and the free-for-all of the independents. For this reason, the Irish Presbyterians have been keen to show that Paisley was not 'properly' ordained. One leading Presbyterian minister said that he was 'self-ordained'.[6] Some of Paisley's followers have been keen to establish that his ordination was Presbyterian in its nature. Thus although Paisley himself has never claimed an Irish Presbyterian ordination, that event has become the focus for considerable rhetorical dispute about the right of Paisley and the Free Presbyterians to the Presbyterian label and heritage.

Someone with no particular stake in the argument has said that

[6] John H. Withers, *Our Past Years: Fisherwick Church, 1823–1973* (Belfast: Fisherwick Church, 1973), p. 172.

Paisley 'was ordained into the Baptist ministry by his father'.[7] This was not the case. The bare facts of the ordination service in the Ravenhill Evangelical Mission Church are as follows. A Reformed Presbyterian minister, Professor T. B. McFarlane, who had taught Paisley in the Reformed Presbyterian Theological Hall, offered a prayer. The Revd Thomas Rowan, an old Irish Presbyterian minister who had worked with the American evangelists Moody and Sankey in their missions at the end of the previous century, 'brought the charge to the congregation': the part of an ordination in which the congregation are reminded of their obligations, especially to pray for their new minister. W. J. Grier, one of the founding ministers of the Irish Evangelical Church, preached and charged Paisley 'to be faithful in contending for the faith that was once for all delivered to the saints'.[8] Kyle Paisley and a number of the elders of the church 'laid their hands upon me and set me aside for the preaching of the Blessed Word of God'.[9]

The elders in question had been ordained into the Presbyterian ministry (which makes no radical distinction between the minister and his elders) when they had been in the Ravenhill Presbyterian Church. Of the four ministers who took part in the service, three were Presbyterians: one from the Irish Presbyterian Church and two from the minority wings of Presbyterianism in Ireland. The only non-Presbyterian involved was Ian Paisley's father. Thus, unless one takes a rather 'high' view of ordination, and a strong current in reformed Protestantism does not do so, Paisley was validly ordained.

However, to treat the question in this way is to discuss it solely in the terms of Paisley's critics. Paisley himself had no great commitment to a specifically Presbyterian style of ordination: 'I don't think that the emphasis is on denominational ordination. I think the emphasis is on a *Christian* minister.' I asked him if the service had not been designed to appear 'Presbyterian': 'Well, I mean, that was the people I was moving among and I was going to

---

[7] Tom Gallagher, 'Religion, Reaction and Revolt in Northern Ireland: the impact of Paisleyism in Ulster', *Journal of Church and State*, 23 (1981), p. 427.

[8] Ian R. K. Paisley, *These 28 Years* (Belfast: Martyrs Memorial Publications, 1974), p. 2.

[9] Ian R. K. Paisley, *Life's Four Windows: a sketch of my life story* (Belfast: Martyrs Memorial Publications, 1983), p. 7.

minister to: a secession Presbyterian church.'[10] The service took its form, not from a clever anticipation of the day when he would have to defend his credentials against the Irish Presbyterians, but rather from a combination of his own inclinations and those of the congregation which had called him. Paisley was more interested in establishing his evangelical credentials than he was in laying the foundations for an argument which had not yet started.

This can be seen in the attention that Paisley devotes to the two elements of his entry to the ministry. In most of his accounts, he gives as much space to Nicholson's presence at his first Sunday service as he does to his actual ordination. He is very fond of repeating Nicholson's remarks to him after the service:

After I had finished Mr Nicholson got up, walked forward to the Communion Table, rapped it and said to me: 'Young man, have you ever seen a cow's tongue?'. I said 'Yes, sir'. He said, 'What is it like?'. I said 'It is like a file'. Then he lifted his hand and prayed, 'Lord give this young man a tongue like an old cow'.[11]

A good example of Paisley's often neglected ability to laugh at himself was given during a BBC television interview when he told the story to Peter France. After he had delivered the punch line, he paused and added: 'And some people would say perhaps that prayer has been answered far more abundantly than we can ask or even think', and burst out laughing.

The Nicholson story is important, not only because of Nicholson's direct influence on Paisley—after all he was an influence on many evangelicals of that period—but also because the name of Nicholson is an important prize in the competition for legitimacy. For many Ulster Protestants, Nicholson was both the voice of orthodoxy against the rising tide of modernism *and* the instigator of the last great religious revival in Ulster. To be able to put oneself in the tradition of which Nicholson was part is to be able to claim an important resource. Paisley wishes to lay claim to the mantle— the Bangor Free Presbyterian Church was named the 'W. P. Nicholson Memorial' — and his opponents, especially the conservatives who remain within the Irish Presbyterian Church, are equally keen to deny his inheritance. In a radio documentary I

[10] This and all subsequent quotations which are not followed by a reference to a published source come from interviews conducted between November 1984 and January 1986.

[11] Paisley, op. cit., n. 9 (above), p. 8.

researched and co-wrote for the BBC, I presented Nicholson as a forerunner to Paisley. Sidney Murray, a historian of the Presbyterian Church and an admirer of Nicholson, wrote to *Evangelical Voice*, a magazine published by a conservative pressure group in the Irish Presbyterian Church, contesting my analysis and attempting to save Nicholson from Paisley by showing that Nicholson was not a 'separatist'.[12] Murray was correct in that Nicholson, although he was highly critical of the liberals in the Presbyterian Church, continued to support the organization. Although he attended Paisley's Ravenhill Mission Church, he also worshipped at the Ravenhill Presbyterian Church when he returned to Belfast in the early fifties. Nicholson's lasting impact on Ulster religious life came through the Christian Workers' Union branches he established and promoted. He was leading a ginger group *within* the church rather than a separatist movement, but I would argue against Murray's general conclusion, which is that Paisley was motivated by beliefs which Nicholson did not hold. A more accurate picture emerges if one considers the *interaction* between a set of beliefs and the surrounding environment. Paisley and Nicholson were very close in theology. What had changed between the world of the late twenties and thirties, and Paisley's world of the fifties was the degree of 'apostasy' in the Irish Presbyterian Church. Nicholson was criticizing what he saw as an emergent trend and he was concerned to stem it and reverse it. By the end of the 1940s, Paisley had come to the conclusion that the rot had set in so firmly that only radical separation would do. Unlike Murray, I see nothing in Nicholson's beliefs which would have led him to act in a manner different from Paisley had he been faced with the same circumstances. But this is to move ahead of the story. The next few years of Paisley's ministry were trying but outwardly uneventful. But in October 1949, Ian Paisley had a profound religious experience. Feeling a definite weakness in his ministry, he called three friends to a late night prayer meeting. They prayed through the first night, the next day, and into the second night. By the close, Paisley felt himself to have been 'filled with the Holy Spirit' and to be the possessor of a new evangelistic power. This new phase in his ministry brought him into some conflict with sections of his congregation. In the first place, he

[12] Sidney Murray, 'Paisley and Nicholson', *Evangelical Voice*, 7 (3) (1984). My reply, 'Nicholson and Paisley', was published in *EV* 8 (2).

displayed a sense of enterprise which offended some members who wanted to be consulted about his work. One day he saw Rico's Circus tent in the grounds of the Ormeau Park and persuaded Rico to let him use it for an evangelistic rally. Without consulting his committee, he had posters printed and handbills distributed advertising the meetings and drew a crowd of almost a thousand people: a record in those days when he was hardly known.

Paisley's evangelical fervour was by no means universally popular with the Ravenhill Mission Church. Like many a group formed as a schism from a larger body and convinced of its own possession of the saving truth, the Ravenhill congregation had turned inwards and there were some members who drew so much satisfaction from being part of a small group of cognoscenti, a select band who knew something the rest of the world did not know, that they had no great desire to see the band extended. While Paisley worked the doors of the small working-class streets of East Belfast and held tent missions on cleared ground, resentment grew. A second source of tension was Paisley's aggressive criticisms of those members whose religion was more formal than experimental.

Well, if my preaching lacked fire it now caught the fire, but I tell you when that happens in a Church you are in for trouble, and I was sure in for trouble. When you meet the Devil in trousers he is very vicious, but when you meet the Devil in a skirt, then you are for it! I met the Devil in a skirt. There was one woman in that congregation and she vowed that she would finish me for good.

Of course that sort of thing has to come to a head and it came to the head one night when I preached a sermon on Hell. Her unconverted father was in the meeting and she was entirely upset that I would dare to talk about Hell and offend her father. Going out she said to me, 'I want to talk with you.' I said, 'All right, in fact I would like to talk with you.' So we went into the little room and we shut the door and she started on me. She said, 'Your ministry is finished here.' I said, 'I'm glad to know it. I would like to get away, there are wider places than this, but I can't get away for the Lord has told me I'm going to be around here for a very long time.' She said, 'You are mistaken, my husband is on the Church Committee, my father-in-law is an elder. We control this Church, and, young man, you are going.'

I said, 'Isn't that strange, because I wanted to tell you for a long time that you were going. Now tomorrow night the elders will meet, and the trustees will meet, and they will make a decision, and it will be very simple. They will either say, 'Preacher, you stay', or they will say to you 'Go'.' She said, 'Right.'

So the night came and I walked into that Church. I had perfect peace. I wasn't afraid of losing a pulpit, for if I hadn't that pulpit I would have preached on the Ravenhill Road. It would not have made any difference to me. We might have had this Church built 20 years before it was. I walked in, and she had her armour on. The greatest weapon a woman has is tears, and she was there weeping. She said, 'Oh, Mr Paisley, do we need to have this meeting?' I said, 'We certainly do, and either you are going or I'm going.' She said, 'Could we not come to an agreement?' I said, 'I'm sorry'. I said, 'You know what you have done? You have criticised every person I have led to the Lord in this Church, and I want to tell you, the little ones will be offended no more. It is now or never.' I walked into that room and I said to the elders, 'Gentlemen, I'm just a boy, a stripling, but I believe the Book, and I want to tell you men, I'm going to preach this Book. I'll either preach it in here or out there. Make a choice, I don't want to be hard, I don't want to be cruel but this woman has got to go.' I left, and in a few minutes I was recalled, and they said, 'She has gone, and you are to stay.' I said, 'Gentlemen, you have made the right decision, let us get down to prayer.'

Of course she didn't go on her own, she visited every member of the congregation, she took a lot of people with her. There was I with more empty seats. So I decided that instead of having a prayer meeting sometimes, we would have a night of prayer every week and we would pray on the seats that nobody sat in. We went up into the little gallery and you could have written on the dust that had accumulated on those empty seats and we prayed at every one of them. It was a dusty prayer meeting I can assure you, but as we prayed at every seat, things started to move. Then, of course, the Lord opened doors.[13]

Important for Paisley's later success was making contacts. His father was a well-known evangelistic preacher and his three years with the Reformed Presbyterians had allowed him to meet evangelicals in Belfast. The world of evangelical Protestantism existed outside and beyond any particular denomination. There was a milieu of conservative members of various denominations who read the same magazines, attended the same conventions, and travelled to each others' churches and halls if some particularly attractive speaker was preaching. They might meet regularly at the Saturday night service at the Coalman's Mission in the docks or at the Monday morning prayer meeting in Berry St Presbyterian Church. The milieu did not exist because its supporters were members of the same organization but because they shared a

[13] Paisley, op. cit., n. 9 (above), pp. 12–13.

common set of beliefs. In his early years in Belfast, Paisley was becoming well known in this world.

A Public Reputation

Evangelical Protestantism spreads beyond the strictly religious into the social and the political. In the first place, evangelicals wish to protest publicly against the errors of competing religious traditions, and in Ulster that generally means protesting against Romanism. In the second place, they wish to promote the social conditions most conducive to the maintenance and spread of their own religious beliefs. Although critics of 'the Orange state' have concentrated on the ways in which the Stormont government pro- moted Protestant interests, they have usually neglected the fact that it was only discriminatory in matters such as employment and housing. It did little to promote the more religious elements of Protestantism. The evangelicals thus always felt the need for some public campaigning organization, and it is hardly surprising that Ian Paisley was involved in the major vehicle for public protests in the late forties.

The National Union of Protestants was initially formed in En- gland to protest against what was seen as a rising tide of ritualism in the Church of England. Anglican evangelicals felt that the church was set on a 'Romeward trend'. Such a platform had little obvious relevance to Northern Ireland where the Episcopal Church of Ireland was rather 'low' and Protestant and had few ritualists. None the less, an Ulster branch of the NUP was formed with an unemployed engineer, Norman Porter, as its full-time general secretary and with Paisley as its treasurer. Ian Paisley would probably have become active in such an organization anyway, but he was invited to become involved by his uncle, the Revd Sinclair Taylor, who was the General Secretary in London.

The NUP concerned itself with defending the Protestant re- ligion and with campaigning against changes which it saw as en- croaching on the dominant position of Protestant culture. Hence rallies were held to protest against growing disregard for the Lord's Day, state funding of Catholic schools, and such matters. It drew support from evangelicals in all the denominations and, until Pais- ley and Porter parted company in 1963, its platforms attracted conservative Irish Presbyterian ministers such as Donald Gillies.

The split was a result of Paisley's development of a more rigorous separatist line and his increasingly strong attacks on the Presbyterian Church. Porter and the evangelicals in the main denominations formed the Evangelical Protestant Society, which continues to this day and which has a more narrowly religious focus. But in the late fifties, the NUP provided a convenient platform for Paisley's articulation of a militant anti-Catholicism and anti-modernism.

The Free Presbyterian Church

For the first few years of his career Paisley was welcomed by evangelicals in the Irish Presbyterian Church. When a mission in Rathfriland became too popular to be accommodated in the Friends' Hall, he was granted the use of the Presbyterian Church Hall. He worked in a joint campaign in Mountpottinger in Belfast with Ivor Lewis and Donald Gillies, two well-known conservatives in the Irish Presbyterian Church. In fact, Paisley was so little seen as a threat that Ivor Lewis tried to help him find an assistant minister for a church extension he was planning in Mount Merrion, a new housing scheme in South East Belfast. Lewis suggested Cecil Menary, a member of his Berry St congregation who was then studying at the Belfast Bible College. Menary turned down the offer.

Although Paisley's Mount Merrion scheme could be seen as the first evidence of a desire to build a denomination that would compete with the Presbyterians, no such plan had yet formed in his mind. The real competition between Paisley and the Irish Presbyterians came six months later in March 1951 when the Presbyterian congregation in Crossgar divided and the conservatives asked Paisley to lead their movement.

The background to the division in Crossgar involves the complex rules of the Presbyterian Church for appointing ministers. The general idea is that ministers should be called by their congregations; in the Irish Presbyterian Church that is taken to mean elected by a two-thirds majority. But that raises the question of just who is entitled to be regarded as a member of a congregation. Hence, when a pulpit becomes vacant, a new roll of voters is drawn up. To be entered on the roll one must be a full communion-taking member, and have paid one's contribution to the minister's stipend. The Lissara Presbyterian Church in the small farming village of Crossgar in County Down was vacant. The congregation was divided between two candidates and neither got the two-thirds vote. One party to the conflict complained of an irregularity in the distribution of voting papers and asked the Down Presbytery to begin the whole process again by once more declaring the congregation vacant. This was done and a new roll of voters was drawn up, after the interim moderater had first said that the roll would not be changed. A new financial year had just begun and a number of names were left off this second list for non-payment of stipend. Those left off naturally claimed that they had been deliberately disfranchised by their enemies.

Prior to this dispute, the evangelicals had invited Ian Paisley to lead a mission in the Lissara Church Hall. Although the Kirk Session had unanimously granted the hall, the Down Presbytery stepped in at the last minute and refused permission. The justification given was that 'the Presbyterian Code restricts the holding of evangelistic missions in church premises to ministers, licenciates, ruling elders or others approved by the Assembly's Committee on the State of Religion'.[14] Although this is strictly true—the Presbyterian Church, like any ideological organization wishes to have some control over what views it might appear to be sponsoring—the rule had usually been operated with varying degrees of flexibility. Paisley was no stranger to Presbyterian pulpits. The conservatives believed that it was used this time because the speaker was Paisley. The liberals were trying to prevent the true gospel being preached.

The liberals could have given another reason for banning the mission. Paisley's credentials apart, there was a well-established principle that one did not encourage special events such as missions during a vacancy. It was well recognized that vacancies exacerbated any tensions that might exist in a congregation, as each side pressed for its favourite, and special events might well increase such tensions. Hence an interim moderator (the senior minister given oversight during a vacancy) would normally ban missions. But on this occasion he had not. Anyway, such an explanation, had it been given, would not have satisfied the conservatives who would, quite

---

[14] The Free Presbyterian version of the Crossgar dispute has been given many times. The first public statement was a press release published in the *Belfast Telegraph*, 13 Mar. 1951. There is an account which includes an interview with Hugh James Adams, one of the founding elders, in the *Revivalist*, Feb. 1969, pp. 6–9.

rightly, have interpreted it as a desire for a quiet life triumphing over a desire to preach the gospel.

Whatever the actual motives of the parties to the dispute, the conservatives read the actions of the Down Presbytery as final confirmation of the sorts of things that evangelical critics such as Paisley had been saying: the Irish Presbyterian Church was now run by people who did not want to hear the true gospel being preached. The rot, first identified in the Davey heresy trial but not then exterminated, had spread. The church was beyond redemption. The only appropriate course of action was that taken twenty years before by the American fundamentalists: separation.

Four elders of the Lissara congregation and a number of families withdrew and constituted themselves as 'The Free Presbyterian Church of Ulster'. They met in the Lissara Mission Hall, a small building erected by one 'Hallelujah' Gibson, a local farmer, and they ordained George Stears, a retired minister of the Presbyterian Church of South America whom Ivor Lewis had introduced to Paisley.

It is noticeable that the press statement released by the elders of the new congregation made no mention of Ian Paisley. His name was first brought into the public parts of the controversy by the Down Presbytery in their repudiation of the new denomination. In their view, the 'Free' in the title meant anarchic and the 'of Ulster' signified a parochial vision. 'Presbyterian' it would not be. Thirteen column inches down the Presbytery's press release comes the mention of Paisley and he is only introduced so that his credentials as an ordained minister can be disputed.[15] The new congregation's coyness about mentioning Paisley might seem like a deliberate attempt to minimize his part in the dispute but more likely it reflected a desire of the elders to establish the general principles on which they had seceded. Obviously Paisley was very influential in the development of the controversy. It seems clear that it was his Baptist background which explained why the new organization did not adopt exclusively the traditional Presbyterian view on infant baptism and instead permitted both infant and adult baptism in its doctrinal statement. Having said that, it would be a mistake to see Paisley as having deliberately planned and stimulated the controversy and the split. Like so many crucial events in Paisley's career, the Crossgar split and the foundation of the Free

---

[15] *Belfast Telegraph*, 15 Mar. 1951, p. 7.

Presbyterian Church of Ulster was an affair with complex roots in which others played a large part in producing the outcome. Although this would also overstate the case, it is perhaps more accurate to see the Free Church as having been formed by others, albeit with considerable influence from Paisley, and then Paisley being invited to assume the leadership of the movement.

From March 1951, Paisley was committed to active competition with the Irish Presbyterian Church. For the Crossgar split to become meaningful, it would have to be followed by others. Paisley's preaching tours of the province thus took on a quite different meaning and purpose from that point. He was no longer an evangelistic preacher holding 'undenominational' rallies. He was now the figurehead and leader of a new denomination which, if it was to mean anything at all, would have to attract other dissident Presbyterians; and it did. In the summer of 1951, two more groups of Irish Presbyterians were added to the Free Church.

Ballymoney is the main market town between Coleraine and Ballymena in North Antrim. The Drumreagh Presbyterian Church, which covered the farming area south of Ballymoney, was attended by Alexander McAuley and his family. After his conversion in a small country gospel hall, Sandy McAuley came into conflict with two successive ministers: John Barkley because he was a liberal[16] and William Hyndman because he was thought to live an immoral life which McAuley felt obliged to denounce. Relations between McAuley and Hyndman became so strained that Hyndman actually assaulted McAuley. In the summer of 1951, McAuley invited Ian Paisley to conduct a series of meetings in the Cabra School House. In addition to promoting the positive virtues of salvation, Paisley also criticized the apostasy of the Presbyterian Church—something readily accepted by the McAuleys—and at the end of the mission, a handful of Presbyterians decided that they could not go back to an apostate denomination. And so another Free Presbyterian congregation came into being, meeting first in the upstairs of a barn, and later erecting its own building right

[16] A story commonly told in Free Presbyterian circles is that the only spiritual advice which Barkley gave McAuley was that he should 'smoke two pipes a day and not worry'. It is only fair to Barkley to record that he gave that particular piece of advice in response to McAuley's concern about whether he could continue smoking now that he had been converted. Although that particular story arose out of two people speaking at cross purposes, there is no doubt that the two men were theologically poles apart.

next to the Cabra School, the site of the mission, which had been closed to them from the moment they had announced the formation of their own congregation.

Of the first three congregations, that of Rasharkin, ten miles south of Cabra, was the one whose formation had least to do with theological disputes. The issue which divided the Presbyterians of Rasharkin was the divorce of the Presbyterian minister and accusations of ill-treating his wife. The town divided between those who supported the wife and those who supported the minister. Paisley was preaching in Cabra at the time of the dispute and the conservatives went to hear him. They were impressed and decided to form themselves into a Free Presbyterian congregation.[17]

It might seem as if the formation of the Free Presbyterian Church had very little to do with theological differences and a lot to do with personal animosities and family feuds. It is certainly the case that such idiosyncratic elements play a part in the various schisms but they act mainly as a catalyst or as an accelerator. Underlying the divisions were genuine differences of belief and, even in the Rasharkin case, the congregation could have divided without one half going to the Free Presbyterian Church. It was only because some respected local men heard Ian Paisley preach and became convinced of his separatist argument, that they joined his denomination. They could simply have travelled a few miles and sat under another Presbyterian minister. That they chose instead to form their own congregation with all the opprobrium that such a move attracted, and all the financial sacrifice it caused, can only be explained in terms of genuine conviction that the Irish Presbyterian Church was so riddled with apostasy as to be beyond redemption.

The formation of the new denomination at Crossgar and not at Ravenhill put Ian Paisley in a rather awkward position. His own church was not yet a constituent member of the denomination he had helped to found! The arguments about whether or not to join

[17] The founding of the various early congregations is described in the following editions of the *Revivalist*: Rasharkin—Feb. 1969; Cabra—Sept. 1951 and Apr. 1969; Mount Merrion—July-Sept. 1969; Whiteabbey—Oct. 1969; and Dunmurry—Jan. 1970. Revd Stanley Barnes of Hillsborough Free Presbyterian Church kindly lent me a large number of issues of the *Revivalist* and Dr Paisley was good enough to lend me three scrapbooks in which an early Free Presbyterian had collected details on the various congregations and their ministers.

were simply a continuation of a feud within the congregation which
had persisted since his ordination. One section wished to maintain
its independence (having clearly lost its sense of 'Presbyterian-
ness' since 1935) while the other was keen to follow its pastor.
Paisley finally convinced his committee to affiliate and the critics
withdrew.

The plan for an extension of the Ravenhill Church into the
Mount Merrion housing scheme which Paisley had proposed to
Cecil Menary in the summer of 1950 went ahead.

In order to build up a congregation an attack was made on the battlements
of hell, sin and apostasy in the neighbourhood: an old time Gospel campaign conducted by the Rev. Ian R. K. Paisley, was held in a large tent.
Here God the Holy Ghost was seen in dynamic soul-saving power and
seventy-six souls hit the cinder track for salvation. Glory to God! Having
received such blessing from the hand of Almighty God in this, our first
Gospel attempt in Mount Merrion, the Spirit led us again in another
hell-shaking, sin-smashing, Holy Ghost mission conducted by a special
commando Team from Ravenhill Free Presbyterian Church, when over a
score of precious souls sought and found God. Hallelujah! From victory
to victory Jesus leads us on, and another milestone was passed when on
Saturday 2 August, 1952, this building was opened to the glory of God,
the quickening of the saints, the salvation of souls, the denunciation of
sin, the exposing of modernistic teachings and soul-damning heresy, and
the defeat of the old serpent.[18]

Mount Merrion gave the Free Presbyterians five congregations.
The sixth was a departure for the Church in that Paisley bought a
building before he had the nucleus of a congregation. A hall on the
Shore Road in Whiteabbey, on the north side of Belfast Lough,
was purchased but the work was always uphill. Even ten years
later, when William Beattie and Ivan Foster were students for the
ministry and given charge of the meetings, it was hardly thriving.
They spent a lot of time touring the area trying to create interest
but despite their best efforts they found that there was far more
interest in the late evening meetings they held in the Orange Hall
in nearby Newtownabbey, and in the late sixties the Whiteabbey
building was given up in favour of moving the church to the
growing Newtownabbey area.

A year after the Whiteabbey building was bought, a more prom-

18 'R. N. C.', 'Mount Merrion Free Presbyterian Church Opens', *Revivalist*
(July–Oct. 1952), p. 1.

ising work began in Ballyhalbert, a small village on the Ards peninsula. A small group of people broke from the local Irish Presbyterian church and applied for admission to the Free Church. As if to atone for the Whiteabbey mistake, the Free Church hesitated to accept this group because the reasons for the secession were not obviously theological, and there was considerable doubt that the Ballyhalbert people were 'saved'. So the group was accepted, almost 'on probation', for preaching, and not as a full congregation. John Douglas, the first student who had been converted under Paisley at Ravenhill, was given oversight of the group. In circumstances which were similar to those of Paisley's first years at Ravenhill although not as acrimonious, some of the audience came to regret their request for preaching offices and drifted away but others, mainly from Portavogie, a few miles down the coast, joined and in 1958 a church was built in Portavogie.

1957 saw two further branches added: one in Coleraine which was largely inspired by the evangelistic work of John Wylie in Cabra, and the other in Dunmurry, a suburb of Belfast. I will explore this point in more detail later but it is interesting to note here that the Dunmurry congregation was always small. Although set in a 'dormitory' area with an increasing population, it made few inroads into the local council estate. To some extent this was a consequence of it having to compete with Paisley's own preaching in Ravenhill, and later, when the congregation was too big, in the Ulster Hall. But largely it was due to the lack of interest in evangelical religion in the urban working class.

The tenth Free Presbyterian congregation was short-lived. A Church of Ireland curate in Antrim and some of his parishioners seceded from the Church of Ireland and were admitted to the Free Presbyterian Church. Although Harold V. Magowan shared Paisley's dislike for modernism and the ecumenical movement, many other things divided them, and four years later in 1963, Magowan resigned at the same time as the Free Church Presbytery decided to sack him, and the work in Antrim dried up.[19]

Only three other congregations were added in the period before Paisley's imprisonment in 1966: Sandown Road in East Belfast,

---

[19] In an advertisement placed in the *Belfast Telegraph*, 4 Jan. 1964, the Magowan supporters gave as their reason for leaving 'the absence of annual election for the Moderatorship', 'the preponderance of a political element to the detriment of spiritual life', and, most implausibly, 'the recent growth of modernism in Presbytery'.

Limavady in Co. Londonderry, and Armagh City. The Sandown Road congregation, like Mount Merrion and Dunmurry, was an extension of Ravenhill. Armagh was a congregation formed from nothing but, like most Free churches, it attracted mainly Irish Presbyterians. The Limavady church was fairly typical of later congregations in the method of its formation. A local farmer who had been a keen Irish Presbyterian left the Dungiven congregation because its minister was a liberal, became interested in the Free Church's separatist stance, and travelled first to Cabra and, when it opened, to Coleraine, to attend the services. He also started holding small Bible studies and prayer meetings in his own house which attracted evangelical friends. Although the distance to Coleraine was not so great as to put off any committed Free Presbyterians, it would have made it very difficult to invite interested local people to 'come to the Free Church' and so he determined to promote a local church. John Wylie was convinced that this was God's will and a site was bought at Limavady.

In 1965, the Free Church had twelve congregations. The most successful ones, apart from Paisley's own Ravenhill Church, were those in the rural Presbyterian heartland. Although Paisley and his aides were working very hard, leading evangelistic crusades here and there all over the province, the Free Church had only been built up to the same sort of size and presence as the Evangelical Presbyterians. Although they prayed hard for revival, there were, in 1965, few signs that it was about to come. This is not to say that the fourteen years since the foundation of the Free Church had been wasted. Although there were few obvious tangible results, the years of evangelism had brought Paisley and the Church to the attention of many evangelical Protestants, and had created a network of contacts who would be invaluable in preparing the ground for the dramatic lift-off which followed the imprisonment.

Recruiting Ministers

One of Paisley's main problems in the early days was finding enough suitable men to pastor the various congregations which were being formed. Menary had turned down Mount Merrion. Stears was an old man and obviously only a stop-gap in Crossgar, and there were three empty pulpits. In July 1951, Paisley again approached Menary and asked him if he would serve Rasharkin and

Cabra. This time he accepted and was ordained in August. Three months later, he passed Cabra over to John Wylie.

Like Menary, Wylie was a disenchanted Presbyterian. As his own religious career and background are similar to those of many other Free Presbyterians of this period, I will spend some time on his biography. 'I was brought up in the Presbyterian Church. I went to church and so on and learnt my catechism. When I got converted—now I had a very Presbyterian life, keeping the sabbath day and so on—when I was nineteen . . . this was a real work in my heart.'

Once people had heard that he had 'got saved', he was invited to address farmhouse meetings and he also attended the Knock Church formed by James Hunter after the Davey heresy trial. There he heard, 'A real firey old preacher and I enjoyed him and I got a real grasp of what had happened and how they [the Irish Presbyterians] had drifted from the principles of Presbyterianism, from the principles of the word of God'. In his own Presbyterian congregation, Wylie tried to engage his minister in argument during a Bible class. The minister refused to be drawn into debate and asked Wylie to leave.

I became a sort of wandering Jew for a while and went here and there. I went to the Methodist Church and then I used to go to the Baptists and I went here and there. Then when we got married we went to the Presbyterian Church in Gransha where the minister was an evangelical. I got to know Ian [Paisley]. We were involved in Protestant rallies. The church was formed in 1951; I must have met him in 49. I got to like the fellow. He was very sincere and he appealed to me.

Although his electrician's business in Dundonald was thriving, Wylie felt a distinct call to the ministry. He was accepted by the Free Presbyterian Church and called to take over Cabra from Menary.

The first minister of Mount Merrion differed from Menary and Wylie in not having been a Presbyterian. Robert Coulter had trained at the Faith Mission College in Edinburgh and was working as an evangelist for the Faith Mission when Paisley, who had shared a platform with him in Ballymena, invited him to take over Mount Merrion. The problems of finding ministers were so pressing that Paisley was only able to be concerned about people's basic orthodoxy. Conservatives who were not Presbyterians were not rejected on that score. As Coulter put it: 'I don't think he was all that worried at the time. I think he wanted the help; people to come in and take charge of these churches that were springing up.'

Coulter did not last long in Mount Merrion, largely because he was not happy with the aggressively controversial style of preaching that was expected. He was himself extremely conservative in his theology, but he preferred to preach the gospel and had little taste for denouncing the apostasy of the liberals and the modernists:

I was later summoned for not preaching against individuals like Dr Davey and so on. My reply was that my first priority was to preach the gospel and, if I had any time left over after preaching the gospel, I would preach against heresy. They had to agree with it. The gospel had to come first in their thinking.

The Presbytery gave him a month to adopt a more aggressive attitude but Coulter had already decided to accept an invitation to work in America and he left the Free Presbyterian Church.

The American invitation came from an interesting individual who played a very minor part in the early days of the Free Presbyterian Church: Hugh Johnson. In October of 1952, the Free Presbyterian Church announced the opening of its own training college with lectures from J. K. Paisley, Ian Paisley, H. H. Aitchison, and Hugh Johnson. This was Paisley's second choice scheme for staffing his church. Initially he had intended to send his students to the Free Church of Scotland College in Edinburgh where Grier's Irish Evangelical Church trained its ministers. For a variety of reasons nothing came of this. There were doubts on both sides. Paisley felt that the Free Church, although itself orthodox, was keeping bad company by associating with other denominations which were not entirely sound. The Free Church for its part consulted one of the theologians of the Irish Presbyterian Church and was told that Paisley's denomination was not genuinely Presbyterian. In any case, as I will argue later, the creation of his own college, although difficult in the early years, provided an invaluable resource for the later church in that it allowed a generation of loyal ministers, sharing not only Paisley's theology but also a strong sympathy with the political implications of Protestantism in Ulster, to be raised.

In the early years it was difficult to find competent lecturers who were willing to be associated with Paisley's unpopular new movement. The backgrounds of Aitchison and Johnson are important for understanding the growth of the Church in that they show both Paisley's reliance on the evangelical milieu and the vulnerability of that milieu to charlatans.

Aitchison was a Scottish Presbyterian minister who had come to Ulster in 1931. After serving two Presbyterian churches in Belfast, he fell out with his kirk session and defected to pastor a Congregational church. His fourth congregation in Ulster, which he was serving when he became associated with Paisley, represented yet another link back to the Davey heresy trial. Whitehead Presbyterian Church called as its minister W. F. S. Stewart, an Old Testament scholar who had been vocal in his support of Davey. A conservative element in Whitehead then withdrew to form its own congregation and Aitchison became the minister. Although no great intellectual or preacher, Aitchison had the paper credentials and the right associations to be at least a symbolic asset to the new Free Presbyterian theological hall.[20]

Johnson was a charlatan, an alcoholic who managed to disguise his drink problem from Coulter and Paisley who shared lodgings with him. He was a reasonably talented preacher and for a few months he made a living from collections taken when he preached. He returned to America.

Other early associations were no more fruitful. The short career of Harold Magowan in the Free Church has already been mentioned. The cases of Magowan and Coulter suggest the general principle that men who had been in full-time Christian work prior to joining the Free Church found it difficult to settle and to remain in harmony with Paisley and the core of the Church. Another man who came to the Free Church with experience of full-time work was Victor Burns, a pastor in an independent evangelical church in England who lasted only a year before returning to England. David Leatham, who was minister in Whiteabbey and Dunmurry, also eventually left the Free Church for the Baptist ministry.

It seemed that the Free Church would only be well served by those who had been entirely trained, and preferably converted, within Paisley's organization. But even this was no guarantee. One

[20] Although H. H. Aitchison's Chester Avenue Presbyterian Church congregation never joined, he personally was admitted to the Presbytery of the Free Presbyterian Church in 1955 (*Revivalist* (Dec. 1955), p. 7).

expects failure in any training programme and perhaps the Free Presbyterians did no worse in this respect than other churches—comparative data would be extremely difficult to assemble—but the early students were faced with the problem of having very quickly to take charge of young congregations. Candidates for, say, the Irish Presbyterian ministry are expected to spend some of their training period in charge of a congregation, but these are generally well established, and students will often be supervised by experienced ministers. The difficulty for a new denomination is that the two enterprises of recruiting congregations and training a ministry have to be run at the same time, and some students fail under the pressure.

Why Did People Join the Free Church?

I have already given a brief account of the key points of Protestant belief, particularly those which most radically separate Protestants from Roman Catholics. But to explain what attracted people to the Free Church, we must consider those things which distinguished the conservative evangelical beliefs of men like Paisley from the mainstream of Protestant teaching and practice.

Men like Sandy McAuley and Bob Wilson's father were not just changing one Presbyterian organization for another. They were also going through a conversion experience. Their new-found faith was qualitatively different from their old religion. Evangelical Protestants believe that salvation requires more than just intellectual assent or the correct performance of religious ritual. No amount of faithful attendance at church will win salvation. What is required is a 'born again' experience. It is difficult to compress a complex faith into a few propositions, but the core of evangelical Protestantism can be summarized in this way. Since Adam's rejection of God's will, man has been in a state of sin. God then sent his only Son Jesus Christ to suffer and die as an atoning sacrifice for our sins. His death pays off our debt. But we have to accept that sacrifice and take it into our hearts. God has chosen some of us for salvation. It is nothing of our doing that saves us. Man, since the Fall, has been in such a state of sin that nothing done by men alone can win back God's favour. His offer of salvation is a free gift and this idea is commonly expressed in the term 'sovereign grace'.[21] But becoming saved is a two-stage process. God has laid the foundation by 'calling' some of us but we still have to respond to that call. The job of the preacher is to make that clear to us; we then respond. We should appreciate our sinfulness (come under 'conviction of sin', as evangelicals express it), appreciate Christ's sacrifice, and then take the gospel into our hearts. This then makes effectual—or cements—the foundation laid by God in our being called. To use a rather irreverent analogy, being saved is similar to those adhesives, such as Araldite, which come in two tubes. Neither element on its own is a glue, but mix the two together and one has a fast hard-setting adhesive. Although irreverent, the analogy is a good one because another element of evangelical Protestantism is the certainty of salvation which follows conversion. Being born again brings the security of knowing that one is saved.

The evangelical emphasis on a personal response to Christ's sacrifice distinguishes it from more liberal interpretations of Protestantism which tend towards universalism. There have periodically been movements which openly assert that all of God's children will be saved and that differences in doctrines between this or that church are, in the final outcome, unimportant. But more common than these avowedly universalistic movements is a general tendency to think in that way. In contrast, the evangelicals insist that only those people whom God has called and who respond to the gospel message will be saved from eternal damnation and hell fire. Behaving well all one's life or performing religious rituals; these things will not do it:

Being a real Christian is not ultimately a matter of things that you *do*. It is a relationship that you enter into, between a holy God and a broken sinner, saved not by anything that he or she can do but only by the blood of Jesus Christ, shed on the cross at Calvary.[22]

People who became Free Presbyterians often reviewed their lives

[21] Different sorts of evangelicals place different stress on the independence of God's 'sovereign grace'. The position described here is that of the 'Calvinists'. Others, such as the 'Wesleyan' Methodists, hold the 'Arminian' position of allowing that men can, to some degree, influence God's judgement. They suppose that one can both 'earn' salvation and lose one's 'saved' status. Those evangelicals who are Calvinists often signal this by having 'Grace' or 'Sovereign Grace' in the title of their church. Jack Glass in Glasgow, who was once a close ally of Paisley, calls his organization the 'Sovereign Grace Evangelical Baptist Church'.

[22] William McCrea and David Porter, *In His Pathway: the story of Rev. William McCrea* (London: Marshall, Morgan and Scott, 1980), p. 15.

in terms of two periods. In the first period, they were good Presbyterians and went to church regularly and lived moral lives, but were not saved. And this lack they blame firmly on the unsaved Presbyterian ministers who did not preach the whole gospel to them and who did not make them aware of their sinfulness and their need for conversion. In the words of a working-class Belfast man who later became a Free Presbyterian minister:

I was completely ignorant of what not only Presbyterianism was but also what the gospel was. I had no idea. Sunday school boy all my life, youth fellowship all my life. Went to church every Sunday practically. Never, never, was confronted with the fact that the Bible condemned me as a lost sinner.

Bob Wilson was converted at the same time as his father who had been an elder in the Rasharkin Irish Presbyterian Church:

It wasn't until February 1952 that I answered an appeal being made in the church to trust Christ as my saviour. I answered that appeal, went through to the enquiry room and . . . I discovered that Dr Paisley was talking to my father, and to his son, at the one time. He wasn't aware of it at the time, but when we had a prayer together after I trusted Christ in that prayer, he asked me to shake hands with the person beside him. Here was my father!

This fundamental difference in theology over the meaning and necessity of conversion explains the desire for a separate organization. Nicholson, who was an encyclopaedia of pithy sayings, used to say 'you never get live chickens under a dead hen'. Sandy McAuley's son uses the same theme to describe the need for the formation of a new church:

I never heard the Gospel really preached in the Presbyterian Church that I went to. Many of the others were the same. They were modernistic in their views and they didn't preach the new birth, that you had to be saved. And we felt, well, to send young converts to churches such as this, well, it would be wrong, so that's why we considered this with much prayer and at the end of the day we felt led of the Lord to commence a Free Presbyterian Church.

The Maura Lyons Case

Given the nature of the Free Presbyterian Church and the reasons for its formation, it is not surprising that its public image was one of opposition: it was anti-liberal, anti-modernist, and, above all, anti-Romanist. A major element of its public activities was 'the protest'. 'To protest' is a verb still used a great deal by Free Presbyterians (and other forms of conservative Protestant). They see themselves as having an obligation to speak out against what they see as error.

Sometimes you've got to—before you can heal, you've got to wound, and, just to be, like, using an illustration: if a person is in a house sleeping and the house is on fire, well, who's going to be that person's friend? The one that goes past and says 'I wouldn't like to disturb them. I'll just let them sleep' or the person that . . . goes in and breaks the door or breaks the window and goes in and raises the alarm and tries to get them wakened up?

Paisley and Wylie were active in Protestant rallies, and in the meetings organized by the National Union of Protestants, but their most public endeavour of the 1950s was, as so many key episodes, thrust upon them.

Maura Lyons was a young Catholic girl from West Belfast. At work she started to attend a lunch-time prayer meeting and one of her colleagues took her to attend the small Dunmurry Free Presbyterian Church. Unwilling to court adverse publicity, David Leatham, the minister, advised her to keep quiet about her conversion until she was legally of age. One evening she returned home to find her parents talking to two priests. Thinking that she would be taken away to some convent for what would now be called 'de-programming', Lyons left the house and sought the sanctuary of David Leatham. A lady missionary working for the Sentinel Union took Maura Lyons to England.

There was a huge outcry in the local press. Paisley and the Free Presbyterian Church were accused of kidnapping an under-age girl. Wylie was contacted and asked to assist in moving the girl from her first hiding-place in Dorset to Preston. Paisley decided to take the initiative and he announced a 'great Protestant rally' in the Ulster Hall and promised some startling revelations. Wylie went to Preston and tape-recorded Maura Lyons 'giving her testimony'. So that Paisley could continue to claim that he did not know where the girl was, Wylie delivered the tape to his doorstep and Mrs Paisley found it the next morning behind the milk bottles.

The tape was played at a large, well-publicized rally in the Ulster Hall in Belfast and there were immediate calls for Paisley to be arrested and charged with abducting the girl. A few weeks later, when she came of age, Maura Lyons turned up at Paisley's house and asked for his protection. The police took the girl and, in a court case in which Paisley refused to give evidence, Maura Lyons was made a ward of court and returned to her parents. For Lyons that was the end of her dramatic career in evangelical Protestantism. She later renounced her Protestant conversion and married a Catholic.

For Paisley and the Free Presbyterian Church the episode generated a great deal of publicity, all of it hostile, but for many evangelicals it established Paisley's public reputation as a man who would stand up to the Church of Rome. For critics of Paisley's style, the Lyons case was a good demonstration of a weakness which he has shown on many occasions since. While they would not deny him the right to represent his religious beliefs as forcefully as he can and hence to protest against those beliefs which he sees as heretical, they would point to the near duplicity in which he engaged to promote his cause. He maintained throughout the police and media searches for Maura Lyons that (*a*) he had not been responsible for her disappearance (which was strictly speaking true) and that (*b*) he did not know where she was and so could not tell her parents. This was only minimally true in that Leatham had been involved in her first move. John Wylie had been involved in her second move, and Wylie had then returned to make the tape-recording. Paisley had only to ask Wylie a simple question and he would have known where the girl was.

Although it is not important for understanding the success of Ian Paisley's movement, it is interesting to speculate on aspects of the character of the man. What the Lyons case demonstrated was that he was capable of taking a very legalistic view of morality and ethics. Like the Jesuits he is so fond of criticizing, Paisley is quite capable of telling the legal truth while not being honestly forthcoming. To his less scrupulous followers, this showed 'that there's no flies on the big man'. To his more thoughtful members, this sort of activity was justified by the nature of the opposition. The Free Presbyterians were battling not only against secular liberalism and the heretics within the Protestant churches, but also against the forces of Rome, and with enemies such as these one must on occasion use tactics which are not as honourable as one might wish them to be.

Protestant Theatre

In these more secular days, when it is almost commonplace for people to change religion, it is difficult to appreciate the public interest which was generated by events such as the disappearance of Maura Lyons and the broadcasting of her taped testimony. In the 1940s and 1950s, an evangelistic rally which had some theatrical element, such as the testimony of an ex-Catholic, was a crowd-puller, as were the staged performances of the blasphemous mass by ex-priests. Even in the late 1950s, Paisley and John Wylie could think it worthwhile to sponsor a tour by an ex-priest who would perform and then denounce the mass. Such performances are now rare and one suspects that the market for them has disappeared. Although it is easy to blame any change in the world on television, it does seem likely that the massive increase in forms of communication such as television and the cinema has removed the attraction of such events. If one is looking for a public display of sin to stimulate one's own sense of righteousness, one does not have to arrange a mimic mass; the modern world, brought by television into almost every rural Protestant home, provides enough sin and apostasy to satisfy any curiosity.

Although this is to move ahead of the historical account, some people now see Paisley as having moderated considerably and point to his abandonment of 'stunts' such as the Lyons affair as evidence of his moderation. I think such an analysis is mistaken. It is not that Paisley has changed. Rather the world has changed so much that what was previously unusual is now commonplace. In an era when the Catholic Church was more solidly monolithic, and when either very few of its priests defected, or their defection was hidden, the presence of an ex-priest was a draw. Nowadays, large numbers of priests leave the Catholic Church and, importantly, most of them do so for 'liberal' reasons. They do not convert from conservative Catholicism to conservative Protestantism, but from what they see as a reactionary organization to a more liberal faith. Hence they are not available to perform for evangelical Protestants.

I would argue that the gradual abandonment of Protestant street theatre has to be seen in the context of several important changes in the general cultural climate and not as a result of a change of attitude by evangelical Protestants. Paisley thinks it as important now as he did then to save any soul from the evil clutches of Catholicism. If such souls have ceased to be an important part of his presentations, it is because there are so many of them that they are no longer newsworthy, and because the general climate has shifted to produce so many other challenges to evangelical Protestantism. It is no longer a straight fight between Protestantism and Rome. The Protestants are beset by so many other threats, most of them related to the liberalization of Protestantism. As Paisley put it:

In those days people were Protestants. It was the natural thing. I mean, even the Clerk of the Belfast Presbytery was one of the referees [of the National Union of Protestants]. In all the denominations there was a sprinkling of good strong evangelical men and Protestants. And almost all the clergymen were in the Orange Order. We're living in a different Ulster today.

And it is an Ulster which probably would not care much if a young Catholic girl becomes a Free Presbyterian or if an ex-priest demonstrates the mass for the entertainment of a Protestant rally.

A Sociological Account of the Early Years

The bare facts of the early years of the Free Presbyterian Church have now been presented. A sociologist is interested in going beyond the particular in search of general patterns of motivation and action. The attempt to 'explain' the origins of the Free Church in any terms other than that it is the result of divine providence or God's good grace may at first sight appear to conflict with the Free Presbyterians' own version of events. They wish to say that this or that work began because God answered prayer; I wish to say that the same actions can be understood in terms of general principles of human social action. Fortunately, there is far less conflict between these two sorts of accounts than there might at first appear to be. Although all Free Presbyterians think that what has happened to their church is the result of divine providence, they do not rule out sociological generalizations. In fact, evangelicals interested in promoting revival have always been interested in making God's work easier for him by creating natural, this-worldly circumstances which are as fertile as possible. It should be made very clear that sociological explanation does not *compete* with religious explanation.[23] The sociologist has no special insight into the supernatural, and if we inadvertently stray into making judgements about the validity of this or that view of the divinity, then we should be ignored. My explanatory generalizations are concerned only with the natural empirical world and as such are quite compatible with most religious world-views. It may well be that the things I extract and offer as explanations are *also* God's providence. The sociologist has nothing to say about that.

Anyway, the test of the value of sociological explanation is not in the programmatic statements in which we say what it is we do, but in the doing of it, and to conclude this description of the early years let us consider whether it is possible to say anything of a general nature about why the Free Presbyterian Church attracted support in one place and not another. Why did these people and not others join?

The first obvious answer is that given by the critics of Paisley's work who are keen to point out that it thrives on divisions. Ravenhill, Crossgar, Cabra, and Rasharkin were all triggered by petty disputes: hair-styles in Ravenhill or a divorce case in Rasharkin. We can readily accept that these contingent disputes played their part, but to stop the story there is to miss the point. Protestantism is prone to such disputes. It is a sad fact that if God does speak to all men, he does not make his message very clear. The basic democratic nature of Presbyterianism encourages disputes and divisions because it has no source of authority other than the word of God, and the Bible is a resource which many people can draw on to justify competing ideas.[24] There is no centralized, well-legitimated structure for settling disputes or exercising social control. What the critics of the origins of the Free Church fail to notice is that trivial disputes in congregations are extremely common. At the same time as the tensions which led to people seceding in Cabra or Rasharkin were developing, there would have been hundreds of

<hr>

[23] For a technical discussion of the relationship between sociological accounts and the accounts of those people whose behaviour they intend to explain, see Roy Wallis and Steve Bruce, *Sociological Theory, Religion and Collective Action* (Belfast: The Queen's University of Belfast, 1986), Ch. 1.

[24] The reasons why Protestantism should be particularly prone to schism and fission are discussed in Steve Bruce, 'Authority and Fission: the Protestants' divisions', *British Journal of Sociology*, 36 (4) (1985), pp. 592–603.

similar conflicts elsewhere. Secondly, as has already been noted, those involved could have withdrawn from their local Presbyterian congregation and gone to another one. There was nothing in the particular disputes which goes beyond their role as catalysts to explain why the seceders went to Paisley. So to point to the conflicts in these congregations is only to explain why some people were disaffected or unsettled: it does not explain why they resolved their problems by moving in the particular direction in which they did.

In this sociological explanation of the origins of the Free Church, there seems to be no good reason to deny the accounts given by the actors themselves which point very clearly to the doctrinal issues. They wished to maintain an evangelical Presbyterianism and they felt motivated to separate from the Irish Presbyterian Church because they thought it was too deep in modernism to be redeemed.

But this raises the question of why only *these* particular groups came to that conclusion. If their reasons were well founded, why did lots of others not come to the same conclusion? There appear to be two answers to that question. The first is rather obvious. The sociological literature on the genesis of new social, religious, and political movements has clearly demonstrated the importance of a catalyst in stimulating in a population the concerns which the movements hope to mobilize. People do not suddenly and individually conclude that they should abandon one set of practices and adopt another: they need persuading. People may be objectively deprived of something or other and feel uncomfortable with some aspect of their world but before they can be recruited to a movement which presses for change to remove their deprivation, they need to become aware of their deprivation.[25] Before Irish Presbyterians could be recruited to a separatist witness, they

[25] The role which 'objective' circumstances play in the generation of discontent, and of collective action as the organized expression of that discontent, has exercised sociologists of social movements. Early work tended to assume that strains in the social structure automatically produced discontent. Later analysts, influenced more by symbolic interactionism than by structural sociology, argued that it was not so much objective circumstances as people's reactions to them which explained subsequent actions. Even something as brutally 'real' as poverty does not automatically produce discontent. People have first to become convinced that they should and can do something about their poverty before they can be recruited to some form of collective action. A new social movement must first convince people that there is a problem and then persuade them that it offers the best course of action to solve that problem. Thus a new movement not only 'taps' what discontent is already present, but also 'creates' discontent.

had to be convinced that their church was apostate. One simple answer then to 'why these people?' is that it was to these people that Paisley preached.

Market potential

Although Paisley's preaching was in theory directed to all sinners and not just to Christians or Presbyterians, it is obvious that his message would have its best reception among conservative Protestants. And such people were more easily found in rural areas. It is a well-reported general observation that secularization has its initial and greatest impact on the cities and on those people most heavily involved in the modern world of industrial production (see chapter 8). The basic pattern can be shown by identifying the three main social groups with the strongest commitment to organized religion in Britain (and most other industrial societies): women, country dwellers, and the *petite bourgeoisie*. In their different ways each of these three groups is removed from the urban industrial world. Women more often than men do not work outside the home. People in rural areas tend to be more remote from cosmopolitan culture and values. And small shopkeepers and 'lesser' professionals are also isolated from the secularizing influences of industrial culture. Ulster is no exception to these basic patterns of religiosity. Thus we would expect Paisley to have found his market in the small towns and villages of the country areas rather than in Belfast and its dormitory suburbs.

But not all country areas were equally fertile. As one might expect from the title of the new Church and the fact that Paisley's attacks on modernism were very much attacks on liberals and ecumenists in the Presbyterian Church, it was those country areas in which Presbyterians were a majority which were most receptive. One has to caution against anachronism here. It would be easy to read back from Paisley's later political successes as the spokesman for militant loyalism to suppose that his appeal would have been strongest to those Protestants who felt most *threatened* by Roman Catholics, nationalists, and republicans. Were that the case, we would expect him to have drawn support from the border areas. This was not so. In part, the 'threat' hypothesis fails because Ulster is such a small country. There are so many interfaces between Catholic and Protestant populations that it would be difficult to argue that certain Protestant populations felt much more threatened than did others. There is undoubtedly some truth in such an idea, and it did become more relevant later in Paisley's career (with, for example, the popularity of his paramilitary 'Third Force' in Fermanagh and Tyrone), but at this stage, when one is considering the early phase of church growth, it is obvious that it was those areas in which Presbyterians were *strongest*, rather than the ones where they were in a minority and hence might have felt more threatened, that Paisleyism had its initial appeal.

But even this analysis is incomplete. To this day, the Free Presbyterians have had only minimal impact on the Presbyterians west of the Bann, and this cannot be explained by the liberal nature of Presbyterianism in Fermanagh and west Tyrone. It is clear that the Presbyterians in these areas are every bit as conservative in their religious, social, and political attitudes as their co-religionists in the areas where Protestants are more numerous. Those ministers who work in this region recognize that their members are very close to the Paisleyites and yet have remained loyal to the Irish Presbyterian Church and rejected the argument that they should separate. Although I do not have overwhelming evidence for my argument, my feeling is that this can be explained by their distance from Belfast and urban culture. In my account of the Davey heresy trial, I suggested that a large number of west of the Bann Presbyterians shared Hunter's critique of Davey's modernism and yet would not vote against Davey, and I explained this ambiguity by pointing out that the Presbyterians who were furthest from Belfast and the apostasy of Assemblies College were in a better position to disagree with it and yet ignore it, than were those with more contact with the 'centre' of the church in Belfast. Their own minister was sound, and their own presbytery was sound, so the doubts about some other ministers somewhere else could be ignored. If that account is basically accurate, it can also offer an explanation for the pattern of initial formation and growth shown by the Free Presbyterian Church. In addition to the stimulating effect of Paisley's preaching, there is the principle of receptivity, and the Presbyterians who were most receptive to the message were those who were located in areas which were rural and hence conservative (the 'Bible Belt') but which were near enough to the 'centre' to be unable to ignore the modernizing influences of the liberals in Belfast and the theological college.

Of course, this underlying dynamic has to be qualified. While the general distribution of 'receptivity' might have followed the lines I suggest, receptivity could not display itself in actual recruitment while the fledgeling church was unable to provide the resources in terms of manpower to recruit people who were attracted by the message. At this stage in the Free Church's growth, its potential was being retarded by its inability to service the congregations which were asking to join. To return to the language of economic theory, the hypothetical demand probably so outstripped supply that a major explanation of the pattern of early growth is the evangelistic endeavours of particular ministers. The reason why new churches were formed in Coleraine and Limavady was part demand but largely supply, in that these works were pioneered by John Wylie from Cabra. Had Wylie been working elsewhere, he would probably have been successful in promoting congregations in Omagh, Dungannon or other such places.

At the start of this analysis it was suggested that supply played a major part in *creating* demand. Potential supporters had to be convinced that there was a problem of liberal apostasy in their church before they would consider leaving it to join another. And even if Paisley was energetic, he was not divisible. He could hold a week of meetings here or there and stimulate initial interest, but he needed a cadre of lieutenants to move in and service this interest on a regular basis. From the foundation of the Free Church, he had problems in recruiting competent professionals. As the careers of those ministers already mentioned show, even if he could find people willing to work with him, he had so little choice that he had to take anyone who shared his core objection to modernism. He could not afford to select only those who agreed with him on the whole range of doctrines and practices which gave the Free Church its ethos. Thus the growth of the Free Church was retarded until it could produce enough young men who had been thoroughly socialized within the Free Church and who were competent to give the new organization a solid foundation.

It should be noted that the quotations above from people explaining their conversion to the Free Church were made many years after the event and represent a refined and well-aired understanding of what they had been doing. At the time they were doing it, their understanding was far less coherent and capable of articulation. Although I have argued that the reasons for schism and attraction to the Free Church were primarily theological, it was clearly the case that the actors involved were unsure and ambiguous about their own motives and it was a number of years before a clear *shared* ideology emerged. Or, to put it another way, it was some time before Ian Paisley and the other core activists had convinced others into a commitment to a clear ideology.

Unlike the process of formation of some other schisms from a major Protestant church—the Free Church split from the Church of Scotland in 1843, for example—the foundation of Paisley's Free Presbyterian Church was uneven because it was not preceeded by a long period of popular and public dispute in which large numbers of people became convinced of the need for schism and then broke away in a concerted movement. In the Free Presbyterian Church case, what one sees is a series of small schisms and individual departures to the new body and an emerging sense of common identity and purpose. And such a process had its counterpart in the changing self-image of many of the key actors. I have already described Paisley's 1949 experience which filled him with a sense of mission. Bert Cooke, who was one of the first men to join the Free Church ministry, enrolled for the training course only reluctantly and only came to think of himself as a committed protesting Free Presbyterian when, as a student in charge of the Mount Merrion congregation, he was challenged by moderates in his congregation to oppose the Free Church's pickets of the Irish Presbyterian General Assembly. After serious thought and prayer, he concluded that Paisley was right: that a genuine Christian commitment required a willingness to publicly denounce apostasy.

As the key activists came to a commitment to aggressive evangelism and public protest, there was a weeding out, as some people who had a tentative commitment found that they did not want to pursue the narrow sectarian ideology of the Free Church. There was a considerable departure of members from Paisley's Ravenhill congregation. People left Mount Merrion when Bert Cooke committed himself to the protesting position. In Ballyhalbert, John Douglas found that many of those who had initially asked the Free Church for preaching offices were not prepared for the preaching they received. To describe the process in general terms, the Free Church was tapping a seam of discontent but the general unease of individuals and groups with what they were getting in the main churches had yet to be channelled into a coherent shared ideology and in the process of refining discontent, some people rejected Paisley's leadership and abandoned the fledgeling organization. Those who stayed through this period became convinced Free Presbyterians.

To summarize the story so far, by the start of the 1960s Paisley had moved from being a free-lance evangelical preacher to being the leader of a small Church largely made up of disaffected Irish Presbyterians. In size, the Free Presbyterian Church rivalled the small Evangelical Presbyterian Church which had grown out of James Hunter's split from the Irish Presbyterians after the Davey heresy trial. To understand the next phase in the history of the Free Church, we must shift our attention from theology and church disputes to the wider sphere of public reputation and political conflict.

3

The Prophet in the Political Wilderness

On the Margins of Unionism

From the first elections for the Stormont Parliament in 1921, the Unionist Party had dominated the politics of Ulster with a virtual monopoly of unionist votes.[1] Given the beleaguered state of Ulster, it is not surprising that there should be a high degree of cohesion among the Protestants, most of whom were members of either the Irish Presbyterian Church or the Church of Ireland. These two populations were then brought together in the fraternal Orange Order and the Order had a major say in the composition and policies of the Unionist Party. However, support for the Unionist Party was neither total nor uncritical. There has always been an independent unionist tradition on the edges and just outside the party, supported by two sorts of people. There was a working-class element, centred on the Shankill Road, West Belfast, which was suspicious of the élite nature of the Unionist Party's leadership and which campaigned for higher wages, better housing conditions, and various welfare provisions.[2] Although populist, this element was staunchly unionist, often more so than the leadership, and expected to be rewarded for the 'loyalty' of the Protestant working class. There was a second marginal element, this time province-wide, which was suspicious of the leadership, not because of its class interests but because of its lack of evangelical piety. This group wished to maintain and increase the evangelical

[1] For a history of the Unionist Party see J. F. Harbinson, *The Ulster Unionist Party, 1882–1973* (Belfast: Blackstaff Press, 1973). Although good on the details of the UUP, Harbinson's short description of Paisley's support is highly inaccurate. He stresses the urban working-class support for Protestant Unionism and fails to notice that both Paisley and Beattie were elected to Stormont for rural seats.

[2] Henry Patterson, *Class Conflict and Sectarianism* (Belfast: Blackstaff Press, 1980); Sarah Nelson, *Ulster's Uncertain Defenders: loyalists and the Northern Ireland conflict* (Belfast: Appletree Press, 1984), pp. 27–47.

religious element in 'Protestantism'. Like the populists, the pious Protestants were profoundly opposed to Irish nationalism and republicanism and hence tended to be aggressive in defence of the Union with Britain.

The two independent unionist members at Stormont during Paisley's early days in Belfast were Tommy Henderson (Belfast North and then Belfast Shankill) and 'D. I.' Nixon (Belfast Woodvale). Nixon was a District Inspector in the Royal Irish, later Royal Ulster, Constabulary who was sacked in 1924 for making a fiercely unionist speech at an Orange function. In 1929 he won his Woodvale seat which he held until his death in 1949.[3] Henderson made his reputation as a spokesman for the working classes of Belfast against the economic policies of the Unionist governments of the 1930s.

Ian Paisley had been born into the rural pious Orange tradition of politicized Protestantism in County Armagh. His grandfather and great grandfather had both been long serving District Masters and his father had been an Ulster Volunteer. Hence it is no surprise that, within two years of arriving in Belfast, Paisley was felt in politics. In 1949, cross-border influences were felt in the Northern Ireland elections. De Valera's Republicans decided to contest seats in the North and thus allowed Prime Minister Brooke to present the election as a plebiscite on partition and the existence of Ulster. The presentation of that election as a popular referendum prevented a new populist attack on the Unionist government. Norman Porter, the general secretary of the National Union of Protestants and at that time still a close colleague of Ian Paisley, had been asked by a number of conservative clergymen to stand against the Minister for Education in order to protest against amendments to the Education Act which increased and regularized state funding of Catholic schools.[4] Once the Republican intervention had made the election into a plebiscite on partition, pressure was put on Porter to withdraw to avoid unionist vote splitting. He did so at the last moment when the Unionists agreed not to oppose Henderson.[5] Paisley, then a member of the Unionist Party, was asked to stand in the marginal Belfast Dock ward seat. He declined but agreed to

[3] Michael Farrell, *Northern Ireland: the Orange state* (London: Pluto Press, 1980), p. 346.

[4] David Harkness, *Northern Ireland since 1920* (Dublin: Helicon, 1985), p. 116.

[5] *Belfast Telegraph* (31 Jan. 1949).

campaign for T. L. Cole, and he and Norman Porter worked hard to produce an unexpected Unionist victory. Paisley was given much credit for the win but his commitment to the party was considerably eroded when the defeated Labour candidate was given a post in the Ministry of Agriculture.

From 1949 to the late 1950s, Paisley remained on the fringes of Unionist politics. His sympathies lay with the independents such as Henderson and Nixon (who at one point in the 1930s constituted, in the absence of the nationalists, the official opposition at Stormont), but the Unionists had not yet shown the degree of liberalism they were to show under O'Neill in the 1960s and Paisley confined himself to promoting various 'ginger group' enterprises on the margins of politics. One of these—Ulster Protestant Action—argued for preferential employment policies to favour loyal Protestants.[6] It also campaigned for what later became a symbolic division between 'extreme' and 'mainstream' unionists: the right to hold parades and marches.

Many of the misunderstandings of the conflict in Ulster stem from a narrow interpretation of the Protestant 'Ascendancy'. Many critics of the Orange state suppose that unionists followed the politics they did in order to maintain and increase their *material* position at the expense of the Catholic nationalist population. It is certainly true that a great deal of the competition between nationalists and unionists concerned the distribution of resources. Nationalists wanted their 'fair share'; unionists, especially in the working class, wanted those who were loyal and who supported the government to be rewarded for their support. But material resources are not the only things that matter to people. Both populations also competed for the prestige of their culture. In such a competition, the right to display or flaunt the symbols of one's own culture, even when it was almost certain to provoke a violent response from the other side, was a crucial right. At various times, the Unionist government attempted to curb such displays either by banning marches or by re-routeing them through areas with the same politics as the marchers. The more militant Protestants saw this as a weakness, a lack of will on the part of the government. It was now illegal to be a Protestant in a Protestant country. The result was periodic clashes between the government and organizations such as Protestant Action which insisted on the right

[6] David Boulton, *The UVF, 1966-73* (Dublin: Torc Books, 1973), p. 26.

to march where they wished. Porter and Paisley were frequently to be found leading such marches and various Ministers for Home Affairs found themselves being denounced by loyalists at Orange rallies.

The first Free Presbyterian involvement in an election was a classically *ad hoc* and reactive affair. Paisley had brought an ex-priest, Father J. J. Arrien, to Northern Ireland and Wylie booked the Ballymoney town hall for a meeting.

I had a poster done out and had it outside the town hall. I had it in big letters—'Father' Arrien (the father in inverted commas!) will preach on the blasphemy of the Romish Mass on such and such an evening—and the priest of the town, he went up to the council and objected to this and said that Wylie's a trouble maker.

Father Murphy, the local priest, was joined by the Church of Ireland and Presbyterian clergymen in his objections and the council decided to cancel Wylie's booking. Paisley's rebuttal of Murphy's claims to speak for the majority of local people was characteristically florid:

Priest Murphy, speak for your own bloodthirsty persecuting intolerant blaspheming political religious papacy but do not dare to pretend to be the spokesman of free Ulster men. You are not in the South of Ireland. . . . Go back to your priestly intolerance, back to your blasphemous masses, back to your beads, holy water, holy smoke and stinks and remember we are the sons of the martyrs whom your church butchered and we know your church to be *the mother of harlots* and the abominations of the earth.[7]

The meeting went ahead. Under the banner of Ulster Protestant Action, Paisley brought a double-decker busload of supporters and a flute band to swell the open-air rally. Before Arrien spoke, Paisley, in Lutheran style, nailed the following 'theses' to the town hall door.

We protest against the iniquitous decision of the Ballymoney Council in closing this hall to the message of Protestantism. We repudiate the lies of Priest Murphy, bachelor agent of a foreign power and brand as traitors all those associated with him and those who hastened to do his will. We affirm Article 31 of the church of our Gracious Lady Queen Elizabeth II that 'masses are blasphemous fables and dangerous deceits'.

It is worth dwelling on that short text, for it contains in brief,

7 *Revivalist*, 3 (11), pp. 1–2.

almost coded, form many of the key elements of anti-Catholicism. The false doctrines of Rome are attacked by repeating the judgement of the mass found in the Articles of the Episcopalian Church of England, of which the Queen is the head; thus correct religious belief is linked to loyalty to the monarch and the loyalty issue is again raised in describing the priest as the agent of 'a foreign power'. Sexual deviance is hinted at in the use of the term 'bachelor' which manages both to describe and to cast doubts on the celibate state of the priest, and the general honesty of Catholic priests is challenged by branding Murphy as a liar. Finally, there is the criticism of 'those associated with him', presumably the Protestant clergymen who shared his objections to the meeting, and there is the suggestion that they and the Ballymoney Council have been manipulated by Rome.

At the next elections to the Council, Wylie continued his protest by standing as a Protestant Unionist and he was elected.

The same year, 1958, Albert Duff, a Belfast Alderman and the superintendent of a small mission hall, stood for the Stormont Parliament in the Iveagh constituency. Duff had sat in the Belfast Corporation since 1946 as an official Unionist but he was now backed by Ulster Protestant Action as a protest against Maginess, the Attorney-General at the time of the Maura Lyons case. He failed to win. The same year Duff and another candidate won seats in the Belfast Corporation as 'Protestant Unionists'. Three years later, Protestant Action fielded six candidates for the Corporation; two were elected.

The sort of people who were attracted to the militant populist Protestantism of Protestant Action can be clearly seen from the occupations of the candidates. Three were shipyard workers, two were self-employed businessmen, and the sixth—Albert Duff— was a full-time Christian worker. The urban working class in an occupational area which had traditionally been dominated by Protestants, the *petite bourgeoisie*, and evangelical Protestants; these are the constituencies from which UPA drew support. What generalized the appeal of Paisley's critique of the unionist élites was the accession to power of Terence O'Neill.

Reformist Unionism

During the 1960s, under the leadership of Terence O'Neill, the Unionist Parliamentary Party found itself devoting an increasing amount of time to questions of economic and social reform. At the central government level at least, the traditional preoccupation with loyalist unity and the constitutional issue seemed to have been superseded by an active concern with setting up 'development' programmes. Indeed, political activity at a variety of levels showed signs of breaking out of the loyalist versus republican deadlock.[8]

Terence O'Neill was the son of a Westminster MP and country squire whose family owned large estates in North Antrim. Educated at Eton and then sent to Europe to improve himself, he worked for a short time in various jobs in 'the city' before becoming an ADC to the Governor of Australia. When war broke out he returned to England and was commissioned in the Irish Guards. At the end of the war, he returned to Ulster hoping to inherit one of the family's traditional seats and a career in politics. He was selected for the Bannside, North Antrim, constituency at Stormont and was returned unopposed to the Northern Ireland Parliament at a by-election in November 1946.

Like most of the Anglo-Irish, the O'Neills were Church of Ireland rather than Presbyterian and moderate in their religion. His autobiography makes it clear that Terence O'Neill had no sympathy with what he saw as parochial unionism. The Orange marches during what his cousin Phelim O'Neill (Westminster MP for North Antrim) called 'the silly season' meant nothing to him. Being a unionist meant being British or, more exactly, English, rather than being anti-nationalist and anti-Catholic. His values were those of cosmopolitan, highly educated, and cultured London society. In his Stormont career, and especially during his period as Minister of Finance, O'Neill gradually developed a liberal reforming unionism in which the pettier aspects of conflict between the two populations would be removed and Protestants and Catholics would work together to modernize the Northern Ireland economy.

Nationalist critics of O'Neill such as Michael Farrell believe that the O'Neill administration was more reformist in its rhetoric than it was in reality. The B Specials were not disbanded, nothing was done to reverse the gerrymandering of local government boundaries, and the great new development plans were side-tracked by traditional Orange discrimination. The new university was not created in the obvious place—Magee College, Londonderry.

[8] Belinda Probert, *Beyond Orange and Green: the political economy of the Northern Ireland crisis* (Dublin: The Academy Press, 1978).

Instead it was put in the Protestant town of Coleraine. The new town development was not sited on Londonderry but between the largely Protestant towns of Lurgan and Portadown.[9]

Certainly one would have to agree that O'Neill did little to change either the reality or Catholic perceptions of their subordinate position in the polity and the economy but his failure almost certainly owed more to his lack of power than to his lack of desire. Farrell uses the fact that O'Neill joined the Apprentice Boys of Derry and the Royal Black Preceptory (two Protestant fraternal organizations similar to the Orange Order) to portray him as a 'closet' die-hard unionist but in so doing misses the glaring point that O'Neill had to join these organizations because he was not *already* a member. Any genuinely orthodox unionist would have been a member since late adolescence! O'Neill's suspect views were known to many unionists and the conservatives did not have to wait for the fruits of O'Neillism, however timid they may have been. They already *knew* that he was a man who could not be trusted to preserve the Union and to safeguard the social superiority of Protestant culture. His subsequent actions in office, however little they may have done to encourage serious Catholic commitment to the Ulster state, were enough to confirm the conservative Protestant suspicion that O'Neill was another Lundy, prepared to follow the original by opening the gates of unionist Ulster's walls to the disloyal Catholics and the Irish Republic.

To appreciate the impact that O'Neill had on Ulster, it is important to bear in mind the power of *symbols*. Material realities may be profound sources of satisfaction or discontent but it is more often symbols which signal to people their own position, their own worth, and their own precariousness. Working-class Protestants had some material advantages over their Catholic competitors and enjoyed preferential treatment in housing and local government employment but these advantages were sometimes marginal and were not often *felt* to be considerable advantages because the Protestants did not sit down to statistical comparisons of their standards of living with the opportunities of Catholics. What was more important was the status of certain symbols. A Sandy Row shipyard worker told Sarah Nelson: 'What did politics mean? Flags, parades, the red, white and blue, that's what you remember.'[10] When Prot-

[9] The case that O'Neill's reformist claims were hollow is made by Farrell, op. cit., pp. 240–1.

[10] Nelson, op. cit., p. 10.

estants did accept that they enjoyed material advantages over the Catholic population, they argued that these were their just rewards for loyalty. Why should rebels who would not commit themselves to the support of the state enjoy its fruits? If Protestants were superior, it was because they deserved to be. They had the right religion, they were hard-working, and had small families which they could afford to keep in decent circumstances. They drank less and saved instead of gambling away their earnings. And they had fought for their country in 1939 when the Irish Republic remained neutral which was, after all, just what one could expect of rebels who had taken advantage of Britain's involvement in the First World War to stage the 1916 Easter Rising.

While O'Neill would have shared some of those views, he was more concerned with the future than with the past and he deliberately set about ending Ulster's 'petty apartheid' by visiting Catholic schools (no previous Ulster premier had ever set foot in one), being photographed talking to priests and nuns, and meeting a cardinal. He then offered the greatest possible affront to traditional unionism by inviting Sean Lemass, the Prime Minister of the Republic, to visit Stormont! Whether Terence O'Neill was committed to promoting the sorts of reforms which might have satisfied the Catholic minority is unknown. What is obvious is that he was sufficiently removed from traditional unionism to be quite happy to ignore its symbols and its sacred history in favour of elements of an instrumental and rational view of politics. Whatever his standing with Catholics (and for a short time it was high), he was set on a collision course with the representatives of traditional unionism and with no representative more so than Ian R. K. Paisley.

Courts and Confrontations

The commitment of Paisley and his supporters to protesting against both religious apostasy and political compromise ensured that the movement would eventually be confronted by the legal powers of the state. In 1957, Paisley and Wylie were charged with causing a disturbance in Donaghadee by preaching through a loud hailer. The charges were thrown out by the magistrate. Paisley's second court appearance resulted from him, Wylie, and Harold V. Magowan, the short-lived Free Presbyterian minister of Antrim,

heckling Donald Soper in Ballymena. Soper was displeasing to the
Free Presbyterians for a number of reasons—his commitment to
ecumenism, his left-wing politics—but more than anything it was
his rationalism which provoked the ire of conservatives. Soper was
firmly in the tradition of those liberals who tried to make the
Christian gospel more acceptable to 'modern man' by explaining
away the supernatural and miraculous elements. He believed, for
example, that Christ had been conceived in the normal way and
then sanctified by God rather than being born of a virgin. The
three Free Presbyterian ministers and their supporters heckled
Soper's open-air meeting in Ballymena so persistently that the
police had to intervene and the meeting was abandoned. They were
later charged with disorderly conduct and fined.

The fines created so much public interest that, on the following
Sunday, the Ravenhill Church 'was packed half an hour before the
service began and throughout the proceedings men climbed onto
the windows to listen and people thronged the open doors and
queued out in the street at the back and side of the church'.[11] The
audience heard Paisley denounce Soper for his blasphemies, the
Methodist Church for not opposing them, and the government for
misusing the law to punish legal protest. In concluding he promised to go to prison rather than pay his fine.

His choice was blocked by the pro-government *Unionist* newspaper which paid his fine for him. In a defence of the action which
recognized the emotive nature of the case, the *Unionist* said:

Dr Paisley could not foresee that he would be in gaol during the throes of
a general election. The cause of Northern Ireland must be greater than
the individual and it would mean a very unfavourable hearing for many
government speakers which would give the wrong impression. Such a
thing would cause repercussions far and wide.[12]

In other words, while leading government spokesmen publicly
derided the Free Presbyterians as a trouble-making minority,
others with the interests of the Unionist Party at heart appreciated
that Paisley's militant stand was popular enough to cause problems
if his challenge was accepted.

Paisley's third appearance in court resulted from a protest
against Rome rather than against liberal Protestants. In June 1963,

[11] *Northern Whig* (7 Sept. 1959).
[12] Reprinted in the *Revivalist* (Sept.–Oct. 1959).

Pope John XXIII, the Pope who had called the second Vatican Council, died. O'Neill sent the following message of condolence to Cardinal Conway, the Vicar Capitular of the archdiocese of Armagh: 'Please accept from the Government of Northern Ireland our sympathy on the great loss which your Church sustained on the death of your Spiritual Leader. He had won wide acclaim throughout the world because of his qualities of kindness and humanity.'[13]

The Lord Mayor of Belfast had the Union Jack on the City Hall lowered to half-mast. Paisley reacted quickly by calling a rally in the Ulster Hall and then leading a march to the City Hall to protest 'at the lying eulogies now being paid to the Roman antichrist by non-Romanist Church leaders in defiance of their own historic creeds'.[14] For Paisley, the issue was both religious and constitutional. The Revolution settlement which formulated the basis for the offering of the British crown to William of Orange in 1689 asserted that British freedoms and liberties could not be safeguarded under a 'popish' prince and closed a number of public offices, including the monarchy, to Catholics. Although the nineteenth century had seen almost all restrictions on Catholics removed, the loyalists of Ulster still believed that to accept the authority of the Pope was to open the way to papal domination and the erosion of civil liberty. When this is combined with the fact that the Republic was an overwhelmingly Catholic country whose constitution recognized the special superordinate position of the Catholic Church, it is easy to see how any state recognition of the Pope or the Catholic hierarchy could be seen as a 'constitutional' issue. The liberals regarded sending telegrams of condolence as a polite gesture. The conservatives saw it as just another step in a 'Romeward' march, and every such step had to be protested.

Paisley, Councillor James McCarroll (a Protestant Unionist Councillor and an elder of the Free Presbyterian Church), and three other Protestant Action activists were summonsed for holding a march without giving the statutory notice to the police and fined £5. For an insight on the complex intertwining of religious, political, and constitutional elements, it is worth quoting at length from a newspaper account which, despite some odd punctuation and grammar, gives the gist of Paisley's speech:

[13] Terence O'Neill, *The Autobiography of Terence O'Neill: Prime Minister of Northern Ireland 1963–1969* (London: Hart-Davis, 1972), p. 50.
[14] *Revivalist* (July 1963.)

He referred to the Bible that had been presented to him by the people of Memel St on July 10 at the opening of their march. He said that 'the powers that be' had presented him with a summons and the Protestant people had presented him with that book and he thought a parallel could be drawn between the two. The rank and file of the Ulster people are still loyal to the core, but he declared 'we have been badly led, both politically and religiously'. He then declared that he and those with him on the platform had pledged themselves to pay no fines and refused to be bound over, 'and we have authorised no one to pay these fines for us. Any Protestant who does so will be a Lundy and a traitor. We are ready to take any penalty Mr Mills desires to place upon us'.

He declared by this determination, Ulster is going to see that Protestantism is neither dead nor buried but is on the march. There was a time, let it ever be remembered, only about 400 years ago, when our fathers were ruled over and tyrannised and when men like Calvin, Knox, Cranmer, Ridley and Latimer broke rather than bend for the Gospel and liberty. Mr Paisley declared that Ulster was in terrible jeopardy. We are losing our liberties and our heritage and he declared 'I tremble what Ulster will be like when the children in our homes reach the years I have reached. Our gospels and their preachers are being assaulted and insulted. Men who have preached for years in the city streets are now under the intimidation of RUC sergeants and police constables'. Continuing a long and impassioned address, Mr Paisley said 'If the Roman Catholic Church flew the Union Jack at their chapel I would have no objection, and when they wished to pull it down was their business and their property, but the City Hall was our property'.[15]

Here then was the world as it appeared to Paisley. Disloyal Catholics did not fly the Union Jack. Protestants who should have known better paid tribute to the Antichrist, the spiritual leader of the disloyal Catholics. Orthodox Protestants doing no more than exercising their democratic right to protest against the paying of tribute to the Antichrist were taken to court and fined. And the final but crucial element: this scenario was contrasted with the government's failure to punish rebels. In the *Revivalist* which carried the reports, Paisley added that, while loyal Protestants were charged for a peaceful protest, rebels could attack an open-air evangelistic meeting in Dunloy and get off. The end of the story is an anti climax. The Free Presbyterians' fines were paid by an anonymous donor.

[15] *Northern Whig* (25 July 1963). The mention of attacks on the clergy is a reference to the assault on John Wylie in Dunloy where he was addressing an outdoor meeting for the Christian Workers Union.

Although this dispute was ostensibly about Protestant dominated councils paying tribute to the Pope, the real contest was
between O'Neill and Paisley. In his biography, O'Neill mentions
his innovation in sending the government's condolences and explains the Lord Mayor's action as 'responding to the general atmosphere'; an atmosphere which O'Neill was helping to create.[16]
When the fines were paid and Paisley's martyrdom postponed, he
responded by sending a telegram to O'Neill: 'Congratulations to
you, the Minister of Home Affairs, the Crown solicitor, the Police
and the Unionist Lord Mayor, on not permitting your own law
to take its course, and on arranging for my fine to be paid. NO
SURRENDER!'

The public confrontations continued. Despite putting up Protestant Unionists against specific Unionists, Paisley was still willing
to work with the Unionist Party provided the candidate was acceptable. In the 1964 Westminster election in West Belfast, Paisley
and Desmond Boal (whose Stormont constituency was en-
compassed by the Westminster seat) backed the Unionist candidate, James Kilfedder. Sinn Fein were contesting the seat and a
tricolour, the flag of the Irish Republic, was flown in the window
of the Sinn Fein election office in Divis St. Although the Flags
and Emblems Act made such displays illegal, the RUC had often
ignored them if they were in nationalist areas. On this occasion,
Paisley made sure that the display was not ignored. At a meeting
in the Ulster Hall, he insisted that if the RUC did not go in and
remove the offensive flag, then he would do it himself. The RUC
moved in and triggered what Farrell describes as the worst rioting
since 1935.[17]

In the same year, Protestant Action again fielded candidates for
the Belfast Corporation. Paisley, with Ivan Foster and William
Beattie, two student ministers of the Free Church, was active in
campaigning for them. After all, one of them was Mrs Eileen
Paisley, who was standing against the outgoing Lord Mayor to
protest his papist flag-lowering. She was roundly defeated by a
ratio of two votes to one and the only Actionists elected were the
two sitting members in the St George's ward, which took in the
fiercely loyalist area of Sandy Row.[18]

[16] O'Neill, op. cit., p. 50.
[17] Farrell, op. cit., p. 234.
[18] Ian Budge and Cornelius O'Leary, *Belfast: approach to crisis—a study of
Belfast politics, 1613-1970* (London: Macmillan, 1973), p. 158.

1966: O'Neill Must Go!

As the general direction of O'Neill's policies became clear, conservative Protestants began to organize against him. The conflict operated on two different levels: in the party and on the streets. Unionists who opposed his policies, such as Sir Knox Cunningham, the Westminster MP for South Antrim, spoke against O'Neill both in public and in the councils of the Unionist Party. Those people who did not have access to that sort of platform took their protests onto the streets and it was here that Ian Paisley and his followers earned their public reputation. As the examples already given illustrate, most of the protests concerned what the conservatives saw as government weakness. Any event which celebrated Catholic, nationalist, or republican culture and history was to be opposed. This was especially the case if it appeared that government legislation was being flouted. The rioting in West Belfast which followed the RUC's removal of a tricolour from Divis St in 1964 has already been mentioned. The loyalists saw the toleration of 'rebel' meetings as being the first signs of weakness which would only encourage the nationalists in their campaign to destroy Northern Ireland. If the government would not prevent such acts of rebellion, then the loyalists would take action themselves. As often as not, the government would then act against the loyalists to prevent the increase in tension. The loyalists would then interpret the government's actions as being proof that there was one law for the nationalists and another for the loyalists.

A classic clash of symbols occurred in April when the government took no action to prevent the 1916 Easter Rising being commemorated in Belfast. This is O'Neill's account:

Considering that Belfast was not involved in that event fifty years previously one might have hoped that those so minded to would have contented themselves with attending the ceremony in Dublin, less than a hundred miles away. But all indications were that there was no prominent Catholic prepared to give a lead in the interests of peace. I decided to form a committee consisting of all former Ministers of Home Affairs under my chairmanship and between us we survived the celebrations.[19]

O'Neill survived but as he goes on to record: 'The Catholic streets in Belfast became and remained a forest of Irish Republican flags for the duration of the celebrations.'[20] Nothing could have been

[19] O'Neill, op. cit., pp. 78–9.
[20] Ibid.

more galling to the Protestants. In their view, the cowardly IRA had taken advantage of the fact that Britain was involved in a world war to stage their rebellion and to murder Protestants. Paisley responded with public protest meetings and a march of over 6,000 loyalists to the City Hall Cenotaph where Councillor James McCarroll, a Protestant Unionist and an elder of Paisley's church, laid a wreath: 'In memory of the members of the UVF, RUC and other civilian population [*sic*] who died in defence of the Ulster Constitution at the hands of Rebel Forces during and since the 1916 rising.'[21]

Although there was as yet no sign that the IRA was capable of mounting the sort of offensive which followed four years later, Paisley had no doubt where O'Neill's reforming policy would lead:

Capt Terence O'Neill . . . will soon have to make up his mind whether he intends to appease the Republican minority or serve the vast so-called extremist majority. Surely he does not seriously think that appeasement will stop the IRA attacks or the cries of discrimination. Or is he secretly selling us to the South?[22]

This latter possibility had been uppermost in loyalist minds since January of the previous year when O'Neill had broken with all previous precedent and invited Sean Lemass to Stormont. While O'Neill and his supporters represented that visit as the Republic's *de facto* recognition that the North did exist as a separate entity and that doing necessary economic business with the North meant the Republic attenuating its claims to the territory of Ulster, the conservative Protestants saw it as an horrendous betrayal of the history and sacrifice of Ulster Protestants. As a betrayal, it had, for the political sphere, the same symbolic quality as leaders of the Protestant churches welcoming the Pope. Opening Catholic schools was bad enough but consorting with the head of the Dublin government was entirely beyond the pale for loyalists.

Symbols were again at issue in the controversy in 1966 over the name for the new bridge over the Lagan in Belfast. The city council planned to call it the 'Queen Elizabeth Bridge' but the more assertive Protestants wanted a memorial to Lord Carson.

So angry was Ian Paisley at the affront to Carson's memory that he increased his tirade of abuse against O'Neill, produced Carson's son to

21 *Protestant Telegraph* (5 May 1966).
22 *Protestant Telegraph* (18 June 1966).

contest the Westminster elections in March (promising four Protestant Unionists in all) and only withdrew when he realised how devoid of constituency organization he then was.[23]

The rudiments of a constituency organization were then provided. As is so often the case in Paisley's career, the crucial step was taken by someone other than Paisley and then offered to Paisley as an opportunity the possibilities of which he could appreciate. Noel Doherty, a committed loyalist, had been a member of Paisley's congregation since 1956. He became a member of Protestant Action and founded Paisley's printing enterprise. In 1966 he suggested the formation of the Ulster Constitution Defence Committee: a body of twelve loyalists chaired by Paisley and quickly nicknamed 'the twelve disciples'.[24] Linked to the UCDC would be the Ulster Protestant Volunteers which would provide a province-wide structure for rank-and-file supporters. Despite adopting some of the paramilitary trappings of the old Carson Ulster Volunteers, the UPV made significant efforts to discipline the movement and separate it from illegal violence. Boulton records that the constitution provided that: 'any member associated with, or giving support to, any subversive or lawless activities whatsoever shall be expelled from the body. The chairman of the UCDC has vested in him full authority to act in such cases.'[25] However good the intentions behind the drafting of that section of the constitution, some members of the Ulster Protestant Volunteers did not share the chairman's stated views about violence. James Murdoch, a Free Presbyterian and a member of the Loughgall UPV, introduced Noel Doherty to James Marshall, a quarryman who said he could provide explosives, and Doherty arranged a meeting between Marshall and a member of the Shankill Road UVF. Although Paisley drove Doherty to his first meeting with Murdoch and Marshall, there is no evidence that he was himself involved in the discussions. The strongest link between the UPV and illegal acts of violence came with a series of bombings in 1969 which, ironically, the *Protestant Telegraph* was quick to blame first on the IRA and then on the Eire government. In fact, they had been organized by members of the Ulster Protestant Volunteers. The explosions in March and April of 1969 at an electricity sub station in Castlereagh

[23] Harkness, op. cit., p. 147.
[24] Boulton, op. cit., p. 28.
[25] Ibid.

and at the Silent Valley reservoir in the Mournes were followed by an explosion at an electricity sub-station over the border in County Donegal. In this case, the device seems to have exploded early and Thomas McDowell, a member of the Kilkeel Free Presbyterian Church and the South Down UPV, was fatally wounded.[26]

Although a number of members of the UPV were charged with these explosions, all the cases failed because juries were not convinced by the evidence of an Ulster Protestant Volunteer who turned police informer. It is important to note that it was only the statements of this man and his wife which contained any evidence of Paisley's knowledge of the crimes, and the juries determined that they were not trustworthy witnesses. The view of Paisley's critics was that he was implicated but was clever enough to avoid any direct contact. Others maintained that, even if he knew nothing of these crimes, he was morally responsible in that he had contributed substantially to the general climate which allowed members of his organization to believe that such acts were justified in order to destabilize the government of Terence O'Neill. This second charge is impossible to evaluate. While it is certainly the case that Paisley was prepared to use militant rhetoric in denouncing O'Neillism, it is also the case that he was a vocal critic of private initiative in vigilantism and of attacks on Catholics. When a young Catholic barman was murdered by loyalists in Malvern Street in 1966, Paisley was quick to announce:

Like everyone else, I deplore and condemn this killing, as all right-thinking people must. Incitement, direct or indirect, must be treated with the full rigour of the law. Under the Special Powers Act the government has the full authority to act and has failed to do so. If it continues to abdicate its responsibilities then the British government must act immediately in its place.[27]

This and other statements were clear enough, and it seems a little one-sided to attribute causal power to one set of statements—those which encouraged Protestants to reject the O'Neill government—

[26] Ibid. Contains an account of these and other incidents involving the UPV which fairly represents what is known from the statements made by Doherty and others. Marshall was found guilty and fined £200 for conspiring with Doherty to provide explosives. James Murdoch was found not guilty of the same charges. See *Belfast Telegraph* (19 Oct. 1966).

[27] Boulton, op. cit., p. 51.

and yet deny causal power to those statements which called for such rejection to be confined within the limits of legality.

If the perceptions of Paisley's critics are revealing of their underlying attitudes, the same could be said for the perceptions of his supporters. Paisley has always provoked strong emotions. To his critics, 'Hell won't be full until he's in it', as one old Catholic lady put it. For many of his supporters he could do no wrong and any semblance of wrong having been done was explained as part of the ecumenical conspiracy to defeat true Protestantism. Thus County Armagh Free Presbyterians, looking back on the explosives cases and the charges laid against Free Presbyterians, recollected that far from supposing these people might be guilty and hence in need of church discipline, they assumed their innocence and believed that the charges were just another part of the plot to discredit Paisleyism.

Such a view was made easy by the reliance of the police on informers of dubious character. In the cases against the Shankill Road UVF, the police case rested considerably on 'verbal' statements, supposedly made to the police, which the witnesses refused to repeat in court. One of these entered the popular literature and is still repeated by journalists, despite the fact that Hugh McClean, who, in admitting his part in the Shankill UVF killings, is supposed to have said: 'I am terribly sorry I ever heard of that man Paisley or decided to follow him', later denied making such a statement to the police.[28] The extensive use of 'supergrasses' in the eighties has made many people sceptical of informers and verbal statements, but such scepticism was far less widespread in the 1960s, and the impression that Paisley was heavily involved in illegal acts became common.

In truth, all that can be said is that, in both the Free Presbyterian Church and in the UPV, there were a small number of people (none of whom were figures of any stature in the Church) who were prepared to abet others in the commission of crimes to further the aims which the vast majority of people in the Church and UPV wished to see promoted by less violent means. On his release from prison in 1985, Gusty Spence, the leader of the Shankill UVF and the man convicted of the Malvern St murder, was asked about

---

[28] According to the police evidence, this statement was made by McClean in custody. In court McClean, through his counsel, denied this and other statements which the police attributed to him. See Boulton, op. cit., p. 54.

Paisley's role and he was frankly dismissive: 'I have no time for Paisley's type of religious fervour or his politics but he had no involvement in re-forming the UVF though he stirred up a lot of tension at that time for his own ends.'[29]

The General Assembly Protest

On 6 June, Paisley, this time wearing his church leader hat, clashed with the police when he led members of the Free Presbyterian Church to picket the Irish Presbyterians' General Assembly. In previous years, the Free Presbyterians had gathered outside the Assembly Hall for their picket, which was almost an annual event. This time, Paisley filed notice with the RUC that he intended to lead a march from his church at the bottom of the Ravenhill Road, across the Albert Bridge, and through Cromac Square *en route* to the city centre and the Assembly Hall. Accounts of why this route was chosen vary. One marcher thought that it had been deliberately chosen to be provocative; others suggested that it was simply the most direct route. Most thought nothing of it, and clearly the RUC did not anticipate any trouble. They did not suggest re-routeing the parade. The fact that many of the Free Presbyterian marchers were women and children suggests that they were equally sanguine.

A mob of young Catholics was waiting at Cromac Square, armed with a good supply of bricks and metal objects to hurl at the marchers. The police called for reinforcements and struggled to keep the rioters back. In view of the subsequent controversy, it is an important point to note that the Free Presbyterians did not retaliate but maintained their composure under a considerable volley of missiles. As film footage of the riot clearly showed, the rioting was exclusively Catholic against RUC.

When the Free Presbyterians arrived at the Assembly Hall in

[29] *Shankill Bulletin* (31 May 1985). A problem with this sort of account, of course, is that it is informed by people's *present* interests, and not simply by a desire to establish a correct record of the past. Some of those loyalists who came to dislike Paisley blame him for their acts of violence. Others play down Paisley's part. Most contemporary observers believe that the attack on the civil rights marchers at Burntollet Bridge was led by members of Paisley's Ulster Protestant Volunteers, and one can even find a student for the Free Presbyterian ministry announcing that the UPV would see the march stopped (*Belfast Telegraph*, 31 Mar. 1969). Yet *Loyalist News*, 2 (51), edited by John McKeague, praised Ronald Bunting for his part in stopping the march and did not even mention Paisley: a reflection of the animosity between Paisley and McKeague.

Fisherwick Place, the police threw a rope across the road and stopped the march. Paisley about faced and led the parade around the block so that it now came upon Fisherwick Place from the west. In his evidence at the subsequent trial, Paisley maintained that he did this to keep the parade moving and hence diffuse tension. The Paisleyites now flanked both sides of a rope-way stretched between the Assembly Hall and the other Presbyterian building across the street. When the Moderator and the other dignatories came out of the Assembly to cross the road, they found themselves flanked by a crowd of Free Presbyterians shouting anti-ecumenical slogans and waving placards.

In retrospect, the events of that afternoon seem trivial, but the combination of stone-throwing rioters and Paisleyites abusing the dignatories of the Irish Presbyterian Church and the Governor of Northern Ireland and his wife triggered a considerable wave of anti-Paisley feeling. The emotions raised by the events quickly led to considerable confusion in the media and Stormont about just who did what. The *Newsletter* ran the story under the headline:

BATONS IN CITY STREET BATTLE: EIGHT ARRESTED AFTER
CLASHES
PAISLEY MARCH MEETS MOB VIOLENCE
GOVERNOR FACES STORM OF ABUSE

Already in this presentation there is the possibility of ambiguity. We have 'clashes' and 'mob violence' but apart from the Governor we have only one named agent: 'Paisley'. There is no specific mention of Catholics as rioters. By the time Terence O'Neill returned from London to face press questioning on what he intended to do to quell the violence, there was a general notion abroad that it was the Paisleyites who had been violent.[30]

The process of attributing the blame to Paisley continued the next day with a debate in Stormont in which a Labour member said:

[30] This fundamental distortion has become part of the historical record. Liam De Paor, *Divided Ulster* (Harmondsworth, Middx: Penguin, 1971), p. 154, says that Paisley and his supporters went to the General Assembly 'to attack and insult Lord Erskine (Governor of Northern Ireland) and Lady Erskine' and that 'a brief but violent riot occurred on the way'. He thus manages to suggest (without any evidence) that the original purpose of the march was the insulting of Lord Erskine and, by failing to mention that the Paisleyites were attacked by Catholics and did not respond, he leaves it open to the reader to suppose that the Paisleyites were involved in the rioting.

The attack last evening was mainly directed against the Presbyterian Church. The parade was making for the Assembly Hall. I am quite sure that the Moderator and his colleagues will be able to withstand any theological attack directed by the Rev. Ian Paisley, but when it approaches physical violence this is another matter.[31]

Here again the images are being confused. A wide variety of things could be construed as 'approaching' violence but to use that expression while condemning the violence of the previous day and to do so in a critique of Paisley while failing to mention the Cromac Square rioters is to exaggerate. News film of the General Assembly disturbance shows much shouting and placard waving but nothing that comes near the sort of heckling and barracking to which present-day government ministers are regularly subjected in visits to the north of England![32]

When O'Neill returned from a meeting with Harold Wilson in London, he reacted in a manner guaranteed to confirm the Free Presbyterians' claims that O'Neill's policies were designed to achieve in the political sphere what the ecumenical movement was trying to do in inter denominational co-operation. He delivered a strong attack on Paisley and sent his Minister for Home Affairs to the General Assembly to apologize for the demonstration and to promise that 'the Government will take all possible steps to prevent a recurrence of such indignities to the Head of this great church and his distinguished guests'.[33]

On 15 June, the House of Commons in Stormont met to debate a motion urging action to preserve law and order. After other speeches condemning Ian Paisley, Terence O'Neill rose and delivered a long statement in which he made it clear that he regarded the defeat of Ian Paisley as a central part of his reforming Unionism. For him, Paisleyism and republicanism were allies, both movements bent on destroying Northern Ireland through the stir-

[31] Stormont *Hansard*, House of Commons (7 June 1966), p. 26.

[32] It is common for critics of Paisley to exaggerate the violence of the gathering outside the General Assembly buildings by referring to Lady Erskine's subsequent nervous indisposition. See, for example, Eric Gallagher and Stanley Worrall, *Christians in Ulster, 1968–80* (Oxford: Oxford University Press, 1980), p. 18. In fairness to the Paisleyites, it should be remembered that the attacks they suffered in Cromac Square involved actual stones. Their own 'violence' was entirely verbal.

[33] 'Speech by Mr R. W. B. McConnell, MP, Minister of Home Affairs, at the General Assembly of the Presbyterian Church in the Assembly Hall, Belfast, on Thursday, 9 June, 1966, at 10.30 am', Northern Ireland Information Service press release.

ring up of community strife. He was able to marshal the support of the Grand Master of the Orange Order who had previously condemned Paisley's extremism. And he reinforced the concern which underpinned his whole political philosophy: the need to placate Westminster:

Do we want or can we afford to alienate our British friends? Do the mindless individuals who use unspeakable language in the streets and hurl vile insults at Her Majesty's representatives and other dignatories ever pause to reflect that our standard of living, our Welfare State services . . . our economic health all depend on our links with Great Britain?[34]

Only one member of the House was in any way sympathetic to Ian Paisley. In a brilliant and witty, though unappreciated, speech, Desmond Boal QC did his best to clarify the events of 6 June. He reminded the House that the police had been given forty-eight hours notification of the proposed route: 'Honourable members on this side of the House who in this respect are charging him [Paisley] with gross civic and social irresponsibility must also charge the police with exactly the same thing.' The critics had argued that the Paisleyites had provoked the Catholic population of the Markets with the anti-Romanist slogans on their placards. Boal reminded the House that the parade did not pass through any Catholic areas:

If their argument is worth tuppence it means that the people in the Markets area must have been aware of the inscriptions . . . before they in fact took the steps they did. It is perfectly clear that long before the procession came into sight, long before the procession had formed, these people in the Markets in their desire to be offended had come down from the side streets and had taken great trouble to be offended, and not only were prepared to be offended but were prepared to throw missiles, stones and other weapons . . . There is not a suggestion that one of these missiles were returned; there is not one suggestion which can be made by anybody, no matter how evilly disposed he is to the organizer of the procession or to the purpose of the procession, that any violence was offered by a member of that procession.[35]

For his pains in defending Paisley, Boal was fired from his lucrative job as counsel to the Attorney-General.[36]

[34] Stormont *Hansard*, House of Commons (15 June 1966), p. 309.

[35] Ibid., pp. 359–62.

[36] W. D. Flackes, *Northern Ireland: a political directory, 1968–79* (Dublin: Gill and Macmillan; New York: St Martin's Press, 1980), p. 28.

Whether or not the procession from the Ravenhill Church and the barracking of the Presbyterian Church Assembly had been designed to constitute a direct challenge to the government, things were moving rapidly in that direction. Paisley, John Wylie, and Ivan Foster, with two others, one a Protestant Action Councillor and the other a staunch old loyalist lady from the Shankill Road, were charged with public order offences. Two thousand supporters marched to the Belfast Magistrates' Court with the accused who were all found guilty. After some discussion, Paisley, Wylie, and Foster decided to refuse to pay their fines and to go to gaol. As had happened previously, the fines were paid anonymously but the magistrates had made it impossible for an outsider to defuse the situation on this occasion by also binding them over to keep the peace. They refused to sign the bond, arguing that to do so would prevent them from making *any* public protests. On 20 July, Paisley, Wylie, and Foster entered Crumlin Road prison.

Someone who had worked closely with Ian Paisley in the 1950s claimed that he had once joked that the only way they would get anywhere would be if they went to gaol for the Protestant cause. Whether or not the story is true, there is no doubt that the imprisonment was a major breakthrough for both religious and political Paisleyism. Different sorts of supporters reacted in different ways. The young urban loyalists took to the streets:

There was a serious riot with Loyalists fighting the RUC outside the prison on 22 July. The next day the RUC tried to block a 4,000 strong Paisleyite protest march from the centre of Belfast, but the marchers broke through and rampaged through the centre of the city breaking shop windows, stoning the Catholic-owned International Hotel and going on to Sandy Row where they tried to burn down a bookie's shop which employed Catholics. That night there was savage rioting outside the jail with repeated baton-charges by the RUC. Only heavy rain stopped it. The government banned all meetings and parades in Belfast for three months, and gave the RUC power to break up any gathering of three or more people.[37]

As with the links between Paisley and the UVF, one must be careful of supposing that Paisley provoked the violence committed by urban working-class Protestants who were active in supporting his attacks on O'Neill but who were generally not members or

[37] Farrell, op. cit., p. 235.

adherents of his Free Presbyterian Church. Mrs Paisley brought a message from her husband in prison, condemning the rioting and asking for it to stop. According to one of the tabloid papers, she said: 'The people who have been fighting the police have no connection with our church. The vast majority of the rioters are just hooligans.'[38]

At first the remaining Free Presbyterian ministers were demoralized and confused. Apparently innocent of the opportunity which had been presented to them, they met in the Ravenhill Church and talked about what they should do and even hesitated about talking to the journalists waiting outside. Beattie argued that they should go out and present their case.

Although O'Neill tried to present the case as one of the law simply taking its natural course to deal with illegal disorder, the Free Presbyterians saw it as a deliberate attempt to use the apparatus of the state to suppress true Bible Protestantism. And once they started to present their case, many evangelicals accepted their interpretation. Here one can see the value of Paisley's province-wide preaching during the 'wilderness years'. William McCrea's family were Presbyterian farmers from Tyrone who had heard Paisley preach in a tent near Dungannon:

We couldn't get seats in the main tent. It was so crowded they had to unlace the side-flaps of the enormous tent and raise them up so that people could sit outside the tent, down the sides, and though we couldn't see him very well, we heard him. The word of God was fully preached that afternoon, and many, many souls were saved. It was a wonderful meeting.

When, after that, we used to hear controversy about Dr Paisley and later heard about his imprisonment in 1966, because of that afternoon when we heard the gospel preached with power and conviction, we found ourselves tending to take his side in the controversy.[39]

There was an interesting difference in the political involvement of different generations of Free Presbyterian ministers. Beattie and Foster were fully involved with Paisley and Wylie in their protests and in electioneering. The slightly older students, John Douglas, Alan Cairns and Bert Cooke, were less often involved in public protests. On this occasion Cooke led a delegation to see O'Neill who had responded to pressure from a Unionist MP, Austin Ardill,

---

[38] *Sun* (25 July 1966).

[39] William McCrea and David Porter, *In His Pathway: the story of Rev. William McCrea* (London: Marshall, Morgan and Scott, 1980), p. 26.

to meet the men. He refused to consider what he regarded as interfering in the judicial process and what they saw as moderating his policy of harassing the Free Church.

The campaign was taken to the country. The remaining ministers and elders found themselves being invited to address meetings all over the province to explain the imprisonment. As Robert Wilson, an elder in the Rasharkin church, recognizes, this was a period of unprecedented interest in the Free Church:

At that time that was a sad day for many people, the day he went to prison. I know people who were in tears as a result of Dr Paisley going into jail, but in the long term God answered prayer. If he hadn't been put into the jail, I don't know what would have been the result today but . . . before he even had his jail sentence served, applications were coming in from town and countryside for churches to be opened up, with the result that in that short space of time about 1966, our church more than doubled in membership and in churches. I think it was very important that he served a term in jail . . . I look on it as a work of God.

But the police harassment did not stop with the imprisonment. John Douglas found himself charged with behaviour likely to lead to a breach of the peace as a result of some remarks he is said to have made at a meeting in Rathfriland. Two plain clothes women constables were in the audience with a concealed tape-recorder. Although Douglas was eventually acquitted of any offence, his initial conviction and the methods of the police—which included presenting in court what they claimed was a transcript of their tape of his speech, but which was only one third of the length of another tape-recording which was played to the court—led many Free Presbyterians and sympathizers to believe that the whole force of the state was being directed against them.

Paisley's whole career has been distinguished by a finely developed sense of symbolism and an event like the imprisonment was not to be wasted. Every Sunday, the huge congregation, gathered in the Ulster Hall, heard either Mrs Paisley or one of the ministers read out a message from their leader in prison. Hitler, Gramsci, and Regis Debray had spent their time in prison writing political treatises. Paisley used his time to hammer home the religious significance of the battle with O'Neill by writing a commentary on Paul's Letter to the Romans, the book which Paul had written while awaiting trial in prison.

Church Growth

For the Free Presbyterian Church the main consequence of 1966 was religious revival. In the period from the foundation of the Free Church in 1951 to 1966 only thirteen congregations had joined and one of those had lapsed. In the eighteen months which followed July 1966, twelve more congregations were formed. On his release Ivan Foster went to Fermanagh and started meetings in Lisbellaw near Enniskillen. John Wylie held a mission in Londonderry and a congregation was founded there. Others were formed in Moneyslane, Tandragee, Dungannon, Lurgan, Portadown, Kilkeel, Ballynahinch, Lisburn, and Magherafelt.

In most places, there was considerable opposition to the Free Church as the local unionist élites did their best to prevent Free Presbyterianism becoming established. But as one might have predicted, such opposition backfired by confirming the very claims which the Free Presbyterians made about the great apostasy and the undemocratic nature of Terence O'Neill's rule. When Beattie tried to hold evangelistic meetings in Hillsborough, he found the Church of Ireland aristocracy who controlled the parish council using planning laws to make it difficult for him to get a site. A land developer, who was not an evangelical but who sympathized with claims to freedom of speech and assembly, offered them land in Lisburn. A site was also secured just outside Hillsborough and thus two more congregations were added to the growing Church by the opposition to one.

This period of growth confirmed the patterns of the earlier period in the support for Paisleyism. Just as Protestant Action had been supported by the almost completely separate constituencies of rural evangelicals and urban loyalists, so the same divisions can be seen in the reaction to the prison sentence. Paisley's standing among the urban working-class 'secular' Protestants was considerably enhanced, and that support was later to be translated into support in elections. At the same time, rural conservative Protestants, especially those from the Irish Presbyterian Church, were attracted to the religious movement. By far the greatest proportion of those joining the new congregations were Presbyterians and they were mostly from rural areas. In occupation they were mostly either farmers or people who worked in agriculture-related industries. In terms of social composition, it is difficult to be more specific because 'farmer' covers a considerable diversity of wealth and social status. My impression, based solely on those farmers whom I have met, is that the supporters of Free Presbyterianism tended to be small to medium farmers running family operations with only one or two labourers. The wealthy farmers were either Church of Ireland in religion or pro-O'Neill in politics and, for either or both of those reasons, were not attracted to Free Presbyterianism.

To return to the second point about church growth made at the end of the second chapter, 'demand' is not the only factor in church growth; one must also consider supply, and the Free Church was gradually coming into the position where it could service the new demand. Had the imprisonment and the subsequent 'religious revival' come six years earlier, it would have produced less spectacular growth because the trained personnel were not then available to lead the movement and direct the sympathy for the Free Presbyterians into recruitment to the Church.

By 1966, the Church was better able to take advantage of the new interest in its separatist stance because it now had a core of Ulstermen who had been converted under Ian Paisley's preaching and who had grown up with his politicized evangelicalism. They had a strong sense of shared identity, had been trained together, and were strongly linked by kinship ties. Beattie, Douglas, and Foster were all in-laws. Cecil Menary had married into the large McAuley family which played a major part in the life of the Cabra congregation and in evangelical culture generally in the North Antrim area. In addition, a greater cohesion was resulting from Douglas, Cooke, and Cairns taking a greater part in the teaching of their more junior colleagues. A reliable cadre had been created which could 'supply' the demand which O'Neill's response to Paisley's challenge had created.

Political Crisis and Religious Revival

An important point in the analysis of Paisleyism is that the religious wing of the movement *predated* the Catholic civil rights movement. The Church did not grow as a result of Protestants reacting to evidence of increased Catholic demands and assertiveness. The political crisis which created fertile conditions for the growth of the Church was that caused by the conflict between O'Neill's reformist Unionism and Paisley's traditionalist stand.

To understand the link between the political crisis and the religious revival, we must separate two elements: the universal and the particular. As was suggested in the previous chapter's discussion of the Nicholson crusades in the 1920s, there is a well-observed connection between political instability and religious revival, *if the culture is already religious*. It is not the case that social dislocation and uncertainty necessarily make people turn to God. Rather, it is the case that people with a fairly strong religious tradition may react to crises by turning back to the traditional patterns of belief which not only made sense of their individual predicaments but which also created a strong sense of communal solidarity. We might suppose that this universal process played some part in the attraction of the Free Presbyterian Church.[40]

But what was much more important was the relationship between the particular nature of this political crisis and the religious recourse which some people took. The point can be made best by returning to the Hunter and Grier schism from the Irish Presbyterian Church in 1927 and its failure to attract popular support, even from those people who shared Hunter and Grier's religious beliefs. I have suggested that they were limited in their appeal because the changes they opposed were confined to doctrinal issues. Paisley's religious appeal was based on the claim that orthodox Protestant beliefs were being 'downgraded' and that, at the same time, liberal Protestants were actively seeking greater harmony with other apostate denominations, in particular the old enemy of Rome. There was a conspiracy to sell out true Bible-believing Protestantism. Even without Terence O'Neill, such claims would have had a better hearing in the 1960s than they had had in the 1920s. The ecumenical movement had become better established and although it would be an exaggeration to say that the major Protestant denominations were heavily committed to a 'Romeward trend', it was clearly the case that many church leaders were seeking better relations with the Roman Church. By 1966, it had become common for Protestant church leaders to visit the Pope and to voice ecumenical sentiments. Even though Rome was giving little in return in terms of moderating its claims to be the

---

[40] The question of the relationship between disruptive and threatening social change and religious revival is a complex one. Some of the problems and the major approaches are discussed in Steve Bruce, 'Social Change and Collective Behaviour: the revival in eighteenth century Ross-shire', *British Journal of Sociology*, 34 (4) (1983), pp. 554–72.

only true Christian church, faint liberal breezes had been blowing through the Vatican since the second Vatican Council. Furthermore, some liberals had pushed their rationalizing of the Christian faith to the extreme point where it was fashionable to argue that 'God is dead' and that the only truly Christian thing to do was to abandon the churches altogether. Although such heresies were far more common in America and in England than they were in Ulster, Ulster Protestants knew of these postures and could see that their own denominations were in formal organizational contact with other churches which did not move to sack ministers and theologians who had obviously given up the traditional beliefs affirmed at their ordinations. All of this meant that Paisley's criticisms of apostasy were being uttered in a considerably more apostate era than the times in which Hunter and Grier had failed to promote their schism.

But what really enhanced the receptivity of the market was O'Neillism. It is always possible to 'compartmentalize' one's life; to separate religion and work and politics so that different criteria are used for decision-making in each compartment. The traditional nature of religion in Ulster meant that such compartments were less water tight than they would be in, for example, America, but the very structure of Ulster society, economy, and polity meant that changes in one sphere would have repercussions in the others. In visiting a Catholic school, O'Neill might have thought he was doing no more than acknowledging that Catholics formed a sizeable part of the population of Northern Ireland and that Catholic schools were largely supported from public funds which his government administered. In such a view, 'Catholic' was simply a term which described part of the population. But for Ulster's evangelical Protestants, Catholic schools were places in which soul-damning heresies were transmitted, and to visit them was to recognize that Catholicism was a permitted variant of the Christian church. And then all the other elements in the complex which bound religion and politics together would pour down. Catholics were rebels who only wanted to destroy not only Northern Ireland but also the Protestant nature of the rest of the British Isles and the only thing which maintained civil liberties was adherence to the Protestant faith. Ulster owed its prosperity, such as it was, not to the accident of a good deep-water harbour and its trade links with Glasgow and Liverpool, but to its sabbatarianism, temperance, and evangelical beliefs. If the Romanists did not destroy Ulster by forcing its people into a united papist Ireland, then God surely would as a punishment for departing from his standards.

What O'Neillism did for Paisleyism was to raise in a concrete way the possibility of change from being a Protestant society and culture (constantly threatened by the old enemy within and without) to being a secular modern society in which religious affiliation would be of little consequence. The spectre of the great apostasy was always a threat to the more ideologically committed evangelicals but Terence O'Neill's reforms, tepid and half-hearted as they were, raised the spectre to a power and status from which it threatened a far greater number of rural Presbyterians who saw the proposed changes as proof that Paisley had been right all along. In Moneyslane and Tandragee and the farming areas around Hillsborough, the Presbyterians rallied to 'the old paths in perilous times'.

4

The Political Rise of Paisley

The Political Rise of Paisley

In retrospect it is clear that O'Neill was in an impossible situation. It is well recorded in the political science literature that the relaxation of an oppressive regime, far from placating its opponents, encourages further opposition as the expectations of the disadvantaged population are raised. O'Neill's minor reforms or, as Utley perceptively describes it, his 'government by gesture',[1] served only to politicize further the frustration of the Catholic population, without making it any more committed to the Northern Ireland state. O'Neill also failed to appreciate the extent of Protestant misgivings, preferring instead to see Paisley and his supporters as a small and unrepresentative rabble. Dismissing Paisley's support as 'a fascist organization masquerading under the cloak of religion . . . deluding a lot of sincere people . . . hell-bent on provoking religious strife in Northern Ireland',[2] he seemed unprepared for the reaction against him within his own party. While attempting to respond to the civil rights movement and to the pressure from the Wilson government in London, O'Neill was being threatened from within the Unionist camp. Although the first revolt was crushed, Desmond Boal could still raise thirteen Unionist backbenchers' signatures for the removal of O'Neill, and Lord Brookeborough, only three years after handing the premiership to O'Neill, was leading a whispering campaign against him.

There is no need to chronicle in detail the conflicts of the last years of O'Neill's administration. That has been done well elsewhere.[3] An example will show the precariousness of his position. In November of 1968, he responded to the demands of Derry

[1] T. E. Utley, *Lessons of Ulster* (London: J. M. Dent and Sons, 1975), p. 41.
[2] Stormont *Hansard*, House of Commons (15 June 1966), p. 338.
[3] For example, Michael Farrell, *Northern Ireland: the Orange state* (London: Pluto Press, 1980).

Catholics by proposing that the Londonderry City Corporation (which since partition had been gerrymandered so that the Protestant minority retained control) be replaced by a nominated body, that housing allocation be removed from political control to be administered on a fair 'points for needs' system, and that the Special Powers Act be re-examined. By then, such gestures were not enough to placate the civil rights supporters who decided to go ahead with a proposed march through Armagh City on 30 November. Paisley and Major Ronald Bunting announced a counter-demonstration.

William Craig, the Minister for Home Affairs, refused to take the advice of moderates to ban the Paisley demonstration and although there was a considerable police presence, nothing was done to stop the Paisleyites blocking the civil rights marchers. Had Craig banned the march, he would have infuriated the civil rights people. Had he banned the counter-demonstration, he would have provoked the Protestants. And so what credit O'Neill might have acquired for his reform package was instantly lost by what Catholics saw as a refusal to confront the loyalist mobs who really ran Northern Ireland.

O'Neill made an impassioned defence of his policies on television and appealed for support for what he saw as the only course that could save Ulster from deepening civil unrest. For a month or so it looked as if he had succeeded in defusing the time bomb, but soon Catholic leaders were arguing that nothing was really changing. In January 1968, Farrell and the other militant civil rights activists of People's Democracy started a march from Belfast to Londonderry, modelled on the famous American civil rights march from Selma to Montgomery. Along the route the marchers were harassed by the RUC and by bands of loyalists, many of whom were off-duty policemen and Specials. The final bloody confrontation at Burntollet Bridge took place before the eyes of the world's media, and united moderate and militant Catholic opinion in a hardening rejection of Unionist rule. To the British government, Burntollet was further evidence of the need to force reform on Stormont. Almost certainly under Westminster pressure, O'Neill announced the Cameron Commission to investigate the causes of the disturbances.

Unionism was collapsing. Bill Craig had already been sacked for criticizing O'Neill's televised plea to the province. Now Brian

Faulkner resigned from the cabinet over what he saw as O'Neill's capitulation to British pressure. Paisley was back in prison, this time for his part in the Armagh demonstrations, but that did not stop him characterizing the Cameron Commission as a betrayal of the Ulster people to the rebels. Under his direction, the Ulster Constitution Defence Committee maintained its traditional line that O'Neill was not responding to the legitimate demands of a disadvantaged section of the population, but giving in to the demands of rebels who would never be satisfied with anything less than the destruction of Northern Ireland.[4] Instead of worrying about how to make the RUC acceptable to the minority, O'Neill should have been using the legitimate power of the state to crush an illegal insurrection.

In January 1969, O'Neill took the only course left open to him: he went to the country to seek a mandate for his policies. For Northern Ireland the election was extraordinary. All previous elections had possessed a ritual quality with the outcome determined in advance by religious demography. Almost all Protestants voted for the Unionist Party and Catholics either voted for nationalists or abstained.

The attempts by O'Neill to change the basic grammar of the language of Ulster politics had left both sides in disarray. Paisley stood against O'Neill in Bannside: the first time O'Neill had been challenged since he inherited the seat in 1946. Other Protestant Unionists were fielded against liberal O'Neillites. But there was also a conservative revolt against O'Neill within the Unionist Party with some 'official' candidates being pro-O'Neill and others being nominated by branches which shared Paisley's politics (and which in some cases were run by Paisley supporters). And on the Catholic

---

[4] In a curious way both traditional loyalists and left-wing critics of the Northern Ireland state agree here. Loyalists insist that the 'reforms' demanded by the CRM—for example, the disbanding of the B Specials—were designed to weaken the state and facilitate the creation of a united Ireland. Left-wing republicans argue, against more moderate nationalists, that the state is fundamentally irreformable because its essence is discriminatory. Hence republicans argued that the CRM had to become republican while loyalists argued that it always was. The historian of People's Democracy gives reason to this latter view when he says: 'It must be remembered that PD had tenuous links with the Republican movement virtually from the outset. During the Burntollet march, Republicans housed and fed the marchers and at one stage a Republican banner was unfurled. . . . Much of the rhetoric, the imagery and the use of traditional music resembled that of Sinn Fein.' Paul Arthur, *The People's Democracy, 1968–73* (Belfast: Blackstaff Press, 1974), p. 112.

side, older nationalist members were opposed by a younger generation raised in the civil rights movement.

When the dust of the election battle settled, Terence O'Neill found himself with a minority government and the support of only eleven of the Unionist backbenchers. Violence on the streets escalated. The civil rights marchers continued their demonstrations. In order to increase the tension and dramatize their fears of an IRA campaign, militant loyalists bombed a reservoir and a power station. The Catholic Bogside in Derry rioted. On 28 April, Terence O'Neill resigned and his cousin Major James Chichester-Clark was elected as leader of the Unionist Parliamentary Party and hence Prime Minister. Under pressure from Westminster, he pledged his government to continue the O'Neill reforms.

Richard Ferguson, the Unionist MP for South Antrim, resigned with O'Neill. Although he had been nominated as a conservative by Protestant Unionists within the constituency, he had quickly become an O'Neill supporter. The two planned by-elections gave the Protestant Unionists the opportunity they needed to maintain the momentum of their electoral challenge. The importance of the contest was well appreciated by the Unionist Party which sent not only the Prime Minister but also a number of other cabinet ministers to Bannside to canvass for Dr Bolton Minford. In the event their prestige was not enough to hold the seat. Paisley added another 1,650 votes to his score against O'Neill and achieved the platform he needed. A reporter described the scene at the count:

In the midst of a victory celebration in Ballymena, Mr Paisley said: 'This is the dawn of a new day for Ulster. Good night Chichester-Clark'. He was given a rapturous reception by a flag-waving crowd of 5,000 when the result was announced shortly after midnight. Speeches, relayed to the milling crowd outside Ballymena Town Hall, where the count was being held, were drowned in deafening cheers, and as the triumphant Free Presbyterian Church leader faced a barrage of questions before TV cameras, an accordion band struck up 'The Sash'. Wearing his now familiar Russian-style hat and white Ulster Protestant Volunteer sash, Mr Paisley was carried shoulder-high through the town hall's main entrance to 'meet his people'. Despite the late hour the town put on the appearance of a miniature 'Twelfth' as he and his wife Eileen and brother-in-law and election agent, the Rev. James Beggs, were paraded on the back of a Land Rover to the Waveney Road, where Mr Paisley was greeted by his

78 year-old father, the Rev. Kyle Paisley who was unable to attend the count. [5]

While the election of Paisley was a major blow to the credibility of Chichester-Clark, who might have been better advised to save face by not becoming personally involved in opposing Paisley, William Beattie's victory in South Antrim was probably more damaging in that Beattie was far less well known, was standing in a more cosmopolitan constituency, and was competing against a man who had previously been a cabinet minister. There could be no explanation for his victory other than that there was considerable support in Unionist circles for the traditionalist positions represented by Paisley and Beattie.

Paisley was developing a distinctive political position which stressed the religious element in the conflict between nationalist and loyalist. While his loyalism gave him urban working-class support, it was the rural Protestants who were most receptive to his evangelical emphases and who made a seat like Bannside obviously attractive. His rural support was again crucial in June, just two months after the Stormont by-elections, when a Westminster general election allowed Paisley to test his wider appeal. He contested the North Antrim constituency (which took in the Bannside Stormont area) and defeated Henry Clarke, the sitting MP, who was a liberal and a member of the O'Neill clan.

It is an indication both of the confusion within the Unionist Party and of the wider appeal of Paisley's politics that the election was punctuated by claims and rebuttals concerning a pact between the Protestant Unionists and the Unionist Party. Paisley asserted that, had he wanted to destroy the Unionist Party, he would have fielded candidates in all the constituencies. Few, if any, would have been elected but the splitting of the Unionist vote would have let in more anti-Union candidates. Eamonn McCann, the 'unofficial Labour' candidate in Londonderry, demanded that the Official Unionist, Robin Chichester-Clark, dismiss those members of his constituency party who had made a deal with the Protestant Unionists or be seen as a puppet on a Paisleyite string. [6] Chichester-Clark denied that any such deal had been made. Whether or not specific arrangements were discussed by the two unionist groupings, the

---

[5] *Belfast Telegraph* (17 Apr. 1970).
[6] BBC Northern Ireland Radio Ulster news, 16 June 1970.

election was more of a success for the conservatives than would be implied by the victory of one of the two Protestant Unionists. In other seats, conservative Unionists who had considerable reservations about the direction of the government—James Kilfedder in North Down and James Molyneaux in South Antrim, for example—were elected.

The Last Stormont

1970 and early 1971 saw the Ulster crisis deepen as the government stumbled on, alternating promises of reform with heavy-handed repression. The Catholics, having come so far in undermining the old Orange State, were not easily going to be satisfied, and the urban working-class Protestants were not about to relinquish fifty years of social and political superiority without a fight. Rioting became common and the British Army had to be called in to replace the overstretched Royal Ulster Constabulary. In an attempt to make the RUC more acceptable to the minority, its leadership structure was radically altered, outsiders were brought in to train and lead it, and the B Special Constabulary was disbanded to be replaced by the Ulster Defence Regiment under army command. But any popular appeal to Catholics that such moves might have had was undermined by repressive acts such as the introduction of internment—imprisonment without trial—for suspected nationalist terrorists.[7] People began to die in riots. Catholics and Protestants in marginal areas were burnt out of their homes and forced to move into their respective ghettoes. In March 1971 Chichester-Clark resigned to be replaced by Brian Faulkner. For all his previous reputation as a hard-line Unionist, Faulkner attempted to broaden his political base with some astute appointments such as that of David Bleakley, ex-Chairman of the Northern Ireland Labour Party, as Minister for Community Relations. He unveiled plans for involving the minority in administration through the creation of three policy-making committees to review government performance in industrial, social, and environmental services. With the already established public accounts committee, this would have

[7] It is interesting to note that Paisley was always opposed to internment. He maintained the constitutionalist position that people guilty of offences against the state should be tried under the existing, and sufficient, laws. He prophesied that internment would soon be turned against loyalist critics of the government.

given four such bodies, each with a salaried chairman, and the Catholics were to be given two of the chairs with the committees being made up to reflect parliamentary seats. This plan was given a cautious welcome by the Social Democratic and Labour Party, led by Gerry Fitt, John Hume, and Paddy Devlin, which had taken over the leadership of 'constitutional' nationalist opinion. However, as Harkness puts it:

It was undone, immediately, by passions once more loosed on the streets of Derry. After sporadic violence there from the beginning of the month, full scale rioting erupted on 8 July and in the early hours of 9th two men were shot dead by the army. One died of loss of blood on his way to hospital in Co. Donegal; the other where he stood in the street. Local opinion denied their involvement in terrorism, and John Hume, local SDLP MP, persuaded his party to demand an official inquiry, failing which it would withdraw from Stormont and set up an alternative assembly . . . No official inquiry could be offered: the SDLP withdrew from Stormont on l6 July; and the IRA campaign increased in ferocity.[8]

Until the middle of 1971, the IRA had played little part in the conflict. It had been largely dormant since the late 1950s and during the communal violence of the summer of 1969, many embittered Catholics had voiced their anger at its lack of action by saying that IRA stood for 'I Ran Away'. At the annual Sinn Fein conference in Dublin in January 1970, a majority broke away to form the Provisional IRA, and in the following years planned and executed an increasing number of shootings and bombings. Internment, introduced in August, was intended to take leaders of the IRA out of circulation, but the information on which arrests were made was often out of date or just plain mistaken. The republican movement flourished.

Loyalist intransigence was bolstered not only by the new IRA campaign but also by the actions of three leading Fianna Fáil politicians in the South who were open and vocal in their support for the IRA. Although they were later acquitted of illegally importing arms and ammunition for use in the North, they were dismissed from the cabinet for their part in the affair.[9] At the height of the troubles in 1970, the Irish Army brought field

---

[8] David Harkness, *Northern Ireland Since 1920* (Dublin: Helicon Books, 1983), p. 168.

[9] Liam De Paor, *Divided Ulster* (Harmondsworth, Middx: Penguin, 1971), pp. 205–8.

hospitals to the border ready for refugees from Ulster. Although the open civil war which so many feared did not then break out, something more important had happened.

The civil rights movement had apparently begun as the vehicle for Catholic claims to full and equal participation in the Northern Ireland state. In its early phase it reflected broad Catholic opinion which wanted acceptance as full citizens of the North and had some liberal Unionist support. The inability of O'Neill and Chichester-Clark to satisfy those demands without destabilizing the state had created the very condition that people such as Paisley had argued had obtained from the first: the rise of old-fashioned nationalist anti-partitionism. The aim was now not assimilation in the Northern Ireland state but its destruction. As the minority population became more vociferous in its demands and more openly nationalist and republican, the stature of Paisley in the loyalist camp was proportionately increased because Protestants looked back at what he had been saying in the early days of O'Neill's reign and saw that 'he had been right all along'. They could see that there was no satisfying the Catholics. Appeasement did not work, because nothing short of a united Ireland had been their 'real' ambition from the start.

It is not the intention of this book to discuss in any detail the shifting politics of the Catholic population. Others have already done that.[10] Furthermore, it is generally the case that what the Catholics were actually doing is far less important in understanding the actions of the Protestants than Protestant *beliefs* about what Catholics were doing. It is Protestant perceptions which explain their actions and those perceptions were amplifying the fundamental divisions between those unionists who remained committed to pragmatic reform, either because they believed in liberal unionism or because they believed that satisfying the Westminster government's demands for reform was the only way to maintain Stormont, and the right-wingers who wanted to preserve traditional unionism.

Ian Paisley was one potential leader of the right wing, but there were others and a key question that has to be asked in any explanation of Paisley's career is 'how did Paisley triumph over other right-wing unionist figures?' In order to answer that we must look

[10] Many of the changes in nationalist politics are described in Barry White, *John Hume: statesman of the troubles* (Belfast: Blackstaff Press, 1985).

closely at Paisley's relationships with other unionists. Once Brian Faulkner had succeeded Chichester-Clark as premier, there were two main groups of 'official' Unionists who were opposed to the general political direction of the Westminster-directed Stormont government. One such grouping was led by Harry West and the West Ulster Unionist Council, which brought together the conservatives west of the Bann. The second grouping centred on William Craig who remained in the Unionist Party despite his constant criticisms of its direction. Craig toured the province building support for what, when it was launched in 1972, was called the Vanguard Movement. He was supported by Martin Smyth, a Presbyterian minister who was the leader of the Belfast Orangemen and about to become Grand Master of the Order, and Billy Hull, the founder of the large Loyalist Association of Workers.

Many activists in Paisley's Protestant Unionist Party insist that they would never have become involved in politics if there had remained one reliable traditional unionist party. This would certainly be the case for someone like Gordon Cooke, the Free Presbyterian minister of Rasharkin, who found himself chairman of the 'parent' branch of the officially constituted Protestant Unionist Party largely because he was a strong supporter of Paisley's political line and a leading evangelical in the Bannside area at the time when Paisley decided to stand against O'Neill. Such people would always have been willing to subordinate their political action to unionist unity, if it could be recreated on a sound basis. Throughout the summer of 1971 there were lengthy discussions between Paisley, Boal, and a number of other dissidents within the Unionist Party about the formation of a new unionist party. Boal sought and received assurances from a number of leading Unionists that they would join such a movement but, when the Ulster Democratic Unionist party was launched on 30 October 1971, many of those who had expressed interest were absent.

Official Unionists, no matter how critical of their leadership, were reluctant to give up their party. As one rather disillusioned Protestant Unionist put it: 'they were a party who believed in their God given right to rule this country' and they were not about to give up that right, especially as they could see signs of regaining control of their own party. With the selection of some anti-O'Neill candidates in the 1970 Stormont elections and the Westminster elections of the same year, the conservatives sensed that they could win back the Unionist Party machine. In such circumstances, they were reluctant to abandon their own positions for a possibly lesser place in a new party in which Ian Paisley would play a major part.

Many Protestant Unionists also had doubts about the new party. In their view, the old party had been doing well. It now had members in Stormont and increasing popular support and, more importantly, it had a clear *Protestant* identity. In many areas, it took the full weight of Paisley's authority, exercised either directly or through loyal supporters such as Gordon Cooke, then chairman of the North Antrim branch, to persuade the Protestant Unionists to dissolve in favour of the new organization.

In the event, the failure of large numbers of Official Unionists to join meant that the new party was more congenial to the old Protestant Unionists than they had initially feared. Protestant Unionists made up about two-thirds of the new Ulster Democratic Unionist Party (hereafter 'DUP'). The two new MPs to join Paisley and Beattie were Desmond Boal and Johnny McQuade. Boal was a successful barrister who combined staunch unionism with a left-of-centre position on social and economic issues. McQuade was a working-class Protestant, ex-soldier, docker, and professional boxer who sat for North Belfast and continued the independent unionist tradition of men like Henderson and Nixon.

Some of the older evangelicals were concerned about the name of the new party, sensing in the dropping of the word 'Protestant' a weakening of its evangelical emphasis, but even among the rural evangelicals there was an awareness of the need for a broader party. Although there is considerable value in the notion that Paisley's political movement always consisted of two elements in tension—rural evangelicals and urban 'secular' Protestants—it is also the case that many evangelicals could be quite pragmatic and recognize that the preservation of things which they valued because of their religious beliefs required them to work in alliance with others who wanted the same things for different reasons.

On 23 February 1972, the DUP took a major step towards establishing its own political identity when the four MPs crossed the floor of the house to take up the position left vacant by the withdrawal of the Catholic SDLP as Her Majesty's Loyal Opposition at Stormont. The period of opposition was almost comically short and its brevity showed how far events in Northern Ireland had passed out of control of Stormont. A month after the DUP crossed the floor, the British government in London gave up the hope that the Northern Ireland government could restore order and suspended Stormont. The politics of the street, which had played such a large part in putting Ian Paisley into Stormont, had now returned him and his supporters to the streets.

Limbo, Power-Sharing, Strike, and Limbo

The first eighteen months of the DUP's existence were not especially auspicious. As the party's official historian admits, recruitment was slow.[11] Craig's Vanguard Movement seemed to be making most of the running on the right wing of unionist politics and the DUP seemed to lack a clear policy direction. Paisley had acquired some further support for his reputation for prophecy by his prediction of the introduction of direct rule and he did not publicly regret the end of Stormont. This was not surprising given that the Parliament was dominated by Faulknerites but even so, it was not clear to Ulster Protestants what it was that the DUP wanted in Ulster's relation to the mainland. Fortunately, Craig's position was not obviously clearer and his credibility was partly undermined by the refusal of some leading Unionists, such as Captain Austin Ardill and Martin Smyth, to follow him when he turned Vanguard from a ginger group into a party.

For most of 1972 and early 1973, the eyes of political observers were focused as much on London as on Ulster. Introducing direct rule had been easy enough; ending it was a problem. Westminster promoted the notion of a power-sharing government in which ministries would be shared between liberal Unionists and the largely Catholic SDLP. It was also suggested that some sort of 'Irish dimension' (to borrow the term of the 1980s) be institutionalized by the creation of a Council of Ireland made up of representatives of the Westminster and Dublin parliaments and members from the to-be-created Stormont 'Assembly'. Although the Council of Ireland proposal was by no means an open door to a united Ireland it would be enough to concentrate loyalist voters in opposition to the new proposals.

Elections for the new assembly were scheduled for June 1973, but before that date there were local council elections. The DUP

[11] David Calvert, *A Decade of the DUP* (Belfast: Crown Publications, 1981), p. 6.

and Vanguard had intended to boycott the local elections, saving their effort for the more important Assembly elections, but activists in both parties thought that the earlier contest should be fought, if only to make use of the free publicity that would be created and to have the advantages of a trial run and an early opportunity to canvass for the more important second elections.

It is difficult to assess the performance of the DUP and Vanguard because there was considerable overlap between the two groups and the affiliation of some candidates was in doubt. Deutsch and Magowan claim that the DUP fielded seventy-five candidates[12] and Fred Proctor, who was involved in the Shankill Defence Association (one of the constituents of the Ulster Defence Association) and instrumental in getting the DUP to contest the elections, made the same claim[13] but that figure includes Vanguard members. It is more accurate to say that the DUP fielded thirty-nine candidates of whom twenty-one won seats (but again there is disagreement with David Calvert claiming only thirteen wins for the DUP).[14]

In the preparation for the Assembly elections, the issue of the relationship between the DUP and the Free Presbyterian Church was again raised. One of the biggest problems for any new party is finding competent activists. Although one might suppose that the creation of a new party offers attractive opportunities for people previously excluded from local élites to establish themselves as leaders, it is often the case that such people do not obviously possess the right qualities. In one respect the Free Presbyterian Church was a valuable resource of the DUP in that it provided a cadre of people who had considerable training and experience in organization and oratory: the ministers and elders. But there were difficulties in recruiting DUP candidates from the leadership of the Free Presbyterian Church. Clifford Smyth stresses the damage that would have been done to the electoral appeal of the DUP if it had been too closely associated with the Free Presbyterian Church and offers this as the main reason why the Presbytery of the Free Church refused to allow ministers other than Paisley and Beattie

[12] Richard Deutsch and Vivien Magowan, *Northern Ireland, 1968–74: a chronology of events* (Belfast: Blackstaff Press, 1974), vol. ii (1972–3), p. 295.

[13] *Belfast Telegraph* (2 May 1973).

[14] Calvert, op. cit., p. 6.

to stand as DUP candidates.[15] While Smyth might be right about the consequence of the Party being too heavily associated with the Church, he is wrong in reading backwards from that possible consequence to the motives of the men who debated at Presbytery. The reason why the Free Church was concerned with the political activities of some of its members was that it saw its main purposes as evangelism and the servicing of church life. It wanted a full-time ministry of people who were first and foremost ministers of the gospel. When Alan Cairns and other leading ministers opposed the candidacy of William McCrea and James McClelland they did so to preserve the interests of the Free Church and not to aid the DUP by reducing the public presence of Free Presbyterianism in the lists of candidates. In his analysis of the links between the Church and the Party in this period, Smyth gets confused by his concern with the question of how 'democratic' the DUP really was. He cites the Presbytery meeting which debated the issue of ministers in politics as an example of the way in which the Church undemocratically affected the policies and direction of the Party. This seems a rather curious reading. There seems nothing at all strange about the Church, which paid the salaries of these men and expected them to serve it, considering the question of whether or not they should be able to engage in an activity which, no matter how acceptable, would have diverted them from their main task. Had the Presbytery been *selecting* candidates and foisting them on the DUP, Smyth's view would be more plausible. As it was, the Church was simply acting to preserve its interests and these were not the same as the interests of the Party. In the event, permission was given for Paisley and Beattie to go forward because they had been members of the Stormont Parliament before it had been suspended.

It was obvious to all participants that the Assembly elections were a referendum on the proposals for the future of Ulster. Those opposed to power-sharing wanted an arrangement to maximize the loyalist vote. Paisley and Craig had spent a good part of the previous year publicly disagreeing about the future of Stormont. Paisley accused Craig of proposing UDI and seemed most committed to the complete integration of Ulster with the mainland if the old

[15] Clifford Smyth, 'The Ulster Democratic Unionist Party: a case study in religious and political convergence', Ph.D. thesis (The Queen's University of Belfast, 1984), pp. 54–7.

majority-rule Stormont could not be reintroduced.[16] However, the need to maximize the anti-power sharing vote convinced both DUP and Vanguard to instruct their followers to vote for the other party as their second or third preference in what was to be a single transferable vote type of proportional representation election. As in the 1970 O'Neill election, the Official Unionists were divided with thirty-nine candidates pledged to oppose power-sharing and forty pledged to support Faulkner.[17]

The DUP's view of the Ulster crisis, its solution, and the Assembly were presented to the Ulster electorate:

The DUP says that Republican violence paid off in the disarming of the RUC, the disbanding of the B Specials, the banning of Orange, Black and Apprentice Boys' parades resulting in the imprisonment of Loyalists, the overthrow of Ulster's parliament, the plan for talks with Dublin to change the status of Northern Ireland within the United Kingdom, the abolishing of the Oath of Allegiance to the Queen in the new Assembly and Executive, the making of such oaths illegal for appointment to government boards, the removal of the Governor, the obliteration of 'On Her Majesty's Service' from official paid envelopes, the attempt to destroy democracy by power-sharing which was a blow at the secrecy of the ballot box and an insult to British citizenship and standards, the proposal to set up machinery for the transfer of Northern Ireland's powers to a body or bodies in or with the Irish Republic, and the continued existence of areas in Northern Ireland where the Queen's writ did not effectually run.[18]

Seventy-two per cent of the electorate decided to voice an opinion. The DUP won eight seats, Vanguard took seven, and Faulkner had twenty-two. But there were also ten anti-power-sharing Unionists elected. This meant that, with the nineteen SDLP members, Faulkner could form a government but he represented only a minority of the unionist voters.

From the point of view of Paisley and the DUP the elections were an important point on the road to acquiring political legitimacy. No longer was Ian Paisley some sort of raving lunatic on the fringes of unionist politics. He was now part of a coalition with people who had held cabinet office in Stormont and, more than that, his party had polled *better* than one led by an ex-Minister.

[16] Westminster *Hansard* (20 Mar. 1972).

[17] W. D. Flackes, *Northern Ireland: a political directory, 1968–79* (Dublin: Gill and Macmillan; New York: St Martin's Press, 1980), pp. 167–70.

[18] *Irish Times* (8 June 1973).

Craig had fielded twice as many candidates and won fewer seats; a result which was probably a combination of public reaction to Vanguard's lack of clear policy and a lack of enthusiasm for some of the Vanguard candidates. It was generally the case that working-class loyalists, especially those connected with the para-military organizations, fared less well in the election than more 'respectable' loyalists and Vanguard had a larger number of such candidates than the DUP.

In the competition with other unionist groupings, the DUP had a major advantage in its *cohesion*. Unlike other loyalist parties, it spoke with a single clear voice: that of Ian Paisley. Even before Desmond Boal stepped down from the chairmanship of the Party to advocate his idea of a federal Ireland, the Party was very much what even DUP activists admit to have been 'Paisley's fan club'. There was hardly any organized party structure. Peter Robinson went so far as to say that until late 1974 'there was no party'. Thus Paisley was free to create party policy and to articulate it without having to convince a large membership. Furthermore, other acti-vists such as William Beattie and Ivan Foster were very obviously his juniors. In the other loyalist groups there were a number of *competing* leadership figures who offered differing responses to events and who were obliged to engage in more extensive con-sultation with their supporters before pronouncing.

The absence of a strong party structure was not something in which the DUP rejoiced. Beattie as deputy leader devoted a lot of energy to trying to build up branches and Robinson, on becoming party secretary, hired the Party's first full-time worker before him-self becoming a paid official. Thereafter all press statements were produced from the party office, but the cohesion advantage re-mained because the leadership of the Party was still very clearly in the hands of one man. This is not to say that Paisley was dictatorial and simply imposed his will on other activists. Rather, he was able to use his considerable personal appeal and powers of persuasion to convince others to take his line. As Robinson put it: 'even with a less persuasive argument he has been able to get a democratic decision in his favour but the democratic process is used through-out the party'.

Quite what the Faulkner/SDLP executive might have achieved will always remain a matter of speculation. According to a survey conducted for the BBC in April 1974 by Professor Richard Rose, sixty-nine per cent of the people of Northern Ireland thought that the executive should be given a chance to govern[19] but this finding was contradicted by the results of a general election two months earlier and may reflect the general tendency of survey respondents to make statements in response to poll questions which are more moderate than their real views.

The first nail in the executive's coffin was hammered in by the Westminster government. In February 1974, just a month after the executive took office, Edward Heath called a general election on the theme of 'who rules Britain?': the elected government or the striking miners. Being entirely devoid of miners, striking or otherwise, Northern Ireland treated the election as a referendum on the power-sharing system and was overwhelmingly convinced by the loyalists. The DUP/Vanguard arrangement of the Assembly elections was extended to take in anti-power-sharing Unionists in a 'United Ulster Unionist Coalition' which fought the election on the slogan 'Dublin is only a Sunningdale away' and won every seat except the West Belfast constituency of Gerry Fitt, the leader of the SDLP and the Deputy Chief Executive in the executive. The loyalists now had the grounds they needed to be able to argue that the executive was undemocratic: the people of Ulster had finally been given a chance to vote on the issue and 50.8 per cent of them were opposed to power-sharing.[20]

However, it was not politicians or election results which destroyed the power-sharing experiment. Since the start of the Troubles, a number of loyalist trade unionists had tried to create a province-wide organization of unionist workers and by late 1973 the plans of men such as Billy Kelly, a power workers' shop steward, Billy Hull, ex-Northern Ireland Labour Party, and Hugh Petrie, a precision engineer from Shorts, were sufficiently advanced for them to propose to the loyalist politicians that the province could be brought to a halt by a strike.[21] The politicians were initially less than enthusiastic, largely because, like the Stormont and Westminster civil servants, they underestimated the power and planning of the Ulster Workers Council. The workers decided to push ahead despite the reservations of West, Paisley and others and the politicians were presented with a *fait accompli*.

[19] Deutsch and Magowan, op. cit., n. 12 above, iii. 43.

[20] Details of these and other elections are given in the appendix.

[21] Robert Fisk, *The Point of No Return: the strike which broke the British in Ulster* (London: Andre Deutsch, 1975).

The strike began on the morning of Wednesday 15 May and
within a week was bringing Ulster close to a standstill. Public
support for the strike was hardly necessary when the electricity
workers could reduce the supply so much that basic economic
activity had to stop. With the paramilitary organizations such as
the UDA, the UVF and the Down Orange Welfare setting up
road blocks and, in some areas, using considerable 'persuasion' to
prevent people going about their normal business, the government
was seriously challenged and it hardly responded. The army refused to become involved in what it maintained was an 'industrial'
strike and, anyway, it was incapable of running the electricity
industry. But most importantly, once the strike had lasted out
its first week, a large number of businessmen and middle-class
professionals tacitly co-operated with the strikers in return for
being able to pursue some of their normal business. All round
there was a lack of shared will to break the strike and maintain
Faulkner's executive. On 28 May, with the electricity all but completely cut and threats of sewage rising in the streets of Belfast,
Faulkner resigned. Power-sharing was at an end.

Paisley played a part in the Ulster Workers Council but, like the
other politicians, he had had to be forced by the workers' action in
starting the strike despite his reservations. He was less prominent
in the action than William Craig and he felt sufficiently distanced
from it to be able to absent himself for a few days in the first week
of the strike when he went to Canada to attend a funeral. On his
return he took a more active part and in the House of Commons
bore the brunt of the hostility of Mervyn Rees, the Labour Northern Ireland Secretary, but the relations between Paisley and the
paramilitaries were never entirely cordial or trusting. The paramilitaries felt, quite rightly as it turned out, that the politicians
would use them when it suited them and then reject them once the
threat of anarchy had achieved the desired end of bringing down
Brian Faulkner. In March of the following year, when the feuding
between the UDA and the UVF reached the point of tit-for-tat
assassination, Paisley called on Protestants to withdraw all support
from the paramilitaries and accused them of committing crimes
'just as heinous and hellish as those of the IRA'.[22]

Fred Procter, by then a DUP Belfast city councillor, was shot,
apparently by the UVF, who objected to his spirited criticisms of

[22] *Irish Times* (20 Mar. 1975).

'gangsterism' on the Shankill Road.[23] The fighting between the UVF and UDA, and the struggles for power within the UDA, did much to damage the reputation of the working-class loyalist organizations and to permit the professional politicians to regain control after the UWC strike. What also helped to undermine their credibility were the claims that the UDA and UVF were 'socialist' or 'communist'. Few accusations, if they can be made to stick, are more damaging in the context of Northern Irish politics where leftism has traditionally been associated with nationalism. Glen Barr of Vanguard and the UDA went to Libya to seek financial support from Colonel Gadaffi for an independent Ulster and was quickly accused of communism by Clifford Smyth, then a leading DUP Assemblyman, who told the DUP's annual conference in November 1974 that Libya was a 'significant springboard for Russian subversion in Western Europe'.[24]

The complexities of the inter-paramilitary disputes need not concern us.[25] What is important is that, having used their muscle to overthrow the power-sharing executive, the working-class loyalists failed to capitalize by creating an enduring political presence and more traditional loyalist leaders returned to pre-eminence in the struggle against nationalism. And in particular the position of Paisley and the DUP was enhanced by having done enough to prove themselves implacably opposed to appeasement of 'rebels' while distancing themselves sufficiently from the working-class loyalists to avoid the opprobrium of being closely associated with thugs and gangsters.

The autumn of 1974 saw the DUP's position further consolidated when Harold Wilson decided to call a general election only seven months after forming a minority government. Once again the three main anti-power-sharing groups—the DUP, Vanguard and the conservative Unionists—fought the election as a coalition. Brian Faulkner, having lost control of the Unionist Party, had formed the new Unionist Party of Northern Ireland which could only field two candidates and won less than three per cent of the poll. The non-sectarian Alliance Party won only 6.3 per cent of the votes cast. The majority of Ulster voters supported the

[23] *Protestant Telegraph* (15–19 Mar. 1975).

[24] *Newsletter* (26 Nov. 1974).

[25] Relations between the paramilitaries are well explored in Sarah Nelson, *Ulster's Uncertain Defenders: loyalists and the Northern Ireland conflict* (Belfast: Appletree Press, 1984).

SDLP, if they were Catholics, or the unionist coalition, if they were Protestant. Power-sharing was dead. Ian Paisley held his North Antrim seat with a massive personal majority of 34,497 voters. Almost half of the eligible voters had chosen Paisley as their representative. He had come a very long way in the decade since his wife had failed to win a Belfast Corporation seat!

And Then There Were Two: The Break-up of Vanguard

The collapse of the Ulster Workers Council and the failure of the paramilitaries to pursue a consistent and popular policy left three competitors for the support of Ulster loyalists: Paisley, Craig, and West. The advantage that Paisley enjoyed of being master of his own house has already been mentioned. But he remained only one of three competitors for the leadership of the loyalists. The competition was soon simplified with the fall from grace of William Craig. Craig was an intriguing character. A Lurgan solicitor who could speak menacing words in a slow quiet voice, he had come close to the leadership of the Unionist Party, had held cabinet office and retained good links with the paramilitaries and the workers' leaders who had planned and organized the 1974 strike. But his good loyalist credentials could not save him when he departed from the narrow path. In 1972 he had suggested independence as Ulster's best course and been severely criticized by Paisley and others. Vanguard had performed well in the 1974 elections but, as Sarah Nelson notes, 'The VUP's future was bound to be in doubt once it shed its two distinctive Vanguard features: militant opposition to British domination and alliance with workers and paramilitants.'[26] None the less it performed well in the elections for the Convention, the constitutional debating chamber established in May 1975 to find an agreed political structure for Ulster. What caused its collapse was Craig's conversion to something which could be presented to loyalists as power-sharing. Craig proposed an emergency voluntary coalition with the SDLP because he saw it as the only way in which some sort of devolved government could be maintained. He managed to persuade the central council to accept the policy but, led by the deputy leader Ernest Baird, a majority of the fourteen Vanguard Convention members broke away from Craig. Paisley had Craig expelled from the unionist

[26] Ibid., p. 166.

coalition. Although the confusion of shifts in allegiance within the various loyalist groupings made it difficult for contemporaries to see the underlying direction of change, with hindsight we can see a simplification of unionist politics. The liberals had been defeated and the Unionist Party was once again being led by traditional unionists. Vanguard was breaking up and its supporters were either rejoining the Unionist Party or moving to Paisley's DUP, which was consolidating its position as the more militant and more populist loyalist party.

As a footnote to the Assembly and Convention periods, it is worth making two points about the Democratic Unionists. Although I have described the events in terms of the DUP's success in displacing other Unionist groups, the leaders of the DUP were not fixed on personal aggrandizement at *any* cost. At a number of points, Ian Paisley and others had tried very hard to create a new party which would embrace all traditional unionists. When the DUP was being planned in late 1971, Desmond Boal kept pushing Unionists such as Austin Ardill to join the new party and received assurances from him and a number of others that they would join. It was only their reluctance to abandon their own party which prevented the creation of a mass anti-appeasement party. At a number of times since, there has been a genuine willingness among some of the DUP members of the United Ulster Unionist Coalition to merge their party into a new wider organization. Although Ian Paisley had unfailing faith in his own leadership qualities—a faith that was shared by his supporters—he was willing to work in coalition with the other unionist leaders, and the continued divisions within the unionist camp cannot be laid entirely at his door.

The second footnote is related to this point and it concerns the career of William Beattie. The voluntary coalition plan floated by Craig also temporarily damaged Beattie in that many DUP members felt that he had failed in his duty more clearly to oppose such a scheme in the discussions at which he was DUP spokesman. He was demoted from deputy leader and replaced by William McCrea, the Free Presbyterian minister of Magherafelt in Londonderry.[27] This suggests an important theme which will be taken up in a later discussion of Paisley's leadership style. Observers who have been taken by Paisley's personal influence over his followers have often

[27] David McKittrick, 'Beattie Ousted as DUP Chairman', *Irish Times* (10 Feb. 1976)

missed the point that those who supported Paisley only did so *conditionally* and the condition was that he continued to articulate traditional unionist positions. Although formal channels for the rank and file to influence Party policy may have been either weak or entirely absent in the early years of the Party, this did not mean that Paisley was free to lead the party wheresoever he wished. There were clear lines beyond which he and the other senior figures in the Party could not go without forfeiting the support of the members and the ordinary voters and, in appearing to have countenanced the idea of an emergency coalition with the SDLP, Beattie had crossed those lines and he paid the price.

To connect these two points, I would stress the obvious point which may be forgotten when one simply looks at the fortunes of particular party organizations. Whatever initial reasons people had for being attracted to Ian Paisley as a politician, the main reason for their support was their commitment to the principles he enunciated. In the end they were committed, as he was, to the preservation of a Protestant Ulster, to the suppression of what they saw as a republican rebellion, and to the restoration of majority rule in Northern Ireland. The leaders and the activists were no doubt also motivated by personal ambition and by a jealous regard for their own organizations but, at various crisis points, many were willing to subordinate their own ambitions to the greater goal of 'saving Ulster'.

The 1977 Strike and the Collapse of the Coalition

Most of the leaders of the 1974 strike felt that they had achieved their goal when Faulkner's power-sharing executive was forced to resign. Others, perhaps with greater foresight, wanted the strike to be continued until they had created an acceptable alternative political structure. The end of power-sharing had left a vacuum, which the constitutional convention had failed to fill, and Ulster staggered on with a vicious IRA campaign, tit-for-tat assassinations, unconvincing direct rule, and no obvious sense of direction.

In an attempt to generate some sort of political movement, Paisley led the DUP into a United Unionist Action Council with the remnant of Craig's Vanguard (now called the United Ulster Unionist Movement and led by Ernest Baird), the paramilitaries, and smaller groups such as the Down Orange Welfare and the

Special Constabulary Association; in effect, the 1974 strike leadership without the Official Unionists. The aims of this new coalition were to press the British government into acting more forcefully against terrorism and to force a return to something like the old majority rule at Stormont. In May 1977, the coalition attempted a repeat of the 1974 strike. Billy Kelly, the power workers' leader who had then been instrumental in halting industry, promised that the electricity workers would again bring the province to a halt. This time Paisley led from the front. And, as one loyalist joked: 'Were the people behind him? Aye, miles behind!' The UDA made some half-hearted attempts to block the roads but they were unpopular enough for the RUC to have little trouble in shifting them. Some of the power workers refused to act as a militant vanguard and said that they would only come out when it was clear that the majority of people supported the stoppage. Paisley stood on a picket line outside the Ballylumford power station in Larne and tried to persuade workers not to go in. The next day, four Official Unionist MPs—Bill Craig (now back in the fold), James Molyneaux, Harold McCusker, and Robert Bradford—went to Ballylumford and asked the workers to keep the supply flowing. The pan-unionist coalition was clearly ended.

In the wake of the 1975 UDA visit to Libya, it had been the DUP who had played the red card and accused the paramilitaries of flirting with communists. This time the Official Unionists made the red scare claims, asserting that the Protestant paramilitaries were in league with the Provisional IRA to create a socialist republic in Northern Ireland.[28] Such accusations resonated with considerable middle-class fears about the power of the UDA and UVF. After all, these people had paralysed the country three years earlier! In 1974, the threat of working-class mobs had been moderated by the presence among the strike organizers of old Unionist leaders like Harry West. With the Official Unionists opposed to this strike, the respectable middle classes had far less assurance that the working-class 'Prods' would be kept in their place.

Furthermore, there was a challenge to the legitimacy of the strike from within the leadership of the working class. A number of the more left-leaning activists from the first strike, such as Bob Pagels and Glen Barr, made clear their opposition to this second stoppage. For once, Paisley had misjudged the climate. As a detailed opinion

[28] *Irish News* (11 May 1977).

poll conducted in May showed, there was considerable support for the general aims of the strikers—better security and majority-rule devolved government—but there was also a strong sense that the strike was ill advised and would only play into the hands of republicans.[29] Within ten days the strike collapsed. However, for the DUP, ignominious defeat produced a surprising increase in their popularity. Given that Paisley's ability to predict political events had always been a major part of his public image, one would have expected the electorate to turn against him, especially when he had committed his personal prestige to the extent of offering to resign if the strike did not change British policy. But when the electorate went yet again to the polls on 19 May, this time to elect their local government representatives, the DUP did quite well in what was the first genuine free-for-all among unionist parties. The OUP took 29.6 per cent of the vote, the SDLP 20.6 per cent, the Alliance 14.4 per cent and the DUP gained seventy-four seats with 12.7 per cent of the votes cast. The main sufferers were the small parties.

That the strike did not cost the DUP support suggests an important point about Paisley's political appeal. Because he was still *ideologically sound*, strategic and tactical mistakes could be forgiven. This particular campaign may have failed but Paisley had demonstrated that his heart was in the right place. He was at least trying to do something. The DUP had the advantage over other politicians of not being in the game of pragmatic compromise. The party stood for certain unchanging principles. It managed to sustain a comparison of itself as the resolute party to the OUP's vacillation. With that as its dominant posture, particular schemes could fail and it would still retain and perhaps even enhance its support, if it could claim that it pursued a course which was known to be difficult but which was still the ideologically sound thing to do.

The day after the elections, Enoch Powell, the Official Unionist MP for South Down, put the formal touch to the end of the coalition by announcing to the Speaker of the House of Commons that Dr Paisley would no longer be welcome in the office used by the Official Unionist members.

Protestant politics were being simplified. The power-sharers, relocated in the Unionist Party of Northern Ireland, were wiped

[29] NOP Market Research, 1977, 'Political Opinion in Belfast—UUAC strike May 1977'.

out, as was the Baird-led remnant of Vanguard. The competition was now between Ian Paisley's DUP and the Official Unionist Party. In 1979, the DUP received a major boost to its fortunes when it gained two more Westminster MPs. One of its gains was at the expense of Bill Craig. Craig had first won the seat for East Belfast as a member of the coalition. But at that and the second Westminster election, he had been put in office by the DUP. Vanguard had little organization in East Belfast and the Official Unionists gave very little assistance. Craig's campaign manager therefore was the young leader of the DUP in East Belfast, Peter Robinson. With the collapse of the coalition, Robinson felt free to challenge the man for whom he had previously campaigned and he won the seat by the extremely narrow margin of sixty-four votes.

When asked about his victory, Robinson was surprisingly frank. He thought that Craig might have lost some votes because people had not forgiven his voluntary coalition heresy but recognized that, had Craig emulated Paisley and created a reputation as an active constituency MP, he would have retained the seat.

The second new DUP seat was won by Johnny McQuade who had moved to contest North Belfast after failing in earlier elections to unseat Gerry Fitt in West Belfast. While it would be dangerous to build too much analysis on the characteristics of the three main public representatives of the DUP, Paisley, Robinson and McQuade between them represented the full spectrum of DUP support. Paisley was the evangelical preacher, embracing the religious and the political in his two careers and he was backed by the Protestant farmers. McQuade represented the old working-class independent unionist combination of militant loyalism and a populist critique of the ruling élite. Robinson was the first of a new generation of supporters of Paisleyism. As a teenager he had been attracted to hear Paisley because he shared his evangelical religion. He quickly became convinced of the need for political action and founded a branch of the Ulster Protestant Volunteers. Better educated, brighter, and more articulate than many of the older men who had supported Paisley since the 1950s, Robinson gave the party managerial and organizational skills it had previously lacked.

Establishment

Winning three Westminster seats gave the DUP an important edge in the first direct elections to the European Parliament. When the United Kingdom had entered the EEC, it had asked the major parties to nominate representatives to the Parliament. In 1979, British voters were given their first opportunity to elect representatives. In order to ensure that the Catholic population won at least one of the three seats allocated to Northern Ireland, the whole of the province was treated as one constituency with three members. The election could hardly have been better designed to promote the DUP. Although Robinson and others were achieving success in building a province-wide organization, the DUP's greatest asset was its leader. Treating the whole province as a single constituency gave Paisley a chance to cash in on his considerable personal support.

Paisley was the sole DUP candidate and John Hume was the candidate for the SDLP, but the Official Unionists made the tactical mistake of fielding *two* candidates. Supporters in the west were asked to give their first preference to Harry West and their second to John Taylor; those in the east, vice versa. Paisley's view of the EEC will be discussed in chapter 8. It was hardly important for the election where, as in almost every other Northern Ireland election, the main issue was the constitution. Although some Catholics (and fewer Protestants) voted for the socialist platform of Paddy Devlin or the militancy of Bernadette McAliskey (née Devlin), most voted for Hume. The interesting competition was between Paisley and the Official Unionists for the title of spokesman for the Protestant people, and it was a contest which Paisley won comfortably. He took 29.8 per cent of the first preference votes, Hume took 24.6 per cent and John Taylor did not pass the quota until West was eliminated and he collected his transfers. Together both the Officials took only twenty-two per cent of the first preferences.

In an opinion poll conducted in 1967, ninety per cent of the people asked said they preferred Terence O'Neill to Ian Paisley as premier. One can assume that all the nationalists preferred O'Neill but even eighty-four per cent of those who called themselves unionists were opposed to Paisley.[30] Now, twelve years later in the first province-wide 'beauty show', the majority of Ulster unionists chose Ian Paisley as their spokesman.

[30] *Belfast Telegraph* (12 Dec. 1967).

United Again?

The last five years have seen the DUP establish itself as the voice of about half of the unionist population. They have also seen the electoral rise of Sinn Fein, the political arm of the IRA.[31] The two things are connected. The political climate reacts like a see-saw. Increased weight at the republican end calls for increased weight at the loyalist end and the rise of Sinn Fein has added to the appeal of Paisley's political postures.

In terms of proportions of votes cast at elections, the Official Unionists have recently regained the advantage but they have done so by becoming more and more like the DUP. In November 1981, the IRA assassinated the Revd. Robert Bradford, an Independent Methodist minister and Member of Parliament for South Belfast. Like Paisley, Bradford was extremely conservative in theology and sufficiently opposed to the ecumenical movement to be forced out of the Irish Methodist ministry. Although an OUP member, he had been active in Vanguard and was well to the right of the Party. The DUP's first reaction to the murder was to suggest to the OUP that a joint candidate, acceptable to both parties, be found. When the OUP rejected such advances, the DUP fielded the Revd William McCrea, minister of Magherafelt. McCrea polled very badly against the OUP candidate Martin Smyth, and some journalists hailed this as the turn of the tide in the DUP's electoral fortunes. But Martin Smyth, although a minister of the Irish Presbyterian Church, was active in conservative and anti-ecumenical Pres-

[31] The Sinn Fein policy of not contesting elections was gradually abandoned. In 1981, Frank Maguire, the independent nationalist MP for Fermanagh and South Tyrone, died during the IRA prisoners' hunger strike and Bobby Sands, the leader of the strikers, was nominated. With the SDLP not contesting the seat, Sands won it. When his death created another by-election, Owen Carron (who absconded in 1986 while on bail for arms charges) stood on behalf of the prisoners (whose own candidacy had been prevented by a hurried legislative act) and was elected. Encouraged by these successes, Gerry Adams and his supporters persuaded Sinn Fein to pursue an 'armalite and ballot box' strategy. In the 1982 Assembly elections, Sinn Fein won 10% of the vote as compared with the 18.8% of the SDLP. In 1983, Adams won the West Belfast Westminster seat from Gerry Fitt and the following year Danny Morrison won 13.3% of the poll in the European Parliament elections, as compared with John Hume's the SDLP's 22.1%. But the psychological breakthrough for Sinn Fein came with the 1985 local government elections which gave them 46 council seats. The elected representatives took their seats and unionist councillors, refusing to sit with Sinn Fein, began a campaign of disruption and abstention. This was the first stage in the development of the DUP–OUP alliance which the Anglo-Irish accord turned into a united front.

byterian circles. He was also Grand Master of the Orange Order. He had been active with William Craig in Vanguard. All in all, he was the closest thing the OUP had to a DUP man.

In the last six months, inter-party rivalry has been subordinated to the need for a united unionist front. The Sinn Fein successes in the 1985 local government elections were dramatically symbolized in the election of a Sinn Fein councillor as chairman of Omagh District Council. Unionists responded by either boycotting council meetings or trying to exclude Sinn Fein councillors, depending on whether or not there was a unionist majority. Although one or two local DUP and OUP groups continued to squabble about tactics, the leadership of the two parties managed to present a common front and the signing of the Anglo-Irish accord in November 1985 gave unionists a very good reason for laying aside their differences.

On a wet January afternoon in 1986, Ian Paisley and James Molyneaux walked around the North Down seaside town of Bangor with the local MP and Speaker of the Assembly, James Kilfedder. As usual on such occasions, Molyneaux looked a little embarrassed and out of place, as if he did not particularly relish the 'glad-handing' of strangers. Paisley was in his element, at one point stopping two old ladies to say 'We're here to introduce this young lad to you 'cos you'll not recognize him, will you?', laughing and nodding in the direction of Kilfedder, who, with a 13,000 vote majority, needed no introduction in North Down. In the twenty-two years since Ian Paisley had campaigned for Kilfedder in West Belfast, the world had been turned upside down more than once and the three men had crossed and re-crossed each other, like figures in a bizarre dance. Paisley had broken with Kilfedder because he had not been sufficiently outspoken in his criticism of O'Neill. Paisley had supported him again once he had broken with the Official Unionists. Kilfedder had been Paisley's choice for Speaker of the Assembly. Kilfedder and Molyneaux had once been close but Kilfedder's desertion of the OUP had divided them. When Molyneaux was first elected to Westminster for South Antrim in 1970, he had been regarded by Paisley as a conservative ally. But when he became leader of the Unionist Party, he also became the target for accusations of vacillating leadership. Now, faced with the Anglo-Irish accord, the three unionist leaders were again united and Paisley and Molyneaux were working the main street of Bangor to boost Kilfedder's support.

The initial aim in forming the DUP had been to create a united unionist party which would be as orthodox in its constitutional position as the Unionist Party of Craig and Brookeborough. It would be a stronger party because it would win popular support from all sections of the unionism by advocating equitable social and economic policies and by removing power from the undependable unionist élites. The DUP failed to achieve its goal, largely because conservatives recaptured the Unionist Party. However, if one forgets for a moment the organizational structures of the two parties and considers their policies, one sees a relatively united unionist movement. In this sense, the DUP has succeeded in establishing its view of the constitutional crisis and the proper reactions to it. Whatever the future holds for Northern Ireland, it is clear that Ian Paisley has moved from being a prophet crying in the wilderness to the centre of the unionist stage.

5

Church and Party

Free Presbyterian Unionism

In the first chapter I argued that the fact that the Scots settlers and the Irish natives were respectively Calvinists and Roman Catholics had profound consequences for the development of social conflict. Specifically, it established a cleavage along religious and ethnic lines which prevented other sorts of conflict, such as those of economic interest, developing. The preservation of the basic Ulster divide of Protestant and Catholic into the age of nationalism ensured that competing political ideologies would be added to the religious and ethnic divisions: the Irish Catholics became nationalists while the Scots Presbyterians and the Anglo-Irish drew together as unionists. If most Protestants in Northern Ireland are unionists, are Free Presbyterians especially committed to the Union with Great Britain?

The reasons for unionism can be placed in two broad categories: those specifically concerned with religion, and those which are concerned with a wider range of social, political, and economic considerations. The first category is easy to describe. Putting it bluntly, many Protestants fear that they will be unable to continue to practise and promote their religion in a united Ireland. In discussion, they point back to the Spanish Inquisition or the St Bartholomew's Day Massacre as evidence that the Roman Catholic Church is set on persecution of dissenters. Older Protestants can point to examples of Catholic persecution from their own lifetimes: in Spain under Franco or in a number of Latin American countries in the 1940s and 1950s.

The sceptic might argue that the modern Roman Catholic Church in civilized societies no longer acts in this way but the convinced anti-Catholic can turn Rome's own claims to be unchanging back on the Catholic Church and insist that the basic aim remains the same. Only the tactics have changed. It is certainly the case that, a deviant fringe aside, the core of Catholicism maintains the claim to be the only true church, insists that church unity must mean unity with Rome on its terms, and, in such practices as insisting that the children of mixed marriages be raised as Catholics, continues to behave in an 'intolerant' fashion. So even those Protestants who do not believe that the Catholic Church would actually sanction a return to the thumbscrews if it thought it could get away with it view with profound misgivings the decline of the Protestant population of the Irish Republic from 330,000 in 1911 to 130,000 in 1971. By 1981, it had fallen from being four per cent of the population in 1971, to just 3.49 per cent.[1]

In addition, the Catholic Church's reaction to the recent IRA campaign—in particular the refusal to excommunicate convicted murderers and to condemn for mortal sin the hunger strikers who committed suicide—has been taken as confirmation that the Church does not really mind if other people exterminate Protestants. It is difficult to exaggerate the strength of Protestant feeling about this issue and it is worth quoting Allister's statement of the views expressed by many of the people I interviewed:

For those republicans who lose their own lives in advancing their struggle, there is available the full solace of their Church as IRA murderers are buried with no lesser Roman Catholic Church rites than the very priests of that Church. Glorification rather than the more seemingly fitting excommunication is the response of the Roman Catholic Church to the IRA terrorist. It is this insoluble marriage of Roman Catholicism to militant Irish republicanism, where the latter is seen as the 'political' expression and promoter of the former, which makes what should otherwise be possible, namely the co-existence of the political expressions of Protestantism and Roman Catholicism impossible in Ireland.[2]

No amount of public condemnation of terrorism by cardinals, bishops, and priests has altered the basic perception of many conservative Protestants that, by its refusal to deny religious ordinances to terrorists, the church subtly countenances such actions.

[1] Maire Nic Ghiolla Phadraig, 'Religious Practice and Secularization', Ch. 7 in P. Clancy, S. Drudy, K. Lynch, and L. O'Dowd (eds.), *Ireland: a sociological profile* (Dublin: Institute of Public Administration, 1986).

[2] James Allister, *Irish Unification Anathema: the reasons why Northern Ireland rejects unification with the Republic of Ireland* (Belfast: Crown Publications, n.d.), pp. 20–1.

If this is what happens in the North now, how much worse then would things be in a united Ireland?:

The people of Northern Ireland naturally and rightly reason that if what they have suffered at the hands of the southern-spawned IRA, they have suffered while a majority, how much greater would that persecution not be if they ever entered a state in which they were a perpetual minority.[3]

It is difficult to put a percentage figure on the proportion of Ulster Protestants who would accept this perspective. It is probably a minority, but a *general* feeling that the Roman Catholic Church is a threat is widely shared. Only nine per cent of Moxon-Browne's survey described themselves as evangelicals, but 74.5 per cent gave 'fear of the power of the Roman Catholic Church' as their reason for being unionist.[4] The offensive section of the 1937 constitution of the Republic which recognized the special position of the Catholic Church has been removed but this is largely irrelevant to Protestant perceptions. When ninety-five per cent of the population of the Republic professes to being Roman Catholic, the Catholic Church does not need a constitutional commitment to dominate moral and social legislation. The Irish Republic is a Catholic country and even those Protestants who do not expect to be actively persecuted doubt that they will have full civil and religious liberty when the major religious institution refuses to engage in fair competition by, for example, permitting the parents free choice of their child's religion in the case of mixed marriage.

Free Presbyterians would differ from other Protestants in their attitude to the above reasons for unionism only in taking them more seriously. If they do have a distinctive perspective it comes from their belief that Rome and terrorism are further linked in a more roundabout fashion through the ecumenical movement and the World Council of Churches. In the 1970s, the WCC launched a programme to combat racism and, as part of that initiative, gave money to a number of African liberation movements. The funds were designated for humanitarian rather than military aid, but given that such funds freed existing funds for arms purchase, it was not difficult for critics of the WCC to argue that it was supporting terrorism. At the same time, a number of leading liberal church

[3] Ibid., p. 16.
[4] Edward Moxon-Browne, *Nation, Class and Creed in Northern Ireland* (Aldershot: Gower, 1983), p. 38.

leaders in Northern Ireland became involved in negotiations with the IRA to establish a cease-fire.[5] Thus the conservative Protestant critic of the ecumenical movement can equate ecumenism and terrorism and, given that the ecumenical movement is on the road to Rome, Rome can be equated with the IRA. So Free Presbyterians and other evangelicals critical of the ecumenical movement can add a further set of elements to their ideological objection to a united Ireland.

It is possible to identify a second cluster of reasons for unionism. These could loosely be described as 'secular' Protestantism. In talking about what is good in the Protestant way of life, even evangelical Protestants go beyond theology and begin to list things that are thought to be the results of the right religion. These would include loyalty, diligence, honesty, affluence, a lower crime rate, families small enough to be supported by one's own labour, a certain independence of mind, democracy, and so on. Obviously different social groups have a varying ability to articulate these concerns, but there is a widely shared general notion that there is something valuable—'the British way of life'—which would be undermined by translation into an overwhelmingly Catholic country. Generally this is perceived, not in the abstract, but by listing the failings of Catholic countries. Spain and Portugal are poor. The Republic is poorer than Ulster. Franco was a dictator. The Republic has more alcoholics. Or comparisons are drawn between Protestants and Catholics in the same country. If Protestants are better off than Catholics in Ulster, it is because they work harder and have fewer children. If Catholics figure disproportionately in the crime statistics, it is because Protestants are more law-abiding. Thus, beyond the specifically theological reasons for unionism, there is a broader penumbra of social concerns. Protestants believe that Protestantism produces better people and a better society, and this belief is held by even those people who have ceased to have any active religious commitment.

Again, this second set of reasons would be subscribed to by Free Presbyterians, who would only differ from the bulk of the Protestant population in being more consciously committed to such arguments. While non-evangelicals and atheists might agree that there have been historically specific benefits from Prot-

[5] Eric Gallagher and Stanley Worrall, *Christians in Ulster, 1968–80* (Oxford: Oxford University Press, 1982), pp. 69–71.

estantism, and that we ought to preserve such benefits, the evangelical adds a more direct link with the belief that God will punish us if we deviate further from his commands. A failure to defend the Protestant heritage will cause God to remove from us what benefits remain.

Is the Free Presbyterian Church Democratic Unionist?

The detailed history in the previous chapters has given an account of Ian Paisley's personal combination of religion and politics. Against those who see his political career as stemming from mundane and this-worldly considerations such as a desire for power, I would argue that there is no good reason to reject his own understanding of the connection between the two. In his view of the circumstances in which he found himself, the preservation of his religious culture required a political response. Given his initial assumptions and central beliefs, his political involvement has been rational. From where he stands, it makes sense.

To what extent do other members of the Free Presbyterian Church, especially other leaders, share Ian Paisley's politics? And how important has the Church been in promoting Paisley's politics? These are the questions which I wish to address. Some ministers fully endorse 'the Doc's' politics. In fact, a number were attracted to the religion and to the ministry by the political conflict. For someone like William Beattie who was raised in a tradition which firmly linked the preservation of a religious culture with the maintenance of a Protestant and unionist polity, changes in the political world acted to reinforce his religious commitment. In his explanation of how he became involved in the Free Presbyterian Church, he combines two elements: the appointment of O'Neill as premier and his attention being drawn to a biblical text which talked of the 'evil to come'. He believed that God was drawing his attention to this particular message from Scripture and that O'Neill was a harbinger of the troubles that lay ahead. So from the very outset, before O'Neillism was widely recognized as a new force in Ulster politics, Beattie was committed to the politicized evangelicalism which Paisley promoted.

Unlike Beattie, who was socialized into evangelicalism and unionism, Ivan Foster was recruited after a more dramatic conversion. Although his uncle was a keen Pentecostalist, his family had a strong Orange background, and his parents were 'saved', Foster had little interest in religion or politics. He was working as a trainee film editor with Ulster Television in Belfast and, like most young men, pursuing an active life of sin when he felt the Lord speaking to him. Once saved, he entered into the life of the Free Presbyterian Church with gusto. Immediately after hearing Paisley, he wanted to become involved: 'I was mad keen. I rang the Big Man up the next day after I had talked to him and said: "When's the next meeting?". I was bursting for meetings, bursting for meetings!' He simultaneously became an enthusiastic supporter of Paisley's politics:

I didn't divorce the spiritual battle in Ulster from the political and I still wouldn't. So I felt that our heritage was basically a spiritual heritage. . . . I went to Gaelic matches in Dublin. I went to Croke Park and I had not the slightest interest in Protestantism but I did come from a Fermanagh family where you did live cheek by jowl with republicanism so I had imbibed it undoubtedly and it resurfaced, the inherited knowledge of the heart of the controversy in Ulster. It was there all the time but I had turned my back upon it in a sense, so when I got converted, and of course I was listening to the Big Man's comments on events and I recognized the validity of what he was saying. I don't come from an evangelical background, I came from a raw environment straight into the contentions of the Big Man and you couldn't have been too extreme. It didn't bother me. Up the Shankill Road in the riots! I had no problem relating to the roughs and whatnot.

For Foster the resurfaced family tradition of unionism and his newly acquired loyalty to Paisley made him an active and enthusiastic supporter of his political activities.

Other early ministers were pushed into politics by the reaction of others to what they saw as religious activity. John Wylie's experience in Ballymoney is a good example. He saw nothing political about inviting an ex-priest to publicly denounce the mass as a blasphemy, and took the council's refusal to let him use public property for this purpose as the state interfering in valid religious activity. The liberals wanted to promote a modern secular understanding of religion as a largely private matter which should be pursued in such a manner as not to offend people of other religions. Wylie's desire to maintain a more traditional notion of religion as a matter of truth and falsity (where those with the truth have an obligation publicly to denounce falsity) brought him into conflict with the state and he responded to that challenge by standing for election to the council.

The experiences of 1966 and the imprisonment of the three ministers politicized a number of ministers and elders in this way. Some, such as Cecil Menary of Crossgar, remained largely un-involved, but most found themselves becoming increasingly in-volved in public criticism of O'Neillism. Even those men, such as Bert Cooke and John Douglas, who were later critical of ministers becoming professional politicians, found themselves acting in the political arena as they tried to explain to an increasingly interested audience why their spiritual leader was being sent to prison. One can best describe their position, in contrast to that of Paisley and Beattie, as being one of reluctant and short-term involvement in politics. Where possible, they emphasized the spiritual side of the conflict and used the interest in the Paisley–O'Neill conflict as a means of 'religious revival'. Bert Cooke describes the im-prisonment rallies which he addressed with Alan Cairns:

Alan and I took a lot of meetings . . . in Londonderry, Coleraine, Port-glenone. We were involved in a large one in the Ulster Hall. Alan set up the legal part of it and the political side and I would come in with the more spiritual side of it: the demand for separation from the Irish Presbyterian Church that was operating in cahoots with O'Neill at that time. Because this was our charge; that the government linked up with leaders of the Irish Presbyterian Church in order to silence Paisley. And so we were involved a great deal in what we would call 'protesting' but as far as political activity, that was never my thing.

The Free Presbyterians can be divided into a very small group of what one man called 'the bible college—God bless you brother—every blessing' types who remained distant from politics; the ma-jority who saw themselves as being unionist, but not especially so, who were forced into political activity by the alliance of O'Neillism and the ecumenical movement; and a small circle of fully poli-ticized ministers.

It was this last group which provided Paisley with the resources necessary to launch his campaign against O'Neill. In the absence of a well-organized party machine, it was his friends and colleagues who were called on to turn out for hurriedly organized dem-onstrations. When he decided to challenge O'Neill in Bannside in 1969, he asked Jimmy Beggs, the Free Presbyterian minister of Ballymena who had married his adoptive sister, to act as election agent. The minister of the Rasharkin congregation, Gordon Cooke, became the chairman of the Bannside branch of the Protestant Unionist party. Of the six Protestant Unionists who stood in that election, three were Free Church ministers (Paisley, Wylie, and Beattie) and a fourth was an elder. Nevertheless, Paisley was keen to establish a public distinction between these two roles. At an early election meeting in an Orange Hall in the Bannside constituency he arranged to have a friend ask him if Protestant Unionism was just Free Presbyterianism by another name. He replied that he recognized that 'there are those who agree with me politically but who disagree with me religiously' and said he wanted their political support. Ironically, his reliance on Free Presbyterians for his early support is demonstrated by that story. The stooge who set up the question was a local Free Presbyterian elder!

There are two separate elements to the Free Presbyterians' support for Paisley's politics which in practice reinforced each other. As I have tried to demonstrate, there were good ideological reasons for Free Presbyterians to be Protestant Unionists, but there was also an element of personal loyalty. For the early Free Presbyterians, who had joined the Church when it was still small and there was still a great deal of personal contact between Paisley and his followers, there was a strong personal commitment to Paisley's political analyses because they had come to trust and respect his judgement and ability as a spiritual leader.

The fact that the major period of growth for the Church was a result of the political conflict with liberal unionism meant that most of those who were attracted to the Church were aware of its high political profile and either positively endorsed it, or at least did not find it offensive. Controversy had two major advantages for the Church: considerable free publicity, and such a negative public image that only those who were strongly committed would join. I have very little knowledge about why ordinary members joined, but my knowledge of why those people who later became ministers joined should be fairly representative of the core support. Again, the cases can be grouped in types. There were those who did not like the Church's controversial image. Most of them left the ministry and moved to other evangelical outlets for their vocation. There were some who were initially repelled by the controversy which surrounded Paisley, but who overcame that revulsion and became committed supporters. Although Bert Cooke, shortly after his conversion, became an active supporter of Paisley's evangelistic work, he was less than enthusiastic about the public image of the Church: 'When I started thinking about full-time service, I didn't want to be a Free Presbyterian. I wanted to be non-controversial, popular with people.' His complete acceptance of the 'protest' in 'Protestant' did not come till a few years later when some leading members of his Mount Merrion, Belfast, congregation insisted that he object to the Church's 'street corner boy' activities of picketing the Irish Presbyterian Church General Assembly. He considered this for a short time and concluded that he had to make a public stand for those things which he believed. From that point on he was 'a real dyed in the wool Free Presbyterian'.

The third group consists of those who were positively attracted by the controversy and some of these were unionist before they were 'saved' Protestants. Harry Cairns first met Paisley in 1958 when he was promoting Albert Duff as a Protestant Unionist candidate against Maginnis, the then Attorney-General, in the rural Iveagh constituency. Although he had recently been converted, it was Paisley's conservative attack on unreliable unionist leaders which first drew him to Free Presbyterianism. When the 1966 imprisonment again gave Paisley a high profile, he attended meetings being led by Beattie in Hillsborough and became a founding member of the Free Presbyterian congregation there. He then felt called to the ministry.

If that is the biography of a rural evangelical Free Presbyterian activist, the following is the urban working variant:

Way back in the 1960s, when the tricolour flew in Divis St, I was only sixteen at the time. I thought the man was crazy really but in 1966 I did develop an interest and started to attend the services . . . I went to him for the political because I was a red hot loyalist at that time. Doc Paisley was the first man I ever heard preach to me directly that I was sinner, that God loved me and that Jesus died for me . . . It was shortly after that I was converted, in my own home, 5th November 1966.

He went on to add that, had his interest not been channelled into the evangelical Protestantism of the Free Church, it would probably have led to him getting in with 'a bad crowd' and joining the tartan gangs of loyalist youths.

Of course, it was possible for people to accept Paisley's political analyses and the need for evangelicals to be politically involved and yet not support the particular organizational expressions of those views which Paisley led. The Church was always broad enough to include such people. Cecil Harvey was one of the founding elders of the Free Presbyterian Church. He sat as a Unionist councillor and, when the Unionist Party became dominated by powersharers, he moved to Vanguard, then to Baird's United Ulster Unionist Party, and only switched to Paisley's Democratic Unionist Party after the demise of the UUUP. It may have been that Harvey enjoyed such seniority in the Church that in his case such deviation was permitted, but given that two or three other committed Free Presbyterians have been active in the Official Unionist Party (in 1985 there were two Free Presbyterians in local government as Official Unionist councillors), it is more likely that the Church leadership was genuinely able to maintain some distance from Paisley's politics.

So far I have been suggesting ways in which the Free Church benefited from the political activities of its founder and other leading members. There have also been corresponding costs.

The first and most general cost has been to give the impression that Official Unionists would not be welcome in the Free Church. Despite their best efforts, the ministers have not been able to break the public association of Church and Party. In the early days, when unionist politics were in a state of flux, some people may have been alienated from the Church by their dislike for Paisley's political image, but they would not have felt that the Church was a DUP church. It may have been a controversial church, but its image as a party church dates only from about 1977 when Vanguard disappeared and unionist politics became a straight fight between the Officials and the DUP.

There was a time when I felt that the Free Church could present a broader appeal to the Protestant people, while there was greater harmony among the unionist parties as such. Now when you find a lot of political infighting between the Officials and the DUP, a lot of people, wrongly in my opinion, suspect that the Free Church is just the religious arm of the DUP. I would like to think that my ministry would appeal to a cross section of the population, that Official Unionists could come to my services and not be insulted by anything I might say.

They almost certainly could go to the services of any Free Church and not be insulted. None the less, in many congregations, many

of the elders are DUP activists or members, and in some congregations all of those members who vote at all would vote DUP.
And at times of crisis the Church has rallied to the political position
of the Party, and ministers such as Bert Cooke who are not normally politically active have supported the DUP's initiatives from
their pulpits. The call for a day of action to protest against the
government's security policies in the wake of the murder of the
Revd Robert Bradford, MP for South Belfast, in 1981, is an
example.

This close association of Church and Party may well have had a
cost to the Church in limiting recruitment to people who are not
committed supporters of the Official Unionist Party but, given that
the DUP support is twenty times the size of the Free Church and
that there is a large uncommitted population, this is probably not
something which explains why more people do not join the Free
Church.

A second cost to the Free Church of its political involvement is
a drain on leadership resources. I have already mentioned the
debate in Presbytery in 1974 about ministers going forward in
elections. The arguments had actually been rehearsed on many
occasions:

The Presbytery has not encouraged party political participation and it has
only been because we felt certainly that Dr Paisley's position, that the
country needs it and we felt that he should be allowed to go. For years we
had requests from political people, parties, you know, around the country,
to allow other ministers to go forward and we said 'No'. The Free Church
had got its hands full. We are not going to have all our ministers in
politics.

Alan Cairn's view was echoed by most other ministers I talked to.
Even those who are active in the Party expressed concern at the
diversion of energies from their primary task of building the
Church. It is interesting that Cairns saw the pressure for ministers
to run for office coming, not from ambitious ministers, but from
party activists who thought that certain ministers would make good
political leaders. We should not forget the general point that, in
many communities where religious affiliation plays no part in political decisions, the clergy are still seen as leading figures who can
be called upon to lead and organize activities outside the narrow
remit of religion.

The political involvements of Free Presbyterian ministers can be described as follows.[6] No minister is a member or is active in any party other than the DUP. But of forty-nine ministers in Northern Ireland (which includes one retired man and three students), only six have held elected office, only eleven in total have been office holders in the DUP, and only fifteen in total are members. That is, less than a third of the clergy are members of the DUP. Although the Free Presbyterian clergy are probably more politically involved than the ministers of the Irish Presbyterian Church (unfortunately data for comparison are not available), there is certainly not the tight connection which many outsiders assume.

A further problem for the Church is that it may be seen by some people as a stepping-stone to a political career. In the second part of this chapter, I present evidence from a survey of the denominational affiliation of DUP activists. Much of the information was gathered by asking Free Church ministers if any of a list of local DUP people were members or attenders of their church. In these conversations, an interesting sub-theme emerged. In a very small percentage of cases someone was described as *having* been a Free Presbyterian. Although some of these may have been cases of a genuine change of religious commitment, in many I was given the strong impression that these were people who had come to the church regularly at the time when they were building their political careers but who had subsequently fallen away and now professed no strong denominational attachment. Although the ministers were too polite to commit themselves, even when I pressed them on this point, it was clear to me that they felt they, and their church, had been used. Still, this is hardly unusual or unique to the Free Church. Although its connection with a political party, and the fact that some of its ministers and elders are leading figures in the DUP, provides some people with a good ulterior motive to participate in the life of the Church, it is often the case that people have more than one motive for church involvement. Many people attend churches in order to foster an image of respectability, to make business contacts or to make friends. What makes the position of the Free Church more problematic is that, where the

---

[6] The bulk of this and other information about Free Presbyterian ministers was solicited in interviews with 23 of them. A brief questionnaire was sent to the rest and was completed by 22. Only 6 people who were not interviewed did not complete and return the forms.

ulterior motive is connected to a set of strong commitments outside the Church, then changes in those commitments can cause disruption in the Church.

The already mentioned case of Cecil Harvey suggests that active membership of another party is not a problem for Free Presbyterians, provided one has been consistent. There are, however, problems when someone who was active in both Church and Party leaves the Party. Arguments started outside the congregation may spill over into it. When Clifford Smyth was persuaded to resign from the DUP, he also felt obliged to leave the Free Presbyterian Church, not because the leadership of the Church suggested it, but because he felt a tension between himself and other congregation members who had previously been political colleagues. When conflict between Ken McFaul, a founder member of the DUP and an ex-mayor of Carrickfergus, and other DUP members reached the point of McFaul being expelled from the Party (and simultaneously resigning), he also left the Free Presbyterian Church of which he had been an elder.[7]

William Belshaw was another founder member of the Party who has recently left. As in all such cases, the actual sequence of events and the combinations of motives is complex. Belshaw seems to have been disappointed that he was not selected to fight an Assembly seat. For whatever reason, he chose to break the DUP's stance on relations with representatives of the Republic's government by attending a dinner at which Garret Fitzgerald, the Republic's Prime Minister, was guest of honour. After falling out with the Lisburn DUP, Belshaw resigned his office of treasurer in the Lisburn Free Presbyterian Church and began to attend the church only rarely.

To summarize: although Paisley and the other ministers of the Free Presbyterian Church have always maintained a clear division between 'constitutional' and 'party' politics—the Church has a position on the constitution but does not back any particular party—the close historical and biographical links between Church and Party have made it impossible for the Free Presbyterian Church to avoid either being tagged with the label of being the DUP at prayer or on occasion being disrupted by the spill-over of tensions from the Party into the Church. Although the overlap in personnel is less than many commentators might suppose, the

[7] *Newsletter* (18 Feb. 1984); *Belfast Telegraph* (21 Feb. 1984).

presence of Ian Paisley is such that, despite his best efforts to keep his roles as Church and Party leader distinct, the simplifications of unionist politics into just two parties has left the Church firmly associated with the DUP.

Is the DUP Free Presbyterian?

In the early stages of his political career, Ian Paisley depended a great deal on the Free Presbyterian Church, largely because it was through his evangelistic work that he had become well known. Most of his friends and close supporters were Free Presbyterians. But there was always a second non-evangelical element in his political support which drew on the independent unionist populist tradition. Especially in the Belfast area, people would work for him, not because he was an evangelical who denounced apostasy and promoted sabbatarianism and temperance, but because he was a strong loyalist who articulated their suspicions that the leaders of the Unionist Party—'the fur coat brigade'—were rather more interested in looking after themselves than they were in protecting working-class Protestants.

The DUP was formed with the intention of increasing the non-evangelical element in the movement,[8] but it had little initial success in broadening the recruiting base. Almost half of the seventeen DUP candidates for the 1973 Assembly were Free Presbyterians. For the 1975 Convention election, the proportion rose to almost eighty per cent: fourteen out of eighteen. Scrupulous analysers of elections might argue that the proportion of Free Presbyterians in these contests was artificially inflated by the election pact with Vanguard. Vanguard was stronger than the DUP in urban working-class areas and, as the pacts were designed to maximize loyalist votes by giving the strongest party in any area a clear run, this would have reduced the number of DUP people standing in urban areas. So the DUP candidates would have been drawn predominently from rural areas, the places where the evangelical influence on the Party was greatest. However, the 1977 local government elections were a free-for-all. Of the seventy-two DUP members who sat on councils in 1978, sixty were Free Pres-

[8] Clifford Smyth, 'The Ulster Democratic Unionist Party: a case study in religious and political convergence', Ph.D. thesis (The Queen's University of Belfast, 1984), has a good account of the intentions of the founders.

byterians: eighty-three per cent! The growth of the DUP in recent years has seen that proportion fall. Sixty-two per cent of the 218 candidates fielded in the 1985 local government elections were Free Presbyterians.

Many of the newer activists who are not Free Presbyterians are members of other small evangelical denominations.[9]

The presence of Free Presbyterians increases as one moves up the party hierarchy. All twelve of the 1975 constituency party chairmen were Free Presbyterians. Apart from the brief chairmanship of Desmond Boal, the senior party leadership was drawn exclusively from Free Presbyterian circles until the early 1980s, when Peter Robinson started attending a gospel hall and Sammy Wilson, an Elim Pentecostalist, replaced Jim Allister as press officer.

The Protestant Unionist Party and the early DUP were overwhelmingly Free Presbyterian for the obvious reason that the first activists were recruited through their friendship with, and loyalty to, Ian Paisley, and such qualities tended to be concentrated among Free Presbyterians. These activists then recruited their friends, who were likely also to be Free Presbyterians. The fact that the early DUP was Free Presbyterian explains why the senior leadership still is. Promotion is related to seniority in the Party.

This still leaves a problem. The membership of local DUP branches now includes lots of non-Free Presbyterians. It may be that this will gradually work through and become apparent in the activists in about five years. But even now, some senior DUP men are slightly perplexed at the apparent willingness of non-evangelicals to 'take a back seat and push the others forward', as one man put it. This suggests an important point which will be taken up in detail in the final chapter but which should be mentioned here. Some commentators suppose that there is a considerable Free Presbyterian presence in the lists of party activists because the leaders of the Party favour people who share their religious affiliation. Of course, this is possible but there is good reason to suppose that it is not the case. One area which the leaders unambiguously control is the hiring of staff, and the full-time staff of the DUP is now drawn widely from all the major denominations.

Let us suppose for a moment that the over-representation of

[9] A detailed analysis of the denominational affiliations of DUP activists is presented in the appendix.

Free Presbyterians (and other evangelicals) exists because even those members who are not evangelicals wish it. Is it possible that 'secular' Protestants have a good deal of respect for evangelical beliefs and values even though they do not share them? In the final chapter, I will argue that this is the case. In the meantime, I will turn to potential conflicts within the DUP.

Tensions in Party Support

In the absence of extensive survey material on the attitudes of DUP voters, we can only reason backwards from the platform of the Party to the interests of the people who support it. The manifesto for the 1982 Assembly elections has fifteen paragraphs. The first and second call for the end of direct rule and a return to 'Ulstermen in control of all major government functions by means of legislative as well as executive devolution'. The third and fourth promise that the DUP 'offers the firmest stand against all attempts to force Ulster down the Dublin road', while the fifth section calls for an all-out war against the IRA and the return of the death penalty as 'the only suitable punishment for the heinous murders committed in our Province'. The second section of the manifesto outlines the DUP's social and economic policies, which are moderately Keynesian, calling for 'additional but sensible public expenditure on a sustained jobs creation offensive', cheaper energy through a link to the British mainland's North Sea gas network, and major investment in housing. The strong rural support for the Party is recognized by a call for 'a realistic return for the farming community, with special measures to offset the disadvantages, especially in the intensive livestock sector, resulting from our isolation from Great Britain'.

The manifesto then proposes more democratic control over education and leisure, an end to the financing of two distinct educational systems, an increase in old-age pensions, and more facilities for the handicapped. It is only in the very last paragraph that there is a distinctly evangelical position in the Party's platform. Under the heading 'Moral Matters—Morals Matter', the Party promises that:

A strong and forthright stand will continue to be taken in accordance with Christian principles on the great moral issues of our day. We utterly deprecate the imposition by Westminster of alien moral standards upon

Ulster. The DUP will lead opposition in the Assembly to such matters as the legalising of homosexuality, opening sex shops and Sunday opening of public houses. Ulster should decide its own moral standards and codes of behaviour.

It is clear from this manifesto, and from other DUP election litera-ture over the years, that the Party is mainly known for, and hence presumably supported for, its hardline unionism. With some mi-nor deviations—such as Paisley's preference for fuller integration with the mainland in the early 1970s—the DUP has maintained the image of being the most traditional of the unionist parties and the one with the record of consistent opposition to any changes in the political structures of Northern Ireland which could be seen as compromise with nationalists and republicans. Especially since the demise of Vanguard and the simplification of the inter-unionist competition, the DUP has stressed its own reliability ('for trust-worthy leadership, vote DUP') and made much play of divisions within the Official Unionists and the continued presence in the Unionist Party of some people who were tainted by O'Neillism and power-sharing. Many 1983 Westminster election advertisements mention only law and order, job creation, and the Union. It does not seem implausible to suppose, therefore, that it is the loyalism of the DUP rather than the evangelicalism of many of its leaders that accounts for its support, especially in the greater Belfast urban area.

This poses what is potentially a serious problem for the DUP: the 'Christian principles' which are dear to the leaders of the party may cost them popular support. Certainly some commentators see the unpopularity of the DUP's stand on Sunday opening as part of the reason for its fall in votes in recent elections.[10] What prevents sabbatarianism becoming a major vote-loser for the Party is the absence of serious competition from any group to the right on the constitution.

The DUP and Working-Class Loyalists

The Democratic Unionist Party is in the curious position of being

[10] A number of DUP activists felt that a local press campaign against the sab-batarianism of Carrickfergus DUP members was a major cause of their poor per-formance in the 1985 local government elections in Carrick. Ironically, the leader of the Official Unionists in Carrick, who managed to blame the DUP for the Sunday closing of leisure facilities, was Jim Brown. In 1975, Brown had been a student for the Free Presbyterian Church ministry!

dominated by evangelicals and hence being more favourable to
temperance and sabbatarianism than the Official Unionists and at
the same time being better supported than the Officials by
working-class loyalists who are not known for their piety and who
are prepared to support acts of criminal violence. Critics from both
the nationalist and the loyalist side have attacked the DUP (and
its predecessor, the Protestant Unionist Party) for using working-
class loyalists to further its aims. It encouraged them to break the
law and used the threat of a 'backlash' to discourage the British
government from compromise with Dublin, and then denounced
loyalists for law-breaking. To quote the UDA's magazine *Ulster*:

No body established by the two parties will do anything outside the law
to halt any sell out; what they will do is to engineer situations and emotions
that lead other people to break the law. They are the mirror image of the
Eire politicians who use the IRA. Thousands of Ulster citizens have taken
the law into their own hands to save their country, many of these people
were encouraged by the speeches of our 'leaders'; many were frustrated
that speeches were all they made.[11]

While it is easy to see how those people who took the aggressive
martial language of Paisley and others as justification for violence
can feel used, such an analysis over-simplifies and fails correctly
to identify the 'respectable' Protestant's view of the law and the
genuine dilemmas of loyalism. In this section I will look in some
detail at the DUP's role in recent illegal demonstrations and
marches, the party's attitude to law-breaking, and the complex
relationship between the DUP and working-class loyalists.

Parades are the very stuff of Protestant politics. Public marches
permit the display of one's symbols: the flags, the banners, the
open Bible, and, on occasions, the uniforms which hint at potential
violence. The flaunting of symbols has so often been the occasion
for counter-demonstrations and rioting that the government has
often banned parades or re-routed them away from particularly
sensitive areas. Bans on parades are always seen as a sign of weakness, and as such have frequently given militant Protestants a
chance to show, by defying the bans, that they will not be a party
to any 'sell-out'. In the 1950s, Paisley and Norman Porter led
banned parades. William McCrea was imprisoned in 1971 for tak-

[11] *Ulster* (Sept. 1985), p. 7.

ing part in a banned march in Dungiven.[12] Paisley's second prison term was the result of his organizing a blockade of Armagh to prevent a civil rights march. In Protestant history there is good precedent for such opposition to bans. In 1866, William Johnson of Ballykilbegs led a banned march, was sent to prison, and on his release was elected to Parliament by Protestant voters.

In the summer of 1985, bans on a number of parades led to rioting, loyalist attacks on the RUC, and a revival of interest in DUP views on illegality. A loyalist band parade through the at least ninety per cent Catholic County Down town of Castlewellan was banned. Local DUP councillor Ethel Smyth called for defiance of the ban. The RUC surrounded the town with a cordon of divisional mobile support units. Ivan Foster announced that the Third Force would take part in the march. Although the RUC succeeded in preventing the march, twenty-two people, including Ethel Smyth, were injured, and Foster and another DUP Assemblyman, George Graham, were among those arrested. The DUP view was that the ban was intended to placate the Dublin government. If Protestants could not parade wherever they liked in Ulster, then the day was not far away when they would be sold into a united Ireland. As George Graham put it: 'The day has come when we see that the country has gone to the dogs. We have lost everything that we cherish and hold dear. Our backs are to the wall and we must fight.' Ivan Foster added: 'We are declaring war. If we didn't do what was done at Castlewellan we would have had a complete sell out.'[13] DUP Assemblyman Jim Wells was also present but apart from the DUP politicians, the only other leader who was present was George Seawright (of whom more later).

The following night there was a similar confrontation between loyalist marchers and RUC in Cookstown and again the DUP was prominent, this time in the figure of William McCrea, the local Westminster MP.

The major scene of confrontation was to be Portadown. There the 12th of July parade had been re-routed to take it away from the 'Tunnel', part of the traditional route which had become a Catholic area. This time the Orange Order, which had distanced itself from the Castlewellan and Cookstown incidents, was

[12] William McCrea and David Porter, *In His Pathway; the story of Rev. William McCrea* (London: Marshall, Morgan and Scott, 1980), p. 56.
[13] *Newsletter* (29 June 1985).

involved. Senior Orange leaders, DUP representatives and Official Unionists held a series of negotiations with the RUC and the Secretary of State to have the re-routeing order lifted. On 4 July, 30,000 Orangemen gathered in Portadown 'to demand the right to march anywhere in Ulster'.[14] This time the leadership of the OUP joined Paisley in lending political weight to the demonstration, which passed without incident. The Chief Constable of the RUC added confusion to the parades policy by announcing that he would permit an Orange church parade on the Sunday before the Twelfth to pass through the Tunnel because it would be a 'peaceful, dignified, church parade' but insisted that the Twelfth march had to be re-routed.[15] When the first parade passed off without serious incident (but with a massive police presence), the Portadown Orangemen reaffirmed their determination to go through the Tunnel on the Twelfth. At this point, the Orange leadership began to retreat, suggesting that they had made their point with the church parade and calling on the Portadown loyalists not to break the law.[16] While Martin Smyth was trying to persuade the march organizers to relent, Ian Paisley was promising his support. Although committed to the Independent Orange Order's rally in Ballycastle, he announced that he would begin the Twelfth by visiting Portadown to add his support to the planned march.

The marchers did not walk through the Tunnel. The massive RUC presence prevented them, but over that weekend fifty-three police officers and at least nineteen civilians were injured in serious rioting which wrecked shops in the town centre. At least forty-eight loyalists were arrested, two of whom turned out to be full-time members of the Ulster Defence Regiment. To make matters worse, the Dublin government complimented the RUC on their firm stand against loyalist agitation. Over the following weeks, Portadown loyalists harassed the police in retaliation for what they claimed was police persecution. In Portadown and Cookstown, RUC officers were driven out of their homes in areas which had once been safe because they were loyalist.

In response to demands for figures of loyalists arrested, the police first announced that 130 nationalists and seventy-five loyalists were arrested. The next day, they admitted that they had

14 *Newsletter* (4 July 1985).
15 *Sunday Times* (7 July 1985).
16 *Guardian* (9 July 1985).

miscounted and that 'in the period June 27–August 9 . . . the numbers of persons detained for the whole range of offences connected with public order were loyalists 468; republicans 427'.[17]

All Protestant politicians were agreed that, in theory, Protestants should be allowed to march anywhere in Ulster and there was agreement that marches should not be banned or re-routed simply because nationalists would be offended or would attack the marchers. However, there was a significant difference about the extent to which loyalists should break the law to exercise their right to march if the RUC decided to ban or change the route of a march. As has consistently been the case, Paisley and other DUP politicians were prepared to go further than the Official Unionists and the provincial leadership of the Orange Order. It has also always been the case that Democratic Unionists have been more willing than Official Unionists to try to prevent republican marches. After her Castlewellan protest, Ethel Smyth was arrested in Downpatrick while trying to stop a Sinn Fein march and was roundly condemned by the local Official Unionist Assemblyman for trouble-making. However, the DUP has consistently criticized loyalists who attack the RUC or wreck shops. Pushing at a line of policemen or refusing to be moved on is acceptable; throwing bricks is not. This is precisely the sort of position one would expect given the combination of their respectable backgrounds, in almost all cases their membership of the Free Presbyterian Church, and their belief that the appeasement policies of the government and the Chief Constable have to be opposed publicly. The interesting point is that the really quite moderate and bourgeois position of the DUP is often over looked, not just by its critics (one would expect that), but also by its supporters. Because the DUP is more willing to court confrontation with the police and the forces of law and order than is the OUP, working-class loyalists seem to suppose that the DUP endorses and shares their willingness to go even further in seeking confrontation. When DUP spokesmen give their view of the conflict, which is that the rioters were clearly in the wrong but their actions were understandable, and that the fault really lay with the leadership of the RUC, the loyalists seem to hear only those parts which marked the DUP as being more supportive of their acts than was the OUP.

This selective hearing was clearly demonstrated in a meeting in

[17] *Belfast Telegraph* (16 Aug. 1985).

Portadown on 22 August. Some 400 loyalists had gathered to explain their grievances about police action in the town and to call
Ken Maginnis, the Fermanagh and South Tyrone MP who was
the OUP law and order spokesman, to task for his description of
the rioting as 'orchestrated thuggery'. He had said, of those who
wrecked the town centre in rioting on the sixteenth, that 'they were
not loyalists in any sense of the word but despicable rebels in the
same mould as those in Sinn Fein'.[18] Maginnis had been listening
to almost two hours of complaints about the police when a woman
announced that she would clap her hands if she heard of an RUC
constable's death. He walked out of the meeting to jeers and cat-
calls. Just as he was leaving, Paisley arrived and the meeting broke
into cheering and clapping. When Paisley was later told about the
woman's remark, he immediately condemned it and rebuked her,
but this made little impression on the basic loyalties of the audience. As far as they were concerned, Paisley and the DUP were on
their side, the side of the common Protestant people being
squeezed between the nationalists and an RUC directed from
London to enforce the government's compromising policies.
Maginnis, and by implication the Official Unionists, were weak and
failed to stand up for the common man.

One can identify a similar pattern in the DUP's relationship
with the Protestant paramilitaries. Paisley has gone on record time
after time to condemn the assassination of Catholics and has insisted that the potential violence represented by the old Protestant
Volunteers and more recently by the Third Force should only be
exercised in a defensive manner and in the event of a complete
breakdown of law and order. However, the DUP still enjoys better
relationships with the paramilitaries than does the Official Unionist
Party.[19] When the loyalist prisoners were campaigning for seg-
regation from republicans (a campaign which involved the tactic
so loudly condemned when used by republicans: the hunger
strike), DUP spokesmen were conspicuously more active than the
Officials in the promotion of the prisoners' case.

[18] *Belfast Telegraph* (17 Aug. 1985).
[19] A number of prominent DUP activists (some of whom have now left the Party)
were active in the various local 'defence committees' which were amalgamated in
the UDA. While he was in prison, William McCrea launched an appeal for
Christmas hampers for loyalist prisoners and their families. In January 1983, the
DUP members of the Assembly were prominent in supporting the loyalist prisoners
in their desire to be segregated from republicans (*Voice of Ulster* (Jan. 1983), p. 14).

When Vanguard was a force, its leaders, rather than those of the DUP or the OUP, were most active in courting the paramilitaries.[20] With its demise, the DUP retained the greater working-class loyalist support. Because it appeared more resolute in its unionism, it was taken to be more trustworthy by those who were prepared to break the law for their unionism. It is clear then that the DUP will receive the votes of the working-class loyalists so long as it retains an image of being more unionist than the Officials, unless there should be an alternative to the right of the DUP.

George Seawright and the Ulster Protestant League

In 1984, the beginnings of an alternative were offered when George Seawright was expelled from the DUP. I have already mentioned the failure of the paramilitaries to create and sustain a political initiative. The voters of the Shankill Road in Belfast, traditionally the home of working class populist independent unionism, had supported Johnny McQuade rather than the UDA or UVF and McQuade had taken that vote into the DUP when he joined it in 1971. George Seawright is a Scot who had developed an interest in Ulster politics while still in Springburn, near Glasgow, where he was one of the few Scottish members of Paisley's Ulster Protestant Volunteers. When he moved to Belfast he joined the DUP and campaigned for McQuade, and he became an elder of the John Knox Memorial Free Presbyterian Church in North Belfast. From the start, he was in conflict with the DUP's leadership who tried to persuade him not to accept the local branch's nomination to stand for the Assembly. His view is that he was unacceptable because he was working class, lived in a council flat, and was in debt to the Housing Executive. Underlying the objection to Seawright's lack of respectability was the fear 'that they could not control us'. The debt problem was solved by someone he hardly

[20] The differing attitudes of the unionist parties to the paramilitaries was neatly symbolized by their reactions to an anniversary dinner to commemorate the UWC strike organized by the Ulster Army Council (which then consisted of the UDA, the Red Hand Commando, the Down Orange Welfare, Orange Voice, and the Ulster Volunteer Service Corps). William Craig and Ernest Baird attended the dinner and appeared to enjoy themselves. Harry West of the Official Unionists went but left early. Paisley sent back his ticket and no representatives of the DUP attended (Conor O'Clery, 'Loyalists With Still More Uneasy Coalitions', *Irish Times*, 31 May 1975).

knew paying his debt and Seawright was elected to the Assembly where he turned out to be a thorn in the DUP's flesh.

The problem with Seawright was that he openly voiced what many people took to be the true feelings of Democratic Unionists, often to the embarrassment of the DUP spokesmen who were presenting a more moderate position. When Protestant gunmen tried to kill Gerry Adams, the President of Sinn Fein and Westminster MP for West Belfast, Seawright applauded. Although the DUP condemned the use of uncorroborated evidence in the 'supergrass' trials, it was Seawright who went to the court day after day to offer sympathy for the families of loyalist prisoners. Eventually, in June 1984, Seawright went too far when, during a meeting of the Belfast Education and Library Board, he suggested in regard to Catholic schools that 'taxpayers' money would be better spent on an incinerator and burning the lot of them. The priests should be thrown in and burned as well.'[21] Sammy Wilson, the DUP press officer, dissociated the party from Seawright's remarks: 'The DUP has always made it crystal clear—as Protestants we believe in civil and religious liberty for all men, and no one should be persecuted for their religious beliefs.'[22] Seawright was first suspended and, when he failed to withdraw his remarks and apologize, was expelled from the Party.

It has generally been the case that people who leave the DUP see their political careers terminated. Only those who move to the Official Unionists have continued to win elections. But Seawright revived the 'Protestant Unionist' label and won a convincing victory in the 1985 local government elections. Where the three DUP candidates in his area of Belfast could win only 1.25 quotas, Seawright took 1.7 quotas in first preference votes.

Belfast loyalists did not vote for Seawright because he wanted to burn Catholics but because he lived in a council flat, spoke up for those loyalists who tried to kill IRA men, and was not prepared to abandon working-class Protestants in order to appear respectable.[23] Like the young Paisley, he talked straight and was prepared to *act*. In a piece of street theatre almost copied from Paisley's early days, Seawright climbed on the roof of the Whiterock Leisure

---

[21] *Newsletter* (1 June 1984).

[22] Ibid.

[23] It must be significant that a number of the DUP candidates standing in working-class areas of Belfast actually lived in the pleasant suburban surroundings of South Belfast and North Down.

Centre and removed the tricolour which other unionists had complained about. And although he is a teetotal sabbatarian lay preacher who now attends the Church of God, Seawright has not allowed his religious principles to come between himself and working-class loyalists who do not share his temperance and sabbatarianism.

The fact that he won re-election suggested that the working-class independent unionist vote was only temporarily lodged with the DUP while Johnny McQuade was alive. Although Nelson is probably right to say that the DUP had lost its role 'as the articulator of poor Protestants' social grievances'[24] by the end of the 1970s, this would not cost it votes until there was an alternative. The paramilitaries had failed to provide such an alternative. They could not develop an agreed political ideology, they were tainted with the 'red' smear, and they had less success than the IRA in making themselves acceptable to their own communities.

The failure of the DUP to endorse the illegality of working-class loyalists, which stems from a general reluctance to break the law and an evaluation of the present situation which argues that such extreme acts are not yet justified, should have made it unpopular with working-class loyalists and to an extent it has. Yet until someone like Seawright can build a province-wide alternative, the DUP will remain the home of the loyalist vote. If the DUP's criticisms of 'gangsterism' have made it unpopular with some sections of the working-class Protestant population, its view on the sabbath and alcohol consumption have further widened the divisions and it is to this sort of issue which I now want to turn.

Evangelicals in Politics

It should be clear from the preceding chapters that the Free Presbyterian Church is no ordinary evangelical sect (using that term in its sociological rather than pejorative sense). The political crisis which vastly increased its recruitment could not help but give it an unusual character. Other religious organizations, such as the Dutch Reformed Church in South Africa, have played important parts in providing religious legitimation for political ideologies,

[24] Sarah Nelson, *Ulster's Uncertain Defenders: loyalists and the Northern Ireland conflict* (Belfast: Appletree Press, 1984), p. 167.

but few modern churches have had so many of their personnel actively involved in one particular political organization.

This close association of religion and politics has also given the organizational vehicle for the politics—the DUP—an unusual character which I now wish to explore by examining the tensions caused by the presence in a political agenda of religious attitudes.

In theology, Free Presbyterians are Calvinists. However, they are not Calvinists when they come to think about politics. Knox and Calvin were not democrats. They believed that society ought to be ordered, not according to how sinful men wished to live, but in accordance with God's divine commandments. They believed that the saints had a divine obligation to rule and to impose righteousness, even if the mass of the people showed no particular desire to live righteously. Ivan Foster, in an attempt to show that Knox and Calvin were democrats, pointed out that they sought such popular mandates as were available in their societies. Calvin left Geneva and only returned to lead the city when the city council asked him to return. Knox tried to create as wide a base as possible for his theocracy. But even making allowance for the circumstances of their times, it is impossible to save the Protestant reformers from their own political philosophy, which finds its clearest statement in the old Scots Covenants, documents much loved by Ulster conservative Protestants and the model for many unionist statements of political faith. The Covenants called for the state to 'extirpate' and 'suppress' heresy, popery, prelacy, and diverse superstitions and blasphemies. That is, they believed that the civil state could and should be used to enforce religious conformity.[25]

No modern conservative Protestant holds that position. Whether because they have genuinely changed their political philosophy or because they simply realize that they will never get away with it in a modern pluralistic society, for whatever reason, conservative Protestants have preferred to follow the democratic inheritance of the Reformation. In passing, one might note that democracy was never an intention of the reformers but rather an unintended consequence of their theological reformation. Once they had established that all men were equal before God and that all men were theoretically capable of finding out, for themselves, what God demanded of them, they could not confine that principle to the religious

[25] J. G. Vos, *The Scottish Covenanters: their origins, history and distinctive doctrines* (Pittsburgh: Crown and Covenant Publications, 1980).

sphere, no matter how much they may have wanted to. Luther took fright at the anarchy he had loosed but could do little to prevent it, even when he threw his weight behind the German princes in their crushing of revolutionary movements.[26]

Many of the Free Presbyterians to whom I talked are themselves confused about their political philosophy. Most begin by asserting their commitment to democracy, yet few would commit themselves completely to the notion that if the people want to wallow in sin, they should be permitted to do so. Some would take this view, arguing along the lines of the story of Christ healing the lepers, that some of God's gifts are given free to men who may then go and abuse them. Thus benefits such as a welfare system or a national free education system should be given to all people who may do with these things as they wish. The Christian has an obligation to try to persuade the sinner to give up his or her sin but he has no right to prevent the determined sinner from following his chosen course. The quite understandable confusion comes in the area of just what is meant by persuasion and permission. What one person would construe as simply permitting a sinner to dig his own pit, another would see as encouraging further sin. Thus the Free Presbyterians (and other conservative Christians) who picketed a newly opened sex shop on the Castlereagh Road in Belfast (so successfully that it closed) saw themselves, not as denying anyone their basic right to sin, but as preventing further incitement and encouragement to sin.

These issues need not bother the ordinary Free Presbyterian, but they do concern those Free Presbyterians who are also active in the DUP. The conventional political party exists to promote certain key principles. These are seen as essential and other parts of the party's platform are negotiable: things that may be changed in order to increase popular support for the party. Obviously, if a party changes its central principles, it becomes another party. In most modern societies, parties have key positions on economic and social issues or on constitutional matters. Thus, for example, the Labour Party in Britain supposedly stands for the redistribution of wealth, the maintenance of a national health and social security

[26] One of the best discussions of the radical social and political impact of the Reformation is Michael Walzer, *The Revolution of the Saints: a study in the origins of radical politics* (Cambridge, Mass.: Harvard University Press, 1965). See also Ernst Troeltsch, 1976, *The Social Teaching of the Christian Churches* (Chicago: University of Chicago Press, Midway Reprints, 1976).

system, considerable government intervention in the economy and so on. The DUP is one of two unionist parties. Its *raison d'être* is the preservation of the Union with Great Britain. The other positions it takes are presumably negotiable. Its strong defence of farming interests is designed to win the support of the large rural community. If only ten per cent or less of the Protestant population were engaged in farming, one would expect the DUP to reduce its interest in farmers. That would be sensible politics.

This is where the special evangelical emphasis in the Party becomes interesting. The DUP can argue that part of what is meant by being a unionist is that one should be teetotal and sabbatarian, opposed to homosexuality and divorce. They can argue that they make their position on these things perfectly clear, and that if people vote for them then they know what they are going to get and have no right to claim that sabbatarianism is being forced on them. But what if sabbatarianism costs the DUP votes? Some members would abandon the evangelical parts of the platform, while others would rather give up politics.

This argument is usually presented in the media as a battle between the Free Presbyterians in the DUP and the secular working-class loyalists. While there is some truth to this, it is an over-simplification. Some of those active in both the Church and the Party, who hold the combined ideologies of evangelicalism and unionism as being inseparable, are quite pragmatic. They are so strongly committed to their unionism that they are prepared to go some way towards moving some of their evangelical principles into the area of private life and personal choice, rather than alienate non-evangelical unionists. This can be seen in the way in which the sides lined up in recent arguments about sabbatarianism in the DUP manifesto.

The 1985 manifesto shows an interesting change from previous documents. It again begins with strong positions on the need for government action to 'smash Sinn Fein', for a rejection of the Anglo-Irish 'sell out', and an end to cross-border collaboration. Less than half-way through the document is the paragraph headed 'The Republican Sunday':

Recognizing the laws of God and the inherent benefits of the Ulster sabbath as part of our heritage, the DUP is opposed to the introduction or promotion of the Continental and Republican Sunday in Northern Ireland.

As it is the ratepayer who funds and owns Council facilities, the DUP believes that any change to Sunday opening of Council provisions should only be undertaken following the test of the electorate's opinion in a local poll held for that purpose in the district of the council. If the Government seek to deny this facility to a Council, or if other parties successfully oppose such a democratic test of ratepayers' views being held, then DUP councillors will vote, as in the past, against a Republican Sunday.

In one way this statement is more conservative than the previous one in that it has elevated the popular usage 'Republican Sunday' to a part of party language and thus confirmed the belief that Catholicism and republicanism are the same thing, but it represents an important departure from previous positions in clearly tying the DUP's position to that of the electorate. In practice, the issues may never be put to the test because it is very likely that other parties would succeed in preventing referenda, but it is still enough of a departure for some evangelical DUP activists to have been initially opposed to the change.

Although it is difficult this long after the crucial debate to reconstruct correctly people's positions from their own and others' accounts, it does seem that, while some Free Presbyterian ministers in the party were opposed, others, including Paisley and Beattie, supported the new position. Ivan Foster took the unexpected but reasonable position of arguing that sabbatarianism should never have been in the manifesto: 'I do not believe that that particular one is something for parties to legislate on. If I had been standing I could have put it in my personal manifesto that I was a sabbatarian but when the Party committed itself to that, it was placing itself in the position of a church.' However, given that it had been DUP policy, he was opposed to changing it, even to the extent of the local option position, because he thought the change would be seen as a weakening, as a change of principle. Gordon Cooke reluctantly accepted the change but only on the understanding that the DUP was not committed to encouraging local option votes. But while some of the most vocal opposition to change came from the Free Presbyterian elders and laymen in the party, other members of this group, in particular Beattie and Paisley, supported it!

It is difficult to capture accurately the complex patterns of motivation that produce an individual's actions but I think the position of Paisley, Beattie, Foster, and others can be better understood if we distinguish motivational background and front stage. The background to, or fundamental source of, political ideology and action is an indissoluble mix of evangelicalism and unionism. They are committed to each because they are committed to the other. But they are prepared to act on the political stage according to a script which permits pragmatic compromise up to the point where further compromise would endanger the fundamental evangelical principles of the background. Fortunately for their own consistency, the dimensions of the conflict in Northern Ireland do not encourage such a degree of pragmatic compromise. In the slightly similar American case of the Moral Majority, evangelicals have no choice but to work in political alliance with secular conservatives, conservative Catholics, and conservative Jews. They entered politics because their Baptist fundamentalism has produced certain moral and social positions which they see as threatened and which they wish to preserve or re-establish. While Baptist fundamentalists are powerful in the 'Bible Belt' of North and South Carolina and Virginia, they can only ever succeed at federal level by working in alliance with other conservative blocs, of which the biggest is that of American Roman Catholicism. To pursue political objectives seriously, they must work with the very people whose religious beliefs are most antithetical to their own. In order to do this, Jerry Falwell and the other Baptist pastors in the movement have to operate with almost watertight compartments for, on the one hand, their religion (in this box Catholics and Jews are doomed sinners), and on the other, their politics (we are all part of a shared Judeo-Christian tradition).

That sort of compartmentalization has been roundly denounced by Bob Jones University and those sections of American fundamentalism with which Paisley is most at home but we will never know if his religio-political system would permit such pragmatism because the constitutional issue so overrides everything else in Northern Ireland that there is no expectation or need for him to work with conservative Catholics. This does not mean that Paisley would not be glad of the support (such as he had in his campaign to 'Save Ulster From Sodomy'[27]) of individual Catholics, but he

[27] 'Save Ulster From Sodomy' was the arresting title given to the DUP's campaign to prevent the extension to Northern Ireland of the British mainland's laws which permitted adult male homosexual activity. The 'order in council' which brought law in Northern Ireland into line with the more liberal law of the mainland was passed in October 1982 after the British government's earlier position of exempting Ulster had been judged by the European Court of Human Rights to

would not work with Catholic organizations or officials of the Catholic Church because that might dilute his separatist witness.

The Evangelicals and the Orange Order

The only problems of alliances and compartmentalization faced by Free Presbyterian Democratic Unionists are those which concern the 'fraternal' orders. To what extent the Orange Order, Apprentice Boys of Derry, and Royal Black Preceptory have ever been thoroughly evangelical is debatable. Nevertheless they were considerably more evangelical at the turn of the century than they are now.[28] The problem for the Free Presbyterians is that the fraternal orders have always seen themselves as linking the broad Protestant religious tradition with the main unionist party, hence the common arrangement of Orange Lodges holding their annual church parades at each of the Church of Ireland, Presbyterian, and Methodist churches in turn. As the main churches have become more liberal, Free Presbyterianism emerged to challenge the lack of 'real' Protestantism and hence offered an implicit challenge to the fraternal organizations to purify themselves by breaking their ties with the main, and now apostate, denominations.

Ian Paisley was once a member of the Shankill Road Lodge of the Orange Order and a lodge chaplain, but he resigned from the Order when the County Grand Lodge refused to expel Sir Robin Kinahan for attending a funeral service in a Roman Catholic chapel.[29] Another Free Presbyterian minister, Austin Allen, resigned from the Order because it would not accept Free Presbyterian ministers as district chaplains. His district stuck to the tradition of only accepting chaplains from the three main Protestant churches. A third Free Presbyterian minister said: 'Perhaps the main reason [for leaving the Orange Order] was that in 1969 I was saved by the grace of God and therefore felt that I could not sit and be associated with members of the Orange and Black while they consumed alcohol in their meetings on the 12th and 13th mornings each July.'

infringe basic human rights. Although there was no contact between the Free Presbyterian and Roman Catholic churches over the issue, many Catholics signed the petitions organized by Free Presbyterians.

[28] D. A. Roberts, 'The Orange Order in Ireland: a religious institution?', *British Journal of Sociology*, 22 (3) (1971), pp. 269–79.

[29] *Newsletter* (9 Apr. 1970).

Given the Free Presbyterian Church's high political profile one would expect that many of its ministers would be active in the Orange Lodge, Black Preceptory, and Apprentice Boys. Of forty-four ministers whose affiliations are known, twenty-one have never been members of any fraternal organization. Ten have been members of the Orange Order but nine have resigned. Three have been members of the Independent Orange Order and one has resigned. Ten ministers are known to be members of the Apprentice Boys of Derry.

It would be easy to exaggerate the extent to which the lack of genuine evangelicalism in the fraternal organizations creates motivational problems for Free Presbyterians who wish to be active in politics. Some districts are clearly sympathetic to the Democratic Unionists and are willing to invite Free Presbyterian Democratic Unionists such as William McCrea to preach at their church parades. Some have church parades to Free Presbyterian churches. Nevertheless, the fact that Paisleyism in both its religious and political forms is a reactionary movement which seeks to purify Protestant religion and politics creates a background tension which regularly produces public arguments. For example, in 1977 the Revd Ken Elliott, the Free Presbyterian minister of Portadown, offended many Apprentice Boys by refusing to take a collection for the restoration of the St Columb's Church of Ireland Cathedral in Londonderry, which is regarded by the Apprentice Boys as their spiritual home. His argument was that the Church of Ireland was 'poisoned by ecumenism' and as such he, as a Free Presbyterian, could not take part in fund-raising on its behalf.[30]

To place these observations in the general context of the special qualities given to the Democratic Unionist Party by its close links with Free Presbyterianism, we can summarize by saying that, were the Democratic Unionist Party a 'secular' political party, it would certainly cultivate links with the fraternal orders to strengthen its ties with the ordinary Ulster Protestant voter. Some Democratic Unionists do precisely this by, for example, listing their active involvement with the Orders on their election literature. However, the evangelical element in the DUP refuses to cultivate such links and occasionally offends the ordinary Protestant voter by taking what appears to the general unionist public as an 'extreme' stand. For example, in 1976, three DUP councillors in Ballymena boy-

[30] *Belfast Telegraph* (7 Oct. 1977).

cotted the Remembrance Day service (an event they would normally have been very keen to support) because a Roman Catholic priest who had served in the Royal Naval Reserve was reading a lesson. It seems likely that a local commentator is right in thinking that the boycott cost the DUP votes in a subsequent by-election.[31]

However, and this is the point which will be argued in detail in the concluding chapter, the Free Presbyterian critique of the laxity of the Orders is not as damaging to the DUP as one might suppose because there is no legitimate direction in which the liberal or lax element in the Orders can go without, for other reasons, losing the support of the ordinary Ulster Protestant. There is no sound ideological position from which the more liberal elements can challenge the 'enthusiasts' of the DUP because all the DUP is asking for is strict adherence to the constitutions and traditions of the Orders! If the Orders are not anti-Catholic, what are they? Their history, the interests of their members and the circumstances of conflict in Northern Ireland do not permit the evolution of Orangeism into something which would still have meaning if it abandoned its evangelical Protestant symbols and stated beliefs. It may, and does, tolerate considerable neglect of those symbols and stated beliefs, but those people who find the Free Presbyterian/DUP element petty in their refusal to help restore a Church of Ireland church or attend Remembrance Day services cannot promote a coherent ideology which would justify their criticisms. The middle-class Protestants of an O'Neillite or Alliance Party persuasion must take the logic of their dislike for Paisleyism to its conclusion and resign from the Orders. Most of them did. The working-class Protestants who totter back from the Twelfth field, obviously drunk but still marching behind a 'Total Abstinence Lodge' banner, will continue to be annoyed by the evangelical ideologues, but will respect the fact that the evangelicals' hearts are in the right place. Although the evangelicals in the DUP are clearly out of step with most Ulster Protestant voters, they still represent the ideological centre of unionism, of what it means to

---

[31] The *Newsletter* (9 Dec. 1977) said: 'In the election run-up, the Remembrance Day furore and the DUP's announced intention to close the town swimming pool on Sundays were prominent issues.' The DUP lost the seat by 15 votes but retained control of the council.

be a Protestant. Like the Israelite prophets, they may not be honoured in their own country but they are recognized as belonging.

The Young Professionals: A Generational Conflict?

I have already mentioned the common reference in the media to conflicts between the evangelical and secular elements in the DUP, or between Church and Party, and I have argued that such a simple distinction does not accurately describe the situation. A number of journalists have overlaid the evangelical/secular distinction with a generational difference. Ed Moloney of the *Irish Times* wrote: '. . . a large number of those attracted to and recruited into the party through Robinson's efforts were different in a number of important respects from the traditional Paisley follower of the early rabble-rousing days. . . .'[32] It is generally supposed that while Paisley, Beattie, Foster, and such people wish to maintain the evangelical ethos, the younger generation of Peter Robinson, Jim Wells, Jim Allister, and others recruited through the Queen's University branch of the DUP want to create a mass popular party by playing down the evangelical elements in the party platform and by pursuing more respectable methods of political action.[33]

There is a strong tradition in the sociological literature which would lead us to expect such a change of direction. Based largely on Michels's study of trade union organizations,[34] the model supposes that once any radical organization has grown to the size where it needs to delegate responsibility to professional organizers, and once it has been in existence long enough to produce a complex bureaucracy, then the original radical thrust is lost as the pro-

[32] Ed Moloney, 'DUP Dissenters Soften the Traditional Line', *Irish Times* (19 Feb. 1983).

[33] Peter Robinson was, from 1974, the first full-time secretary of the DUP, a Castlereagh District councillor from 1977, and MP for East Belfast from 1979. Jim Wells was a local councillor in Lisburn from 1981, and for the 1985 elections moved to Banbridge District. As soon as he graduated from Queen's University, he went to work full-time for the Party and was shortly after elected to the Assembly for South Down. Jim Allister was DUP press officer and is now a Newtownabbey councillor and Assembly member for North Antrim. In the 1981 Westminster general election, he contested East Antrim. Both in their thirties, Robinson and Allister are usually mentioned as the main contenders to succeed Ian Paisley should he retire.

[34] Robert Michels, *Political Parties: a sociological study of the oligarchic tendencies of modern democracy* (New York: Dover, 1959). See also S. M. Lipset, M. Trow, and J. Coleman, *Union Democracy* (New York: Anchor Books, 1962), Ch. 1.

fessionals redirect the organization to serve their own ends. Keeping the organizational structure going becomes more important than attaining the initial goals of the movement. For members, there is a shift in the main source of satisfaction. When the movement began they were attracted by a desire to attain certain goals. As it settles down and the chances of ever attaining the radical goals become ever more remote, members begin to shift their attention to the routine satisfactions of just 'being a member'. For the leaders of the movement a dilution of the radical goals is attractive because it will reduce the stigma attached to the movement and reduce the tension between it and the wider society of which it is a part.[35] There are substantial rewards for accommodation to the prevailing consensus. Again Moloney offers such an analysis of the younger DUP activists: '. . . men like Robinson, Allister and Kane who are at the start of political careers know that the negative politics practised for so long by their leader would deny them the office and power that could be theirs.'[36]

What is rarely stated openly but constantly implied is that the younger generation should be less 'negative' because they know better; they are university educated men. Alan Kane, Jim Allister, and Nigel Dodds are law graduates. Jim Wells has a first degree and postgraduate qualification in town planning. Because in the past, upper-class unionists have been less than staunchly committed to the defence of traditional loyalism, it is assumed that others who acquire elements of upper-class status, such as a university education, will themselves be more moderate than their uneducated elders.

At first sight there is some evidence to support this sort of assumption. The younger generation did seem less committed to the politics of the street demonstration and the illegal parade. Willie McCrea, Ethel Smyth, and Ivan Foster are often found in the forefront of such confrontations. While Robinson was involved with Paisley and McQuade in the demonstrations against the invitation of Charles Haughey, then the Republic's Prime Minister,

---

[35] A considerable sociological literature has been built on Michels's work. The key elements in what is often called the 'goal transformation' or 'institutionalization' model are well laid out in Mayer Zald and Roberta Ash, 'Social Movement Organizations: growth, decay and change', *Social Forces*, 44 (1966), pp. 327–40. The same issues are addressed, with more illustrative material, in John Wilson, *Introduction to Social Movements* (New York: Basic Books, 1973), Chs. 4 and 10.

[36] *Irish Times* (19 Feb. 1983).

to the enthronement of the Church of Ireland Primate in Armagh in May 1980, he has not been a conspicuous street demonstrator. Allister, Kane, and Dodds have also been noticeably absent from public confrontations. While Jim Wells was in Castlewellan for the banned parade in June 1985, he preferred to negotiate with the RUC rather than be arrested like Foster and Graham or, like Smyth, lie down in front of a Landrover.

A second source of support for the idea of a generation gap in the DUP is found in the statements of embittered defectors or expellees. When McFaul was expelled from the DUP, he said: 'Dr Paisley is now effectively being swept aside by younger men like Jim Allister, Peter Robinson and Alan Kane on the party executive.'[37] Such a response seems understandable given that it allows McFaul to explain why he is at odds with the Party while still maintaining that he is loyal to its principles and to its founder, but it cannot stand as a general proposition. It assumes a major difference in interest between the founders and the younger men and that, as will be argued, is not the case.

The first point is that, of the five people generally named in any discussion of the generation gap theory, four are Free Presbyterians, which is a similar concentration to that found in the first generation of Paisley activists. Furthermore, they are not nominal Free Presbyterians but people who are active to the extent of giving their testimony in Free Presbyterian pulpits. They are as morally conservative as their parents. Alan Kane turned down an opportunity to explain the Save Ulster From Sodomy campaign on television because the studio discussion would take place on a Sunday. Wells has been active in opposing the opening of a Banbridge disco which will operate on the sabbath. Apart from the fact that they have an arrest rate lower than that of some of the older generation, there seems nothing of substance to distinguish them from the founders of the DUP party.

Furthermore, there is little about splits in the various branches which makes them understandable as a product of conflict between moderate younger activists and older extremists. William Belshaw, and Roy Beggs of Larne before him, left the Party because they moderated and abandoned the party's policy of non-recognition of the Republic's representatives, and they were part of the founding generation. Although the complex divisions in the DUP's North

37 *Newsletter* (18 Feb. 1984).

Belfast branch accord slightly with the view that there is a basic conflict between old extremists and new 'moderates' in that McQuade, while he was alive, supported Seawright against the executive, the departure of Seawright has seen some of the founder members, who left when he became a force, returning.[38]

It is important not to concentrate too much on ideology. Although the DUP has a strong ideological identity, its members are also motivated by the complete range of normal human emotions and interests. They have ambitions and they have pride. Most of the disputes within the DUP can be understood better if they are seen as 'personality' clashes rather than if one attempts to find major ideological rifts. Focus on the personalities involved, albeit with the addition of one important shared characteristic, also offers a better explanation of the supposed generation gap. What the younger men have in common is competence. They are well-educated, competent managers and articulate spokesmen. In addition to their orthodoxy on the issues, this is what makes them an asset to the DUP and this is what accounts for their displacing of some of the stalwarts. In the early days, Paisley was so short of support that he press-ganged people into standing for election. One Protestant Unionist recalled that Paisley arrived at his house a month before a Belfast Corporation election and asked if he and another person would be willing to stand. As the Party has grown and recruited more articulate and able activists, a number of the old 'war-horses' have been put out to grass and, quite naturally, some of them have resented this. Yet they could hardly express their resentment in terms of thwarted personal ambition and so preferred to see their fate as a result of ideological changes in the Party. They, the true defenders of orthodoxy, were being pushed aside by unscrupulous and ambitious young men who were more interested in power than in principle.

Instead of the Michels notion of a radical movement being compromised by a leadership more interested in its own future

---

[38] For example, Ted Ashby, a DUP stalwart, rejoined when Seawright was expelled. The complex comings and goings in the North Belfast DUP defy reduction to a simple ideological division. The major schism in early 1983 saw the departure of moral conservatives *and* representatives of the more 'secular' element in the party, and apparently owed far more to 'personality' clashes between Billy Gault and George Seawright (both of whom were elected to the Assembly), and between lots of members and George Haffey, the DUP whip for the Belfast councillors. For details of the tensions within the Belfast DUP, see *Belfast Telegraph* (4 Dec. 1980; 7 Oct. 1981; 18 Feb. 1983; 24 Feb. 1983).

than in the goals of the movement, a more fruitful theme from the social movements literature is Smelser's distinction between various 'means'.[39] A simple reason why the younger activists are not seen as often on the picket line as their elders were, is that they are too busy pursuing the same goals by other means. When the DUP began, the only formal channel through which it could pursue its politics was Stormont and Paisley and Beattie were outnumbered in a very short-lived parliament. As the Party has grown it has been able to achieve representation in local government to the point of having controlling power on some councils, it has had a major voice in the first Assembly, the Convention, and the second Assembly, and it has elected representatives at Westminster and the European Parliament. These avenues have not only taken up a lot of the time and energy of the present generation of activists but they have also reduced the reliance on the politics of the street demonstration by presenting alternative means of expression and action.

However, this should not be taken to suggest that the present generation are seduced by their salaries and expenses to the degree that they will abandon their principles in order to continue to have access to the institutional channels for political activity.

The disputes in the councils which followed the election of Sinn Fein representatives in 1985 has made it clear that loyalists are willing to close down councils rather than work with Sinn Fein, and the younger generation of DUP activists has been fully active in the promotion of that position. They have also been to the fore in the planning of opposition to the recent Anglo-Irish talks even though they know that the collapse of those talks will make it very unlikely that the constitutional Catholic Social Democratic and Labour Party will take its place in the Assembly. And without the SDLP, the Assembly does not have a very bright future. There is thus no evidence to suppose that the younger generation is prepared to act like Michels's trade union leaders and moderate the principles of their movement in return for personal power and prestige.

The main difference between the situations envisaged by Michels

---

[39] Neil J. Smelser, *Theory of Collective Behaviour* (London: Routledge and Kegan Paul, 1962). To recognize the value of the distinction between various methods of pursuing one's goals is not, of course, to endorse Smelser's theory of collective behaviour, which is overly mechanical and, in its method of linking social strain with the generation of 'discontents', reductionist and deterministic.

and the Northern Ireland context is the entrenched nature of the divisions in Northern Ireland. The DUP is working in an environment in which there are no great rewards for compromise and accommodation. This is even more the case since the Anglo-Irish accord of November 1985 which clearly represents the British government's view that 'solutions' to the Northern Ireland problem require the active involvement of the Dublin government. For the DUP to embrace this accord and attempt to make it work would be for it to abandon its opposition to anything which presages a united Ireland. It is usually the case that those things which best suit the Michels model are social movement organizations which have goals which can be 'compromised' because they are things—like an increase in workers' standards of living or an improvement in working conditions—which are divisible. Trade unionists could be persuaded to accept a moderation of their organization's stated goals in return for the fulfilment of part of those goals. The position and ideology of Ulster unionists is such that their goals cannot be divided. They have already lost a great deal of the autonomy and self-determination they possessed under the Stormont regime. If 'what we have, we hold' was a meaningful slogan in the 1920s, it is even more powerful now when the 'what we hold' has been so drastically reduced.

Putting it more generally, I am suggesting a major difference in 'compromisability' between different kinds of goals. In a modern industrial society economic goals are divisible, both because an increased standard of living is such a broad goal that success on one front can be presented to the members as a decent reward for abandoning some other aim, and because the economic goals of competing groups can be simultaneously satisfied provided there is economic growth. Thus, although the Labour movement has had no great success in squeezing the capitalists until the pips squeak, its leaders can point to a variety of real improvements in the living standards of the working class as good reason for continued support for their moderating policy. Political conflicts of the sort which characterize the Northern Ireland problem are of a quite different nature because they are seen as part of a 'zero-sum' game. There is a fixed pot of political power and cultural dominance. If Catholics get something which makes them happy, then Protestants must have lost something. There is no way in which both sides can improve simultaneously. Every street name in Gaelic which goes up is an English street name coming down. O'Neill tried to argue that this was not the case and lost. The Alliance Party insists that the conflict is not a zero-sum game but very few people are impressed by it.[40]

Accommodation and compromise have not characterized the recent history of the DUP, despite journalists' frequent attempts to portray Paisley as a man sufficiently set on personal power to be willing to compromise to achieve it. Accommodation and compromise have not characterized the attitudes and actions of the young university-educated activists of the DUP of recent years because they grew up in the zero-sum game, and even if they forgot its rules long enough to consider shifting the DUP's aims, there is no reason to suppose that the voters would support them in their deviation.

---

[40] The European election results are useful for comparison because, unlike other elections where not all parties are represented in every area, in these contests every registered voter has a chance to vote for any party which fields a candidate. In June 1984, Alliance took 5.0% of the vote. The rest of the vote went to parties which see the Northern Ireland conflict as one in which gains for 'one side' are made at the expense of 'the other'.

6

The Church Established

The purpose of this chapter is to detail the recent history of the Free Presbyterian Church and to examine the various ways in which it has changed since the volatile 1960s. Particular attention will be given to the ways in which the Church has sought to make its operations in such matters as training of ministers more professional and effective, and to recent innovations such as the spread overseas and the creation of independent Christian schools. Towards the end of the chapter attention will be given to the question of whether the basic character of Free Presbyterianism has changed as it has grown and become well established.

The Growth of Free Presbyterianism

One way of describing the recent growth of the Free Presbyterian Church is to count its members at various points in its history. Fortunately the Northern Ireland census differs from that used in the rest of the United Kingdom in including a question about religious affiliation. From this source we know that 7,337 people of all ages were recorded as Free Presbyterians in 1971. Of course, this cannot immediately be taken as an accurate representation of the size of the Church. A lot of people did not complete the form. Of those who did complete it, a large number entered 'Protestant' or 'Christian' and some of these may have been people who regularly attended a Free Presbyterian church. The same could be said for the 1981 census, which records 9,621 Free Presbyterians; fewer than many observers expected. In an attempt to verify this figure I collected information on average attendances at morning and evening services, either by direct observation or by asking the relevant minister, and concluded that there are now some 12,000 Free Presbyterians.[1] Whether this means that the Church has

[1] The Free Presbyterian Church has two categories of 'member'. Congregational membership, which entitles the member to pastoral visitation and use of the

grown since 1981 or that the census under-represented the reality then is an open question. I suspect that the 1981 figures were broadly correct. If we calculate the growth rate for the decade from 1971 and assume a similar annual growth for every year from 1981 to 1985, we arrive at almost exactly the figure which I computed from my survey of present attendance.

The weakness of such data, of course, is that it tells us nothing about turnover. Other evidence, such as that gathered incidentally while asking ministers whether or not DUP candidates at various elections in the 1970s were Free Presbyterians, suggests that there has been considerable turnover with some Free Presbyterians moving to mainstream denominations and some moving to other small conservative organizations such as the Free Methodists and the Independent Methodists. We can leave aside the problem of whether the censuses accurately represent the total membership of the Free Church and suppose that under-representation, if there was any, was much the same on both samplings. Thus we can still talk sensibly about trends. And the basic picture is that Free Presbyterianism has grown by 31.1 per cent in the decade between the two censuses. If we can assume that the Free Church gained as many 'members' through births as it lost through deaths, then in each of those years, 2.74 members were recruited for every existing hundred members. This may not sound like a great deal but it should be put in context. In the same period the Irish Presbyterian Church declined by 16 per cent, the Church of Ireland declined by 15.8 per cent and the Methodists lost 18 per cent of their membership. Another way of looking at the growth or decline of a church is to count its congregations. Since 1969, which I have taken as the end of the period of unusual growth stimulated by the imprisonment of Paisley, Wylie, and Foster, twenty-four congregations have been added to the twenty-four which were then in existence. By and large these 'third generation' congregations have been planted in between the first and second-wave churches. Most of them share a similar pattern of creation. Free Pres-

---

Church's facilities for marriages, funeral services, and so on, is open to anyone who wishes it. Communicant membership is restricted to those 'who are converted to Christ and who are walking uprightly in accordance with His word' (to quote from the Hillsborough Free Presbyterian Church membership card). Only communicant members may attend, speak, and vote at church meetings, and hold office in the Church. When I have referred to 'Free Presbyterians' I have had in mind both groups of members and not just communicants.

byterians who were travelling some distance to attend church found this a considerable handicap to their own personal outreach work. As one of the founding elders of the Bangor congregation put it, one can hardly invite relative strangers to 'come to hear a certain preacher or come to a special meeting' when that involves a fifty mile round trip. In many cases, a tentative start would be made with the hiring or erection of a temporary hall and the holding of Sunday afternoon services. In others a fortnight of mission services would be held in a tent or a hired hall, and if sufficient interest was shown a nucleus would organize services. Once the nucleus felt confident enough they might take on a student minister, purchase land, or perhaps buy a vacant building. Those local Free Presbyterians who had previously travelled to their old church would then constitute the core of a new congregation. For example, the Mulvin congregation was formed as a result of the coincidence of an old Reformed Presbyterian building coming on to the market at the same time as two elders of the Castlederg congregation who lived locally were considering starting a 'work' in their own area.

Thus in addition to slow but steady growth in membership there has also been a shift from Free Presbyterianism being concentrated on a relative small number of major centres to a structure closer to the parishes of the major denominations, with a meeting-house within easy travelling distance of most people in the province. Another element of what might sensibly be termed 'consolidation' has been the replacement of overcrowded and 'temporary' structures by large, modern, purpose-built churches. Building is not just about bricks and wood; there are important sociological consequences of a major building programme. My attention was first drawn to these by ministers themselves who were well aware of the value that church-building has for creating and sustaining members' commitment. If a building is purchased from another denomination or some secular structure is acquired (in two cases, disused cinemas were bought) there will be a ceremony of dedication and some initial pleasure at entering a newly refurbished building, but there the process ends.[2] If, however, one buys land,

---

[2] There are a number of other reasons for not purchasing a redundant church. Firstly, most redundant churches are so, not because the organization has suddenly become unpopular, but because redevelopment has removed a large part of the local population. The Irish Presbyterian Church sold what is now the John Knox Memorial Free Presbyterian Church in Cliftonville, Belfast, because most of its

one can arrange a sod-cutting service, a stone-laying service, and a service to dedicate the completed structure. There are thus three occasions on which the members of the congregation can gather together to celebrate their success and to which they can invite Dr Paisley, visiting fundamentalist leaders, representatives of the Presbytery, and members of other congregations to rejoice in their 'revival'. Although ministers do not arrange matters in this way solely for the purpose of creating and maintaining a sense of social cohesion, they are quite happy to accept that resulting benefit.

To summarize, there has been an increase in membership which, while less spectacular than that which characterized the period from 1966 to 1969, has still been sufficient to take the Free Church beyond the size of other conservative denominations such as the Evangelical Presbyterians or the Reformed Presbyterians. There has also been considerable consolidation with the membership rearranging itself more evenly across the province and most congregations investing heavily in building programmes.

To return to the notion of 'membership' for a moment, it should be appreciated that one cannot simply compare the impact or importance of different religious organizations or orientations by comparing the figures of those who are counted (in different ways for different purposes) as members. The notion of 'membership' is a flexible one. Even within the world of religious organizations, what is expected from a member varies considerably from one organization to another. The general principle of variation is that a sect (defined as a religious organization which sees itself as having an almost exclusive grasp of the salvational truth: see pages 184–5) will tend to require from its members far more commitment than will a denomination. A body which accepts the denominational attitude of allowing that other organizations have as

members had moved out of the catchment area. The Free Presbyterians only manage to stop the building being embarrassingly empty by bussing members from other parts of the west and north of the city. A second problem is that large Victorian church buildings need a large congregation to prevent them feeling cold and empty. A purpose-built modern structure can have a low ceiling and partition walls which can be moved to suit the growth of the congregation so that a small fledgeling congregation does not have to be reminded constantly of its size. A third and less obvious problem with taking over an old building is that, even if the new congregation fills it, there may be the sense that all that has been achieved is a restoration of the status quo ante. In contrast, a new structure suggests growth and real progress even if its capacity is far less than the total capacity of all the redundant buildings in the same neighbourhood.

much of the truth as it does will find it difficult to instil in its members a compelling need to work to promote the organization or its ideology. For this and related reasons we would expect that a Free Presbyterian member is 'worth more' to Free Presbyterianism than an Irish Presbyterian is to his or her denomination. One certainly sees this in the way in which Free Presbyterians participate in Church-related activities. Take the question of attendance. It is clear from the census figures that those people who describe themselves as Irish Presbyterians or Church of Ireland are more numerous than those who actually attend the services of these denominations.[3] The same is even more true for Roman Catholicism. With Free Presbyterians, almost the reverse is the case. My count of people attending Free Presbyterian services produced more Free Presbyterians than did the question of religious affiliation in the 1981 census. As I have already suggested, it may well be that the 1985 figures represent real growth since 1981 but, either way, those people who call themselves Free Presbyterians actually go regularly to Free Presbyterian churches.

And they not only go once: about seventy-five per cent of them attend both Sunday services. This was the common Presbyterian pattern in Scotland and Ulster a hundred years ago when ministers with lax congregations would solemnly denounce the sin of 'half day hearing'. The morning service tends to be the conventional Presbyterian worship service with hymns, a psalm, scripture reading, a sermon, and more hymns; differing only in the length and nature of the sermon which is normally of an hour's duration and designed as Bible exposition. Communion, on those Sundays on which it is taken, would follow or be part of the morning worship. The morning service is for believers and regular attenders. The evening service tends to be designed more for the outsider with a greater emphasis in the sermon on the need for conversion. In Dr Paisley's own congregation, the evening meeting is usually also the

[3] Because Northern Ireland is more traditionally religious than other parts of Britain, the difference between the proportion of the public who claim church allegiance and the proportion who actually support the church is considerably less than it is in England, Scotland, or Wales. For example, the 1981 census (Department of Health and Social Services/Registrar General Northern Ireland, *The Northern Ireland Census, 1981: religion report* (Belfast: Her Majesty's Stationery Office, 1984)) listed 339,818 Irish Presbyterians—of whom 266,906 were 15 and over—and 220,697 people regularly contribute to the IPC (figures supplied by the IPC Information Office). Thus 17% of those who describe themselves as Irish Presbyterians are nominal church supporters.

more topical and controversial in that he will deal with contemporary political issues. In most of the major denominations attendance at evening meetings has declined so much since the Second War that they have either been abandoned or are now shared by a number of churches in a neighbourhood. Most Free Presbyterians attend both Sunday services and committed core members will often arrive an hour or thirty minutes before the services for Bible study or intensive prayer.

In addition to the Sunday activities, the committed Free Presbyterian will spend time during the week at the 'Hour of Power' prayer meeting, the 'Morning Watch', or a mid-week Bible study. Attendance at such additional meetings is expected of a sincerely converted Christian who should display hunger for gospel teaching:

The worldly Church says 'What nonsense to have a prayer meeting, Let us organize, Let us get money in, Let us have discos in the Church Hall, and ping pong and pool and everything else in the Church Hall and get all the young people in and have a jollification'. Utter nonsense. It is not the policy of the church to entertain the goats. It is the policy of the Church to feed the sheep.[4]

If a minister decides to have a week or a fortnight of special evangelistic meetings, the core of his congregation will turn out night after night to support his efforts.

I had initially thought to demonstrate the different levels of commitment in various denominations by comparing the amount of money given to Church work by the average member but this is not really illuminating, because although one can calculate how much the average Free Presbyterian and Irish Presbyterian give to their respective churches and compare these totals, this misses the point of 'the widow's mite'. One would have to compare the percentage of earnings given rather than the gross amount because it may well be that Free Presbyterians are, on average, poorer than core members of Irish Presbyterian congregations. However, what we do know is that Free Presbyterians are encouraged to 'tithe'; to give one tenth of their free income to Christian work. The average Free Presbyterian does not appear to do so, although, given that many make donations to non-Free Presbyterian missionary work, it is difficult to be sure. However, there is no doubt that they come

---

[4] Ian R. K. Paisley, *Revivalist* (Feb. 1982.)

closer to tithing than do members of the major denominations and it is certainly the case that core members such as ministers and elders tithe.[5]

Where one can see a clear difference between Free Presbyterians and more liberal Protestants is in the ways in which they raise money for Christian work. Free Presbyterians will not organize raffles, tombolas, dinner dances, jumble sales, or fêtes to raise money. To do so would be to fall into the sin of 'worldliness'. Paisley has a well-practised and much-loved line in denouncing such methods:

Like these descendants of Tetzel, the notorious pedlar of the Pope's indulgences, many men who have vowed to preach the whole counsel of God have become organizers of dances, parties, stewardship dinners etc in a vain attempt to bolster up the crumbling structure of their Church finances. . . . No Free Presbyterian minister will stoop to such miserable tactics. When we need money we pray and God's people give as unto him.[6]

And give they certainly do. Those people who regularly give to the Irish Presbyterian Church give somewhere in the region of £80 a year. The Hillsborough Free Presbyterian Church had a total income of £62,202 in 1984, which works out at around £200 per person. Averaging the figures for various Free Presbyterian congregations reduces this to around £150 per person but this is still a considerable proportion of their income. Free Presbyterians take obvious pride in their missionary support and their new church building, but as Paisley's judgement on those who raise money by secular means makes clear, it is not so much the *amounts* of money as the *manner* in which it is raised which produces their sense of satisfaction. Unlike the followers of Antichrist who hold raffles and the 'ecumaniacs' who have dances, Free Presbyterians need no motive other than the belief that they are engaged in the work of the Lord to persuade them to support the Church.

Organizing the Clergy

The growth and consolidation of the Church involved the re-

[5] The average Irish Presbyterian gives £80 per annum, which would be a 'tithe' of an annual income of just £800 or £1,600 for a family with only one wage-earner.
[6] *Revivalist* (Jan. 1978).

cruitment not only of members but also of ministers. In an earlier chapter I made the point that the early years of the Church were characterized by considerable turn-over in the ministry, particularly among those men who were recruited from outside Northern Ireland or who had previous experience of full-time Christian work. A factor in the recent stabilization of the ministry has been the Church's ability to recruit an increasing proportion of candidates for the ministry from a membership which has been 'saved' or raised in the Free Church. There have also been important changes in the organization of ministerial training.

When the Free Church was founded, the theological training for candidates for the ministry was provided by Ian Paisley, his father, and Dr. H. H. Aitchison, an ex-Presbyterian and ex-Congregational Union minister whose educational qualifications did not really extend much beyond a good first degree in divinity. His doctorate had been acquired from a rather dubious American mail-order college for a series of lectures on the psychology of religion (published by Pitman as *Psychology Without Sighs*). Although Ian Paisley did his best to impose respectable entrance qualifications on his young ministers (those who did not possess basic credentials in English and arithmetic, for example, were sent to evening classes) and did his best to teach them the rudiments of theology, he was hampered by a lack of assistance. Although personally quite capable of providing theological training of a standard that would be accepted in many Protestant denominations (after all, despite his penchant for qualifications from mail-order colleges,[7] he had successfully completed a rigorous three-year

---

[7] Paisley's penchant for initials has given his critics endless opportunity for ridicule. The bare facts of his educational credentials are these. In 1946, he successfully completed a three-year course with the Reformed Presbyterians. In April and November 1954, he joined the Geographical Society, the Royal Society of Literature, and the Philosophical Society: all organizations which one joins by paying a fee. In March and October 1954, he was given a BD and a DD by Pioneer Theological Seminary, Rockford, Illinois. In March 1958 he acquired an MA from Burton College and Seminary, Manitou Springs, Colorado. Both Pioneer and Burton were 'degree mills': phony postal colleges which offered no tuition. Qualifications were supposedly given for written work but were, in fact, awarded on payment of fees, irrespective of the quality of work submitted. This does not mean, of course, that Paisley did not submit written work of a standard which would have gained the same qualifications from more legitimate establishments. The *Revivalist*, Sept./Oct. 1959, described him as 'working for a Ph.D.' from Burton for his history of the 1859 revivals in Ulster. However, his book on the awakening, which might well have been awarded a doctorate at some universities, was first published in 1958. In 1966, Bob Jones University, an educationally legit-

course with the Reformed Presbyterian Church), he simply did not have the time to devote to the creation of a theological college. Like many of the other factors which hampered the growth of the Church, this problem was gradually resolved by initial growth creating the right conditions for more rapid growth. Once the first generation of John Douglas, S. B. Cooke, and Alan Cairns had finished their training, they were able to devote part of their energies to training the next generation. As the total number of ministers increased, these three were able to devote more time and effort to teaching, as the others shouldered the burden of evangelistic meetings. The enlarged pool also included some men, such as Gordon Ferguson who had a good degree in Classics from London University, with particular skills to contribute.

An indicator of the increased attention to training is the increase in the number of years the students were expected to spend in college. The initial training period was three years, but in 1976 a fourth year was added. Perhaps more significant was the increased delay in putting a student in charge of a congregation. Until the 1970s, candidates were usually placed in congregations as soon as they were accepted for the ministry. Now a student usually studies full-time for two years before being given ministerial duties. In addition to improving the teaching, the Church has insisted that its students pass their examinations. One man who was pastoring a growing congregation in Armagh was reluctant to complete his courses which, after a sixteen-year absence from formal education, he found difficult, arguing that the success of his ministry demonstrated his competence. He was cautioned by the Presbytery and later removed when he continued to refuse to complete his college work.

The above is offered not as a contribution to the arguments about the validity of Free Presbyterian theology or the intellectual adequacy of Free Presbyterian ministers, but as evidence of the improvement in the organization of the Church which was made possible by a combination of: (*a*) the emergence of a cadre of loyal young men who had been fully socialized in separatist conservative evangelical Protestantism to undertake a number of the roles which Ian Paisley had previously performed; and (*b*) the growth in the revival period between 1966 and 1969 which vastly increased the

imate, although thoroughly fundamentalist, 'liberal arts' university, gave Paisley an honorary doctorate in recognition of his services to fundamentalism.

manpower and financial resources of the organization. Even an organization which has a public image as well defined as that of the Free Presbyterian Church has the problem that people are recruited who gradually conclude, for a wide variety of reasons, that they do not wish to continue in the ministry. In the early days of the Church, such disaffection was demonstrated in ministers leaving. The increase in the amount of time spent in training, and the rigour with which that training is supervised, has shifted forward the point of defection or expulsion (depending on whether the individual or the Presbytery takes the initiative) so that, by the late 1970s, one sees fewer ministers leaving and 'drop out' occurring more in the training period.

It is worth adding that Free Presbyterianism is not, as some of its detractors suppose, essentially anti-intellectual. It violently disagrees with many of the specific beliefs offered by modern liberal educational institutions, but it retains the respect for an educated and learned ministry which was so characteristic of Scottish and Ulster Presbyterianism and which separates it from other varieties of conservative Protestantism. Although the social background of its membership has meant that the Church has had to demand less by way of educational qualifications than, for example, Irish Presbyterianism, it has continued to emphasize the importance of learning and has consistently tried to raise the educational standards of its spokesmen.

The reasons for this are fairly obvious and are related to a theme of the next chapter: authority. Conservative Protestants differ from other Christians in the stress they place on the authority of the Bible. For them the Bible is the centre of Christianity because it, and it alone, contains the accounts of the life and teaching of Christ and the information needed for salvation. Free Presbyterians constantly return to the Bible and the study of it, and the preaching of its message is the core of Free Presbyterianism. The problem, of course, is that the Bible is not self-interpreting. Or, to be more precise, even among those variants of Christianity which claim no source of authority other than the Bible, there are always considerable differences of opinion about what the Bible actually teaches. The practical solution is to accept as 'standards subordinate to the Scriptures' documents which clearly express particular interpretations of the Bible. Hence the role played by the Westminster Confession of Faith and the Longer and Shorter

Catechisms: the classic statements of traditional Presbyterianism. Free Presbyterians insist that the 'church traditions' which they use to guide their interpretation of the Bible are quite different to those used by the Roman Catholic Church for the same purpose. In the first place, they claim, their traditions represent the essence of Bible Christianity and Rome's traditions do not. Secondly their traditions are subordinate to the Bible. However, leaving the truth or falsity of such claims to one side, it is clear that, from an organizational point of view, Protestant creeds perform a task similar to that performed by the bureaucracy of the Roman Catholic Church in codifying the faith and in setting the limits to the valid interpretation of the faith. The mastery of the doctrine expressed in such creeds requires considerable study.

Charismatic religious groups, which believe that the Holy Spirit leads believers, can have leaders with little formal training. A religious culture which lays great stress on doctrinal orthodoxy has to lay similar stress on the acquisition of correct doctrine. Ceremony plays so little part in Free Presbyterianism that learning what a minister does, does not take long, but learning what a minister thinks and says is time-consuming. Furthermore, the widespread acceptance in educated circles of 'higher critical' interpretations of the Scriptures has meant that conservatives are under considerable pressure to defend their ideology and, in order to do this, they must become reasonably familiar with Greek and Hebrew so that they can justify to their flocks their refusal to accept modern interpretations of the Bible. From the point of view of the individual who feels called to preach the word, the lengthy and difficult training may seem like an uncalled-for encumbrance, but from the point of view of the organization, it is justified by the greater cohesion produced and by the increased likelihood that the Church will survive as an homogeneous unit after its founder ceases to be active and his personal leadership ceases to be a source of unity.

Free Presbyterian Schools

A recent development with possibly profound consequences for the Church is the establishment of independent Christian schools. In any society which is not culturally homogeneous, education will be an arena for social conflict because it plays a major part in the

socialization of the next generation. A culture reproduces itself
through education. In common with many basically Protestant
societies, Northern Ireland has a system of state schools which was
formed by the union, and by government acquisition, of schools
which had previously been run by the various denominations. The
Roman Catholic Church insisted on maintaining its own schools,
initially at some cost because Catholics were supporting both a
state system through their taxes and a Catholic system through
donations. Gradually the state increased its contribution to the
voluntary schools so that now all teachers' salaries and almost all
costs are paid for by the state.[8] The logic of Catholic education is
that it is not enough to add a few hours of 'Catholic' teaching on
to the end of a secular curriculum: all subjects have to be taught
within the context of Catholicism.

At the outset of the Northern Ireland state, the government's
intention had been to create a national system of non-sectarian
schools. This was sabotaged first by the Catholic Church refusing
even to enter negotiations, and then by a number of Protestant
clerics, in alliance with the Orange Order, successfully agitating to
improve the terms under which church schools would be transferred to state control. Despite the puzzlement of one Minister of
Education who could not see 'why an exhaustive knowledge of
the Apocalypse should necessarily qualify any man to decide the
amount of money to be expended on lavatory accommodation in
any given primary school',[9] the 1923 Education Act was amended
so as to increase the influence of the clergy in the management
of the schools. Whatever the merits of their case, the Protestant
churches won the right to ensure that only Protestant teachers were
appointed, enshrined one hour of 'simple Bible teaching' in each
school week, and forced teachers to give such instruction as part
of their normal teaching duties. One might have thought that these
provisions would have ensured that the ex-Protestant schools remained more than non-Catholic, but they became fairly thoroughly
secularized. The 1944 Education Act had moderated the successes
of the 1920s campaign for greater church control. For example,
teachers could no longer be required to teach Bible study. By the

---

[8] A good account of the organization and financing of education in Northern
Ireland can be found in Patrick Buckland, *The Factory of Grievances: devolved
government in Northern Ireland, 1921-39* (dublin: Gill and Macmillan, 1979),
Ch. 11.

[9] Ibid., p. 257.

1960s most religious education classes had moved away from Bible exposition. In part this drift was inevitable. Clerical representation on management committees could not prevent what religion there was in schools being 'diluted' because the clergy were themselves not united in doctrine. With considerable doctrinal deviation both within and between the Protestant denominations, it was impossible to maintain any strong religious influence, and religion in schools now generally means what one critic called 'vacuous piety of the lowest common denominator type'. The present Northern Ireland school system thus consists of a Roman Catholic sector and a non-Catholic sector over which Protestant clergymen have some limited influence but which, in practice, has become largely secularized.

For conservative evangelicals, the schools attended by their children have become problematic in three ways. In the first place, there are elements of the teaching which offend their beliefs. In biology classes, for example, children may be taught evolutionary theories of the origins of the species. Even if they are not directly confronted with evolution, they will certainly not be taught the Genesis creation story. More generally, children may be presented with views on sex education and related moral issues, or on current affairs, which are at odds with what their parents teach them at home. Secondly, when the state schools are not actually short of religion, they offer the wrong kind. Even when the Protestant clerics were at their most influential in educational policy, the Bible instruction which they had insisted upon was 'to be Protestant in nature but not distinctive of any Protestant denomination', which effectively meant that, as the main denominations became more liberal in their theology, religious education ceased to be dogmatic. This alone would be anathema to evangelicals, but the problem is often compounded by religious instruction being directed by teachers who see an opportunity for broadening children's horizons by making them acquainted with a variety of religious cultures. Religious education has often become education about religion rather than schooling in any particular variety.

The third set of reasons for evangelicals' distrust of the state education system involves vague, but none the less strongly felt, fears about a lack of discipline. Free Presbyterians believe that children need to be taught manners and respect for authority. People who believe in original sin have little reason to want children encouraged to 'express themselves'. Liberal educationalists with their belief in 'child-centred' learning and distaste for corporal punishment are blamed for vandalism, bad language, adolescent sexual activity, and all the other things which evangelicals believe characterize modern youth.

Most evangelicals share the above concerns but find ways of living with the problem. Some work hard at home to counter the malign influence of the school. Others respond by trying to intervene whenever possible. One Free Presbyterian minister recalled the occasion when his children brought home a BBC carol book which contained 'a carol in it that was pure Mary worship'. He went to see the senior teachers, expressed his concern and found the staff willing to accommodate him by passing over that particular carol. In general, he found that he could maintain a working relationship with the staff of the particular school which his children attended, although he did recognize that other schools were less co-operative.

There are, however, some evangelicals who accept all of the above and yet would not consider removing their children because, they argue, young evangelicals will come face to face with sin and apostasy sometime and it is better to let them get used to being surrounded by unbelief gradually rather than have them cocooned until 18 and then thrown straight in at the deep end.

These points could have been made in relation to evangelical parents in most western societies. However, in parts of Northern Ireland, Protestant parents have a particular problem with state schools: their control by Roman Catholics. The Roman Catholic schools are controlled by Catholics. The state schools are controlled by Education and Library Boards which are made up of people nominated from a number of sources, but which basically reflect the make-up of the areas. Thus the Western Education and Library Board now has a Catholic majority and even non-evangelical Protestants in the west of the province are organizing protests against the Board's power to direct schools. The Fermanagh Official Unionist Association said: 'The unionist people cannot allow the future education of their children to be hijacked by those who are committed to the destruction of the constitution of this province.'[10]

It is against this sort of background that the Free Presbyterian

---

[10] *Belfast Telegraph* (29 Sept. 1985).

Church's establishment of four independent Christian schools has to be seen. The first was founded by the Fosters in Kilskeery. Mrs Foster was a well-qualified and experienced teacher in a state school who became so disillusioned with the education being given to her children that she withdrew them and began to teach them at home. It seemed sensible to offer the service to other Free Presbyterians and in September 1979 the Kilskeery Independent Christian School opened its doors.

Kilskeery was followed by Ballymoney, where the minister is a qualified teacher, and Newtownabbey, where the minister had been deeply impressed by a lecture on Christian education delivered at the 1978 World Fundamentalist Congress in Edinburgh. In researching the possibilities, Reggie Cranston visited fundamentalist schools in Ohio and at Bob Jones University in South Carolina, where he took a short course in school management. In 1985, a fourth school opened in Bangor.

The four schools are, as the name boasts, entirely independent. They receive no state funding whatsoever and, within the constraints set by the London University O and A level examination papers, are free to teach what they like. They are, however, subject to government inspection and to date the inspectors' reports have been generally favourable. They have, however, expressed concern about what the Free Presbyterians see as a major advantage of their schools: the well-mannered and disciplined behaviour of the pupils. Such behaviour is fundamental to what the schools are trying to do and all parents sign an agreement with the school in which they accept the following:

I fully realize that the Bible sets forth plain standards for any institution which claims to be Christian. On the question of modesty (1 Tim. 2: 9–10) and of tidiness and length of hair (1 Cor. 11: 13) plain instructions are given. I undertake to see that my child(ren) at all times uphold(s) the standards of appearance set by the Scripture. I understand that learning can only take place in an atmosphere of disciplined obedience to the teacher. In order to maintain discipline a teacher must exercise authority in a fair, firm and kindly manner. Where punitive measures are necessary to maintain authority, I hereby give permission for appropriate corporal punishment to be administered to my child(ren).

In its publicity literature, the Newtownabbey school lists the fundamentalist Christian beliefs of the Free Presbyterian Church, stresses the importance of discipline and authority, and states that

'All members of staff in a Christian school must be born again'. Apart from the children being sufficiently quiet and well behaved for the inspectors to comment on it, the other defining characteristic of the schools is their frequent recourse to religious activities. The week begins with the reciting of the school creed:

I believe the Bible to be the Word of God. I believe that Jesus Christ is God's only begotten Son. I believe that by faith in his atoning death alone I can be saved from sin and everlasting punishment. I believe that all those who fully trust in Him should live holy lives and avoid lying and all things that would dishonour the Lord's great name. I will not dishonour the name of the Lord Jesus or the name of our school by improper behaviour of any kind at home, in church, in class, or in any other place. I will not be ashamed of or deny this statement of my faith.

One of the two full-time teachers at Kilskeery described the place of the Bible in the work of the school in the following terms:

Each school day starts with half an hour's devotion in which the Bible is read and taught. After lunch there is another time set aside for Bible reading. Each pupil learns at least one Bible verse every week, while those in Form 1 learn four. We have two periods of Scripture lesson every week. The Bible obviously is *the* textbook here and, while we must use other textbooks for our many subjects, anything contrary to the word of God is utterly rejected. Rev. Foster uses the Bible almost exclusively when teaching Form 1 Church History but in *every* subject the Bible is our chief reference book.[11]

In addition to Bible reading, there is frequent prayer. When the children in one primary school class returned from playing outside during break, the teacher asked which children wanted to pray. Three of the volunteers (who included almost all the children) were chosen and they all prayed for Dr Paisley and the Independent Christian schools. Tom Tice, an American Free Presbyterian ministering in Calgary, and Hillis Fleming, the Liverpool Free Presbyterian minister, were also mentioned; both had previously visited the school.

Part of the attraction of the schools is their return to what people think schools were like fifty years ago when children respected and obeyed their teachers. Whether the schools of the rural past actually did represent such a pleasant and viable combination of caring and authority is not the point; lots of parents think they did

---

[11] *Truth For Youth* (Mar.-Apr. 1981), p. 7.

and the Free Presbyterian ministers who run schools offer not only fundamentalist beliefs but also traditional schooling. Unfortunately traditional schooling generally meant small classes and the independent schools, even were they to grow, would have to maintain small classes to continue to offer this attraction. Thus they are prevented from enjoying the economies of scale.

To some extent costs will fall as more schools are started and some resources, such as specialist teaching, can be shared between them. At the moment, they rely heavily on the teachers' willingness to regard their work as a missionary calling and hence to accept lower salaries than they could command in the state sector. At the moment, fees are £300 per child per year with reductions for second and third children. What makes the endeavour possible is the free availability of plant. Many of the new churches are built with specially designed Sunday school complexes of halls and classrooms. Apart from the additional heating and lighting costs, the buildings come free to the schools. This has permitted the Free Presbyterians to avoid other cheaper forms of Christian education. In the last ten years, a number of 'schools' using 'accelerated Christian education' (or ACE) packages have been started in Britain. The American ACE system is based on programmed learning. A school buys work-books which allow a child to learn by following self-correcting exercises. The work can be supervised by any untrained adult who simply checks that children have completed their exercises. As the children work on their own, children of various ages can be accommodated in one room. The decision of the Free Presbyterians not to use ACE systems is an interesting example of their rejection of American innovations. In education, as in many other things, Free Presbyterians are profoundly conservative, and while they have been willing to examine new American methods, it is to what they suppose were the practices of Ulster Presbyterianism of a hundred or fifty years ago that they turn for their models.

At present the four schools are small. The biggest, Bangor, only has forty pupils. Newtownabbey has twenty-two children; seventeen being taught by one teacher in the primary division and the remaining five under a secondary teacher. However, other congregations are planning to follow suit once they have freed themselves from the costs of recent church-building programmes. The Portadown congregation, for example, is planning to start a school which, because of its central location, will be able to serve parents from six or seven neighbouring churches.

Although the schools are administered by the local Free Presbyterian ministers and kirk sessions, their description of 'Independent Christian' rather than 'Free Presbyterian' accurately describes their recruitment from a milieu wider than the membership of the Church. Although Kilskeery recruits almost entirely from Free Presbyterian families, the Newtownabbey school has children from Evangelical Methodist, Elim, Brethren, and Congregationalist families. None the less, the schools take their main *raison d'être* from two Free Presbyterian concerns to which I will now turn: problems of recruitment and problems of sustaining commitment.

Free Presbyterian Growth Outside Ulster

There are good reasons to suppose that the Free Presbyterian Church will in the future grow, if it grows, by recruiting the children of existing members. The vast majority of people who joined the Free Church were already 'saved' Christians or were active members of other denominations. In the main, the rise of Free Presbyterianism can be seen as a relocation of conservative evangelicals from other denominations rather than as a movement which has grown by creating evangelicals. Free Presbyterian recruitment has largely resulted from dissatisfaction with liberalism in the other Protestant churches.

The main reason for supposing that this source of new members has dried up is that the issues have been so well aired that there can be few Presbyterians or Church of Ireland members who have not been confronted with the claims that their church is apostate because it tolerates liberals and that they are involved in a 'Romeward trend'. Many Free Presbyterians recognize this, and a number of ministers acknowledge that there is limited value in constantly preaching on 'the great apostasy'. There will, of course, be a constant trickle of individuals who belatedly come to agree with the Free Presbyterian Church's separatist stance but it is now unlikely that this trickle will ever grow to match the flood of new members which the Church acquired between 1966 and 1969 when the 'great apostasy' was made incarnate in the liberal unionism of

Terence O'Neill and the political conflict between Paisley and the government.

The very rise of Free Presbyterianism has undermined the conditions for its future growth by rallying the conservatives within the Irish Presbyterian Church. The obvious popularity of Paisley's critique of ecumenism allowed those evangelicals who remained in the IPC to force it to the right. The IPC withdrew from the World Council of Churches (though it remains in the Irish Council of Churches which is still linked to the WCC), and in recent years has shown considerable evidence of conservatism in, for example, the forcing out of David Armstrong from his Limavady church for fraternizing with his Roman Catholic opposite number.[12] As the IPC has shifted to the right, so the pressure on conservatives within it to depart for the Free Presbyterian Church has been reduced.

Furthermore, there has been little obvious movement in the direction of church unity to frighten conservatives in the major denominations. To date, all the talk of ecumenism has produced only one significant British church union since the war. In 1972 the majority of the English Presbyterians and the English Congregationalists merged to form the United Reformed Church. The more extravagant schemes for uniting Methodists and Anglicans or Anglicans and Roman Catholics have all led to nothing; hardly surprising when one remembers that the sort of changes in the Anglican Church which would make it more acceptable to Rome or the Orthodox churches are precisely the same changes which would make it less acceptable to the reformed churches. Although relationships between individual congregations of different churches may have improved, such local initiatives need not force other members of the same denomination to re-evaluate their affiliation. If one's own minister is too liberal, one can move to another congregation, or, as in the Armstrong case, unseat him.

---

[12] David Armstrong's version of the Limavady affair is given in David Armstrong and Hilary Saunders, *A Road Too Wide: the price of reconciliation in Northern Ireland* (Basingstoke, Hants: Marshall, Morgan and Scott, 1985). The clearest example of the IPC's move to the right was its withdrawal from membership of the World Council of Churches. The IPC had been involved in the ecumenical movement from the 1930s. The reconsideration of membership began in 1971 with a resolution from the Kirk Session of an Ahoghill, County Antrim (Paisley's constituency) congregation. In 1972, the Assembly vote for remaining in the World Council was 219; that against: 168. The 1976 vote was 481 for and 381 against. The 1979 Assembly voted by 421 to 248 for temporary suspension of membership and, a year later, for complete withdrawal by 448 votes to 388.

Although more could be said on this issue, the above is enough to make the point that there seems little prospect of any major shifts in the main Protestant denominations in Northern Ireland which would cause the sort of disaffection which produced the Free Presbyterian expansion of 1966-9.

With Free Presbyterianism in Ulster stable but only growing slowly, expansion outside Ulster has become the main source of growth. There are now Free Presbyterian congregations in England, Australia, Canada, America, and the Republic of Ireland. Some of these resulted from migration. The movement in Australia, for example, was initiated by Ulster exiles. Some of the others, however, were a result of declining local Protestant organizations asking to be taken under the wing of the Free Presbyterian Church.

The Liverpool congregation is a good example. With its large Irish population, Liverpool often displayed the same sectarian conflict as Belfast. George Wise founded the Protestant Reformers Church in 1903 and created a following of thousands for his aggressive anti-Catholic preaching. He was elected to the council for Kirkdale as a 'Protestant' but did not re-contest his seat in 1906 because, as a paid official of a dissenting denomination, he was barred from election. After his death, his combination of evangelistic preaching and political activity was continued by H. D. Longbottom who increased the congregation so that at one time it boasted over a thousand attenders at its Men's Bible Class. Like Belfast, Liverpool was residentially segregated on 'religious' lines and Longbottom's Liverpool Protestant Party maintained a presence in the council for the areas of St Domingo and Netherfields. Although the movement flagged in 1956 with Longbottom failing to get re-elected, he returned to the council in 1960 'after the Education Act aided new Catholic schools and Heenan advanced the cathedral'.[13] After Longbottom's death in 1962, the party, under his son-in-law Ron Henderson, struggled. In the late 1960s, the Ulster crisis gave it a new relevance and Henderson joined Ian Paisley in the British Constitution Defence Committee. But the religious base of the movement had been eroded by secularization and by population shifts which had removed the Protestants who had supported the Church and the Party. What the German bomb-

[13] P. J. Waller, *Democracy and Sectarianism: a political and social history of Liverpool, 1868-1939* (Liverpool: Liverpool University Press, 1981), p. 349.

ing blitz of the Second World War had started, council rebuilding schemes finished, and St Domingo and Netherfields ceased to exist as traditional Orange areas.[14]

By the late 1970s, it was clear to Henderson that the Protestant Reformers could no longer continue as an independent church and, in 1982, the Free Presbyterian Church of Ulster was asked to take the remnant congregation under its wing.

Although the political dimension was missing, the Toronto congregation has a somewhat similar history. As young boys, Frank and James McClelland had attended Paisley's Ravenhill church. James joined the Free Presbyterian ministry and Frank became an aircraft design draftsman. After working for Shorts in Belfast he went to Seattle and later Toronto. In Seattle, he became active in a new Bible Presbyterian[15] congregation where he had the unnerving experience of almost being killed by a disgruntled member of the congregation. As the only elder, he was with the pastor when he was shot dead by a man who had been suspended from membership. Had the man remembered to re-cock the gun, McClelland would also have been shot. Seeing the experience as a major

[14] Apart from ibid., the best sources of information on Wise and Longbottom are various pamphlets written and published by Ronald Henderson: *George Wise: Protestant stalwart twice imprisoned for the Gospel's sake*; *The Startling History of the new Liverpool Roman Catholic Cathedral*; and *Seventy Five Years of Protestant Witness*.

[15] The Bible Presbyterians are a small denomination founded by Carl McIntire in 1937. McIntire left the Presbyterian Church in the United States in 1932 with J. Gresham Machen and the other conservatives who objected to the liberalism of the major Presbyterian body. Shortly after they helped form the Orthodox Presbyterian Church, McIntire and his supporters fell out with Machen and the majority of the Orthodox Presbyterians over their refusal to endorse pre-millennial eschatology and a total abstention from alcoholic beverages. The McIntire faction founded the Bible Presbyterians, and the American Council of Christian Churches and the International Council of Christian Churches as fundamentalist alternatives to the American Council of Churches and the World Council. In 1969 McIntire was removed from the ACCC executive. The Bible Presbyterians accept the Westminster Confession and the Longer and Shorter Catechism, and are pre-millennial, which makes them very similar to Paisley's Free Presbyterians. However, various personal animosities caused a rupture between McIntire and the Bob Jones family. Paisley took the Jones side and helped form the World Congress of Fundamentalists. Recently, however, the rise of a new generation of fundamentalists involved in new Christian right politics seems to have caused the older generation to forget their differences and Bob Jones Jun. has recently addressed a McIntire-organized convention. The most informative source on the tortuous and schism-ridden history of American fundamentalism is J. Gordon Melton, *The Encyclopedia of American Religions* (Wilmington, North Carolina: McGrath Publishing Company, Consortium Books, 1978).

turning-point in his life, Frank McClelland returned to Ulster to train for the Free Presbyterian ministry and became the pastor of the Tandragee congregation. In 1974 he returned to Toronto for a holiday, and while there he was invited to preach to a very small Bible Presbyterian group whose pastor was about to retire because his ministry had seen the number of the faithful reduced to just thirteen adult members. He invited McClelland to take over the ministry. He agreed on the condition that the work was conducted under the auspices of the Free Presbyterian Church.

Apart from loyalty, there were a number of good reasons for this decision. Evangelicals believe in the power of prayer and are loath to engage in any work for which there will not be 'prayer support'. Frank McClelland had few friends in Canada, but he knew that he would be supported by the prayers of the Free Church. There is, of course, a mundane side to 'prayer support' in that people who pray for a work will also be willing to support it financially.

Such support was not needed for long. Although there was con-siderable early opposition to a 'Paisley' church in Toronto (for example, the local authorities prevented the congregation using the hall they had previously rented), the congregation grew rapidly and is now able both to support itself and to assist the newer enterprises in Calgary and Vancouver.

The Liverpool experience reflects a general problem which dogs American fundamentalism and which explains the appeal of the Free Presbyterian Church for declining conservative congre-gations. Independency has the great weakness that it produces one-generation congregations. Individual pastors such as Wise and Longbottom are able to create huge personal followings but when they die or retire, the work declines. Liverpool was unusual in being able to repeat the process but there was a collapse in between the pastorates of Wise and Longbottom and neither of the men who followed 'Longie' was able to command similar loyalty. In his explanation for the survival of the Free Church, Paisley stresses the continuity which the Presbyterian structure provides. Each congregation is under the supervision of all the congregations. If one falls vacant, the Presbytery appoints a senior minister to take charge until the vacancy is filled. So long as the Presbytery remains committed to enforcing its standards, it can ensure that all people who are licensed as Free Presbyterian ministers will believe and preach the same things. Small groups of believers, such as those in Liverpool or Toronto, can rest assured that they will be supported by the resources of the Church and that any minister who comes to them to preach will continue where the previous preacher left off. In the spring of 1985, a new church was opened in Oulton Broad, Sussex. To date it has been 'supplied' by ministers from Ulster taking it in turn to spend a month building the congregation. Although each month brings a new face and a new voice to the pulpit, the message remains the same.

The practice of pooling resources has been taken even further in the organization of training. In 1976, Alan Cairns was invited to take over a Presbyterian congregation in Greenville, South Carolina. Although located in one of the centres of Baptist fundamentalism—Bob Jones University is in Greenville—Faith Free Presbyterian Church has prospered and Cairns remains on very good terms with the Jones family. In recent years, he has recruited a number of young Americans to the Free Presbyterian ministry. He teaches them theology (as he did in Belfast before he left) and S. B. Cooke and John Douglas travel to Greenville each year to spend a month teaching 'sacred rhetoric' and English Bible. Another example of resource-sharing is provided by the foundation of the Vancouver congregation. The interest in Vancouver had been stimulated by Frank McClelland airing his Toronto broadcasts in the Vancouver area. When Ian Goligher went to take charge of the work in 1984, the Toronto congregation continued to fund the broadcasts and the Mission Board guaranteed half of his salary for a year.

To summarize, it may at first sight seem strange that a religious organization that owes so much of its character to the particular nature of conflict in Northern Ireland should be able to expand beyond the area affected by the conflict. In part this is a function of migration. One of the first families involved in Vancouver had come from Northern Ireland. Part of the impetus for the foundation of the two Australian churches came from people who had been members of the Free Church in Ulster before emigrating. But, as the Toronto and Greenville examples show, the Free Presbyterian Church has considerable appeal to people who have very little connection with Ulster because it is able to offer consistent fundamentalism and an organizational structure which provides continuity and strength in numbers. Its foreign expansion will be slowed by hostility to the high political profile of Ian Paisley and by the assumption, common in North America where fundamentalism is almost entirely Baptist, that Presbyterianism is liberal, but one can expect that the gradual process of Free Presbyterianism 'mopping up' small pockets of isolated conservative evangelicals will continue.

Sustaining Commitment

To use the technical language of the sociology of religion, the Free Presbyterian Church began life as a 'sect'.

Typically a *sect* may be identified by the following characteristics: it is a voluntary association; membership is by proof to sect authorities of some claim to personal merit—such as knowledge of doctrine, affirmation of a conversion experience, or recommendation of members in good standing; exclusiveness is emphasized, and expulsion exercised against those who contravene doctrinal, moral or organizational precepts; its self-conception is of an elect, a gathered remnant, possessing special enlightenment; personal perfection is the expected standard of aspiration, in whatever terms this is judged; it accepts, at least as an ideal, the priesthood of all believers; there is a high level of lay participation; there is opportunity for the member spontaneously to express his commitment; the sect is hostile or indifferent to secular society and to the state.[16]

In most discussions of religious organizations, the sect is contrasted with the *denomination*, which Wilson describes as follows:

It is formally a voluntary association; it accepts adherents without imposition of traditional prerequisites of entry, and employs purely formalized procedures of admission; breadth and tolerance are emphasized; since membership is laxly enrolled, expulsion is not a common device for dealing with the apathetic and the wayward; its self-conception is unclear and its doctrinal positions unstressed; it is content to be one movement among others, all of which are thought to be acceptable in the sight of God; it accepts the standards and values of the prevailing culture and conventional morality; there is a trained professional ministry; lay participation occurs but is typically restricted to particular sections of the laity and to particular areas of activity; services are formalized and spontaneity is absent . . . individual commitment is not very intense.[17]

Wilson's models of sect and denomination are, of course, designed

[16] Bryan R. Wilson, 'An Analysis of Sect Development', *American Sociological Review*, 24 (1959). Pagination from Bobbs-Merrill Social Sciences reprint, No. S-316, p. 4.
[17] Ibid.

to highlight their particular features. It should not be expected that any particular organization will possess all of the qualities of one type or the other. None the less, it should be clear that the Free Presbyterian Church is closer to the sectarian than the denominational end of a continuum. One purpose of clarifying these organizational types is to examine change in religious organizations. One only has to think of the British Baptists, Congregationalists, Quakers, and Methodists to appreciate how common is the transition from 'sect' to 'denomination'. As Wilson makes clear in his description of the classic sect, it is the organization's self-image as having 'special enlightenment' which produces many of its organizational properties, such as strict rules about admission to membership. Of course, few sects go so far as to claim *unique* possession of the truth. Most will allow that a small number of other similar sects or small numbers of people in other types of organizations such as churches or denominations may, almost inadvertently, have stumbled upon some of the saving knowledge. This would be an accurate description of the Free Church's self-image. While it condemns the apostasies of Rome, the major Protestant denominations, and a variety of smaller groups with which it disagrees, it enjoys 'fraternal relations' (or, to use the evangelicals' term: 'fellowship') with many fundamentalist groups. Again, this might best be understood by seeing claims about possession of the truth as being ranged along a continuum. At the extreme sectarian end one has the position of supposing that only fellow sectarians are 'saved' (the Exclusive Brethren position, for example). At the extreme denominational end of the range one has 'universalism': the view that everyone, irrespective of doctrinal position, will be 'saved'. On such a scale, Free Presbyterians are clearly more sectarian than they are denominational.

The sect's self-image has many consequences for relationships with people outside the sect and with the 'world at large'. For simplicity, such relationships can be summarized as a rejection of 'worldliness' or 'high tension' between the sect and its environment. Naturally, which particular parts of the 'world' are rejected will depend on the ideology of the sect. For the Christian Scientists, it is conventional medicine. For the Christadelphians, it is war and aggression. For Free Presbyterians, some of the activities which are regarded as anathema are smoking, drinking alcohol, extra-marital heterosexual intercourse, homosexual intercourse, and gambling. Pop music, the secular cinema, television, and much popular literature are also rejected because they promote the already mentioned perverse activities.

When sects gradually moderate and become denominations, the first signs are usually to be seen in the relaxation of the tension between sect and society. Often the sect members will continue to pay lip-service to their distinctive beliefs and will maintain the rhetoric of a sectarian self-image for many years after they have begun to reduce what is distinctive about their lives. It is well-observed that the transformation begins with the arrival of a 'second generation' of sect members: 'It has been remarked again and again how the arrival of the second generation—of persons socialized rather than converted to sect membership—undercuts the intense rejection of the world the first generation established.[18] There are a number of reasons why this should be the case. In the first place, sect members are faced with the problem of locating their own children within the salvational categories they use to describe themselves and outsiders. Surely their own children must have more 'credit' in the salvation bank than have the real 'heathen'? There is a strong temptation to shift towards a theology of salvation which supposes that, in some way, 'elect' status is genetically transmitted. This is the social psychology behind 'covenant' theology: the belief that God struck a bargain not only with the children of Israel but with the children of the children of Israel. Thus the arrival of second and subsequent generations gives the first generation reason to relax the demands made of new members and thus poses problems for the exclusivity of the sect.

A second possible explanation for the gradual moderation of the sectarian position is the initial lack of commitment of the second generation. They did not choose their religion, beyond assenting to what they had been raised in. They made no great sacrifices to create the new movement. Although they may become personally enthusiastically committed to it, their faith initially has the charac-

---

[18] Rodney Stark and William Sims Bainbridge, *The Future of Religion: secularization, revival and cult formation* (Berkeley: University of California Press, 1985), p. 152. Although the Stark and Bainbridge volume has some interesting theoretical observations based on imaginative use of previously untapped sources of data, I have major reservations about their general theory of religion and about the extent to which their data support their arguments. For a comprehensive critique, see Roy Wallis and Steve Bruce, 'The Stark–Bainbridge Theory of Religion: a critical analysis and counter-proposals', *Sociological Analysis*, 45 (1) (1984), pp. 11–27.

ter of being just something they were given, like their surnames. It may also be the case that the second generation has more to lose than their parents because they are more prosperous. An unintended consequence of ascetic religion is that it tends to raise the standard of living of those who adopt it. If people refrain from smoking, drinking, gambling, womanizing, and other sins of the flesh, work diligently, and acquire a reputation for trustworthiness, then, like the Quakers, they may start out doing good and end up doing rather well.[19] There are thus often increased pressures on subsequent generations to moderate their rejection of worldliness because the costs of such rejection have been raised. The opportunities for sensual enjoyment are increased by their own prosperity. In class terms, the second generation has become 'upwardly mobile'.

One reason for expecting signs of change, at least among the ministers of the Free Church, is the increased professionalism in their training, and the increased proportion who have spent some time in higher education. I have alluded a number of times to the strong correlation between education and liberalism.[20] In its early days, the Free Church made much of its identity as the church with the 'saved' ministry as opposed to the Irish Presbyterian Church, which was the church with the educated ministry. Piety, rather than professional credentials, was the criterion for selection to the Free Church pulpit. Although piety is still vital, recent generations of ministers are better educated. The early ministers were by no means ignorant men, but a few of the older generation mentioned a slight sense of inferiority in comparison to newer ministers and to the increasing number of professional people in their congregations. There are now three Free Presbyterian ministers with university degrees; something unknown in the 1950s

[19] This is the thesis advanced by H. Richard Niebuhr, *The Social Sources of Denominationalism* (New York: Holt, 1929). The weakness of Niebuhr's approach is that he generalizes from the 'conversionist' type of sect to all sects. A more sensitive discussion of sect–denomination transformations is to be found in Bryan R. Wilson, *Religious Sects* (London: Weidenfeld and Nicholson, World University Library, 1970), Ch. 12, and *Religion in Sociological Perspective* (Oxford: Oxford University Press, 1982), Ch. 4.

[20] For example, a recent American survey compares the educational attainment of evangelical and liberal Protestants and shows that while 14.4% of liberal Protestants had completed university, only 8.9% of evangelicals had. See James Davison Hunter, *American Evangelicalism: conservative religion and the quandary of modernity* (New Brunswick, N.J.: Rutgers University Press, 1983).

and early 1960s. If the increased exposure to modern liberal culture is one reason for expecting moderation, another is the possibility of an increasing divide between the ministers and the members. In the discussion of the new generation of DUP activists which closed the previous chapter, I referred to the sociological literature on changes in radical political organizations. It is commonly found in such studies that the creation of a full-time, professional, and bureaucratic leadership brings with it a moderation of the movement's more radical goals because the leadership develops interests—such as preserving their own paid positions—which are at odds with the interests of the rank-and-file members. This tendency is recognized by evangelical Protestants who often explain the apostasy of the major denominations by arguing that the ministers who remain in such organizations are more interested in protecting their well-paid positions than they are in standing for gospel truth.

Wilson has drawn on such themes in his descriptions of sects and denominations: the sect is characterized by lay leadership; the denomination has a clear division between the full-time paid leadership and the rank-and-file. If it is the case that the two groups develop conflicting interests, then the increased professionalism of the training of Free Church ministers may signal a move towards a more 'denominational' and moderate position.

Is there any evidence that the Church is moderating? Some older ministers are certainly concerned about signs of 'worldliness'. During one of his frequent visits to Ulster, Alan Cairns cautioned a congregation about declining standards. He remarked that the number of Free Presbyterian homes with televisions had increased vastly since the early days of his ministry. He also noted that 'in the old days, if you wanted a crowd, you had a prayer meeting. Now if you want a crowd, you need gospel music.' He quickly made it clear that he had nothing against sacred music in its place (a good thing given William McCrea's position as Britain's best selling gospel artist) but he was concerned about an apparent decline in the support for more traditional activities such as prayer meetings. Another minister recalled that when he first attended the Free Church in the 1960s 'you got a lot of "Amens" from the body of the congregation'. Now there is hardly any vocal audience response. Like Cairns, he mentioned the possession of televisions and added: 'A number of years ago a Christian would have been stronger against make-up. Now that's slowly creeping in and being accepted. That's only little things but it adds up.' Signs of 'worldliness' should not be exaggerated. It is still the case that no Free Presbyterian would smoke, drink alcohol, go to dances or patronize the conventional cinema, and many ministers reported no evidence of a lack of enthusiasm from their young people. None the less it remains a problem which concerns them, as well it might, for there can be no doubt that young people in Ulster are far more incorporated into transatlantic teenage culture than were their parents. People of the generation of John Wylie, who has just retired, grew up in a very conservative Presbyterian moral and social climate and in joining the Free Church, they really only deviated from the norm on specifically religious and political questions. To use the language of tension between believers and the wider society, the Free Church has been forced to become more sectarian, not because it has changed but because the considerable liberalization of the culture which surrounds the believers has increased the difference between what they stand for and what the rest of the population accepts. The present generation of Free Presbyterians is growing up in a culture which has changed so much that, to continue to stand in the same place as their parents, they need to sustain an even greater rejection of the world which surrounds them.

The view of most ministers is that the Church is succeeding in socializing its young people into the values which their parents held; that is, that there has been no significant shift in a denominational direction in moral matters. However, it may well be that those who cannot sustain the sect's rejection of worldliness are simply leaving the Free Church. Unfortunately, I have no information about membership turnover. It is natural in this sort of research to be presented only with the successes. People do not readily talk about those who have fallen away from the faith. To say this, though, is to identify a common weakness in discussion about the sect–denomination transformation. Two separate issues need to be kept separate: the fate of any particular group of members and the fate of the organization. Although a failure to win over the second generation is painful for the individual families involved, it is not a problem for the organization as a whole unless it becomes widespread, and young people leave at such a rate that they are not replaced by new converts. Then the total membership declines. That the Free Church is still growing suggests that the defection of young people to more moderate Protestant denominations has not reached such proportions.

A lack of commitment to the standards of the Free Church on the part of the membership will only produce moderation if the ministers and elders permit it. Full voting membership is only open to those who convince the kirk session (the minister and elders) that they are 'saved Christians' who have an 'upright walk with the Lord'. In practice, a minister who enjoys the confidence of his congregation exercises the power of selection. He is also in charge of disciplining members who cease to maintain an 'upright walk'. Thus any shift in the nature of the Church would almost certainly have to be led by the ministers.

Are there signs that the increased professionalism in the training of ministers has produced moderation? I think not. One simple reason, of course, might be that the Church is too young for the shift to a more denominational attitude to have yet become apparent. That might be the case but I think it is possible to offer a number of reasons why such a transformation is unlikely. The notion that the divide between ministers and members is dangerous because the clergy will develop interests which are best served by moderation can be considered in two parts. First, we can examine motives for joining the ministry. Second, we can consider changes which may occur in a ministerial candidate's beliefs as a result of a period of professional training.

There are very few reasons for applying for the ministry of the Free Church other than a sincerely felt 'call' to promote the beliefs and values of the Church. There are other Protestant denominations, even quite conservative ones, which permit considerable freedom of opinion, and which are short of staff. Students who train for the ministry of the major denominations are usually awarded bursaries similar to the full grant available to university students. Free Church students have to make considerable financial sacrifices to complete their training. Furthermore, they make such sacrifices with no certainty of paid employment on completion of their studies. Even if there are vacant congregations, a 'call' is not guaranteed. There is at least one man who successfully completed his studies but who was not called by any of the then vacant congregations; he had to return to secular employment. Even if called, a minister will hardly enjoy prosperity. Although no

Christian ministry in this country pays as well as secular 'white collar' occupations with comparable training periods, the Free Church ministry is not one of the better paid and it has very few fringe benefits in terms of social status and prestige.

Furthermore, although the Church sometimes uses its Mission Board to subsidize congregations which are not fully able to support their own minister, such funding is always regarded as 'pump-priming' and is limited in duration. Until the Free Church becomes sufficiently respectable to be in the position of accidentally offering other sorts of rewards to potential candidates for the ministry, it will only attract and ordain people who are entirely committed to its theology and separatist stand.

It is often the case that liberal movements in 'sect-like' Protestant organizations are led by intellectuals. The major shift which took the Free Church of Scotland from being a conservative schism from the national Kirk in 1843 to being in the forefront of liberal thinking by the end of the century was led by the students and teachers of the Free Church colleges. Alan Cairns knows this and made the point that 'most churches go wrong in their colleges first'. The Free Presbyterian Church college is still run by men who were raised under Ian Paisley's ministry. Until control passes out of their hands there is no reason to expect any change in the doctrine which they teach to their students or in the rigour with which they assess the suitability of candidates for graduation.

Let us follow the career of a graduate to the next stage: his actual ministry. The position of the Free Presbyterian Church in the religious 'market-place' gives its ministers good reason to stay on the 'old paths in perilous times'. Although the Free Church is presbyterian in its organizational structure, in one important respect it resembles a 'congregational' or 'independent' movement. In terms of income, it is every minister for himself. Each one depends for a living on his ability to attract and sustain a committed membership. There is no long history of church investment to allow the present generation of clergy to benefit from the loyal support given to previous generations. As the Church has not been in existence long enough for families to support it because 'they have always been' Free Presbyterians, each minister is under constant pressure to earn the support of his congregation and, if possible, to expand it. If he ceases to 'do the Lord's work' he will be deserted. The Free Church has a particular public image and a distinctive 'witness'. Presumably its members support it because they believe in the rectitude of that stand. What then would be the consequence of moderation? Almost certainly it would result in a loss of members. To reduce its sectarian image, would be to reduce what is distinctive about it and to make it a small and weak competitor in a market already well served by the major Protestant denominations. As in any crowded market, the Free Church survives by offering a distinct product which is not already being offered by the 'majors'. Even if the ministers of the Free Church acquired a sudden desire to become middle-of-the-road Protestants, they would find that they were competing with others who possessed better credentials and a longer history of serving that market.

Far from showing signs of moderation, the careers of younger Free Presbyterian ministers almost suggest that they have read the sociological literature on the sect to denomination transformation and are determined to make sure that it does not happen in their ministry. The example of Wesley McDowell in Limavady is a case in point.

David Armstrong is an evangelical who was much influenced in his teenage years by the preaching of Ian Paisley. He felt called to the Presbyterian ministry and gradually shifted from a fundamentalist variety of evangelicalism to a more liberal variety which had 'charismatic elements'. In particular, he was strongly influenced by David Watson, an Anglican priest who argued that an evangelical gospel did not require anti-Catholicism, and that it was possible to have fruitful 'fellowship' with charismatic Catholics. While he was assistant minister in Carrickfergus, Armstrong invited David Watson and his team to conduct a week of meetings and they were picketed by local Free Presbyterians.[21]

[21] David Armstrong's account is given in Armstrong and Saudners, op. cit. Free Presbyterians disagree with Armstrong's charismatic Protestantism on two grounds. In the first place, the charismatic movement seeks to transcend classic denominational divisions (such as those of Protestant and Catholic) which Free Presbyterians hold to mirror crucial theological differences. Secondly, Free Presbyterians do not accept the theology of 'charismata' held by the present charismatic movement. Where charismatics see the Holy Spirit as an alternative source of authority which complements the Bible, Free Presbyterians see it as an ingredient which enables one to correctly interpret the Scriptures. Thus any leading of the Spirit which does not fit in the traditional reformed Protestant interpretations of the gospel is false leading. It should be noted that Armstrong and Saunders contains (p. 80) an almost entirely inaccurate account of the origins of the Free Presbyterian Church.

Armstrong was called to Limavady, a strongly Protestant area in the middle of the predominantly Catholic county of Londonderry. His church, Second Presbyterian, was close to the Free Presbyterian Church pastored by Wesley McDowell, who had known Armstrong well in Belfast; in fact, they had taken caravanning holidays together. However, while McDowell had become a convinced conservative, Armstrong had shifted sufficiently far for McDowell to refuse an invitation to his ordination. McDowell replied to Armstrong's elders explaining why he could not attend the service, and sent a copy of his letter to the local papers where it was published. He also announced that he would be preaching against Armstrong.

What made the disagreement into a *cause célèbre* was the combination of strong Orange anti-Catholicism in the area and the presence, across the road from Armstrong's church, of the Catholic chapel. Armstrong's problems began when he accepted an invitation from the priest to attend the opening of the new chapel (the building of which had been slowed down by it being bombed at an early stage in its construction). Against the expressed wishes of some members of his congregation, he attended and thus initiated a conflict which grew in intensity when the new priest, Kevin Mullan, made the novel gesture of crossing the road on Christmas Day 1983 to wish the Presbyterians a Merry Christmas. Seeing this as precisely the sort of civilized gesture and antidote to sectarian tension which Christians should promote, Armstrong reciprocated. His elders took their objections to the Route Presbytery. Armstrong expected to be supported by his fellow ministers and was greatly disappointed by the Presbytery's failure openly to endorse his stance. In the spring of 1985, he felt he had no alternative but to leave the Presbyterian Church. Although a Presbyterian congregation in Bangor made it known that they would have him, Armstrong had already concluded from the hostile reception to his acts of reconciliation, that there was no place for his version of Christianity in Ulster and he went to Oxford to train for the Anglican ministry.

Overall, Wesley McDowell played only a small part in the Limavady incident. He had precipitated it, and the picket of Armstrong's church by Free Presbyterians at Christmas 1984 attracted considerable publicity, but Armstrong was actually rejected by conservatives within his own congregation. Disaffected Irish

Presbyterians went to other Presbyterian churches rather than to the Free Church. However, McDowell's own reflections on the incident are interesting for the light they throw on the views of younger Free Presbyterian ministers. I asked McDowell if he did not feel sad that he should end up in the position of public confrontation with someone who had once been a friend.

No. I relished the opportunity to protest against him, you know, because the original Free Presbyterians, they had to take a lot of stick. It meant sacrifice. I relished the opportunity because as a relatively young chap . . . I missed all that and I wanted to make my stand. Not that I did it for any ulterior motive. My motive in the whole thing was the Lord's honour and I think the Lord worked the whole thing out because in the end the man was removed.

Here is a second generation Free Presbyterian making the same sort of public protest which made the first generation so unpopular, and recognizing the part that his protests played in allowing him to share in some way in the unpopularity of the founders.

To pick up the theme of education, it was suggested above that the increasing proportion of ministers who had experienced secular higher education might be an indicator of future moderation. In fact, as was pointed out earlier, one minister who has a degree and a teaching qualification has used his skills to *increase* the sectarian rejection of the world by establishing an evangelical Christian school. Worldly credentials and skills, far from causing the person who possesses them to stray from the straight and narrow, have permitted him to socialize the next generation in the old paths more effectively.

'Blessed are Ye when Men shall Revile You'

It is important not to view the Free Church in isolation from its environment. Some sect-to-denomination discussions suggest that the evolution of sects can be explained entirely as a result of their internal processes. This misses the point that the 'high tension' which exists between a sect and its environment is not sustained solely by the sect. The sect creates the initial tension by rejecting the world but the world often reciprocates and acts against the sect in such a way as to amplify the divisions. In its early days, the Free Church was much despised. Its members were reviled. The qualifications, honesty, integrity, and competence of its ministers were frequently called into question in the media. Planning permission for buildings was refused. Minor but none the less annoying harassment was common. To give an example, the first meeting of the Moneyslane church was almost sabotaged by opponents spreading the rumour that it had been cancelled. Such problems simply reinforced the Free Church's self-image as a righteous and persecuted minority. As Paisley put it:

If you are going to be Godly men in a Godless age, you will be persecuted. When this Church *ceases* to be hated, and when this Church *ceases* to be reviled, and when this preacher *ceases* to be [tape inaudible] in this country, he's finished. He can pack it up and go home for ever. But as long as men hate us and as long as men revile us and as long as the newspaper editorials write against us, praise God, we'll be doing something.[22]

If tension between the sect and the environment is a product of interaction, rather than simply the actions of the sect, then an improvement in relationships between the sect and the surrounding society would be both a sign that it was moderating, and reason to expect further moderation. Are there signs that the Free Church is now accepted? There are some. To take the example of broadcasting, the religion department of BBC Northern Ireland now treats the Free Presbyterian Church as a legitimate minor denomination and broadcasts its Sunday morning services in rotation with those of other organizations (although it is noticeable that it is those congregations with 'reasonable' ministers which are invited to broadcast). This degree of acceptance by an important medium has a slightly moderating influence in that Free Presbyterian ministers know that their allocation will be withdrawn if they infringe the norms of 'good taste' and openly attack other denominations during a live transmission. In practice, few ministers would have trouble with this restriction as they are capable of delivering 'sound gospel messages' without criticizing the 'great apostasy' and, provided they know it is temporary, this constraint is not onerous.

Another minor element of the tension between Free Presbyterianism and the surrounding culture has gradually disappeared. Since the DUP became a major force in a number of local

[22] Ian R. K. Paisley, *This Is My Life* (cassette tape series) (Belfast: Martyrs Memorial Publications, 1980), Tape 3, Side 1.

district councils and Ian Paisley established himself as the single most popular unionist leader in Ulster, there have been fewer problems with local authorities being obstructive about planning permission for Free Presbyterian churches. Reading back through newspaper reports, one can also sense a gradual diminution in the degree of hostility shown to Free Presbyterian ministers and congregations. However, as the hostile media and public reactions to actions such as those of Wesley McDowell in Limavady show, the acceptance of Free Presbyterianism is conditional on it eschewing public protests.

In his discussion of sect–denomination transformations, Wilson makes the important point that not all sects are the same. There are considerable differences in belief systems and hence in views of the world and their place in it. It is thus sensible to suppose that the likelihood of a sect gradually accommodating and becoming more denominational will be largely determined by its beliefs. Here one comes to the heart of the matter. While all of the above points about the compact nature of the organization and hence the more efficient social control, the use of membership tests, the concentration on socializing new members into the values of the sect, and relations with the wider society are important, what really makes it unlikely that the Free Presbyterian Church will abandon its sectarian elements is the persistence of the social and cultural forces which gave rise to it.

The Meaning of Free Presbyterianism

Many of the things which could be said now will be presented in detail in the remaining chapters. For this reason, what is said here must remain suggestive rather than complete. Although it vehemently asserts its independence of politics, the Free Presbyterian Church represents a kind of Protestantism which remains popular in Ulster because it harmonizes with the experiences of many Ulster Protestants. The religious world-view 'explains' the precarious position of Protestants in Ireland. It makes sense of the world for its adherents. A major change in that world-view would only be likely if the world itself changed, and changed in the direction of becoming more welcoming, more appealing and less threatening. There is no sign of this happening. All the changes in the moral and religious climate since 1951 have been in a direction which makes the need for the distinctive witness of Free Presbyterianism all the more pressing. If there were good reasons to reject 'worldliness' in 1951, they are even better now. Although the major Prostestant denominations have not amplified their 'Romeward trend', they have not rejected ecumenism and 'reconciliation'. There has been no let-up in the slow, but none the less real, process of dismantling the Northern Ireland state: the political entity that many Protestants feel is a vital safeguard of their religious freedom. There has also been no let-up in the republican campaign. The considerable reduction in the number of people killed and injured in terrorist actions has done little to change perceptions of threat.

On Sunday 20 November 1983, gunmen entered a Pentecostal meeting-hall near Darkley, on the border in County Armagh, and raked the congregation with machine-gun fire. Three of the elders, who were greeting newcomers in the foyer, died. Seven others were wounded. They had been warming up with a few gospel choruses. One of the songs was 'Have you been to Jesus for the cleansing power? Are you washed in the blood of the Lamb?'[23] In his sermon the following week, Paisley presented the attack as further evidence of the work of the 'Antichrist' in the 'end-times'. The Darkley massacre was Bible prophecy fulfilled.

The last sixteen years in Northern Ireland have seen a string of atrocities but even against that background Darkley stands out. By no stretch of tortured logic could the Pentecostal congregation be described as a 'legitimate target'. Three people were killed simply because they were Protestants and they were killed in church.

Put simply, nothing has happened since 1951, and even less since 1969, to make the Free Presbyterian view of the world any the less plausible.

To summarize, a knowledge of the history of previous conservative Protestant sectarian movements gives us reason to suppose that there are strong pressures for sects to gradually moderate, accommodate to the world, and become 'denominational'. However, when we understand how the ideas of Free Presbyterianism

---

[23] Peter Jennings, *An End to Terrorism* (Tring, Herts.: Lion Publishing, 1984), pp. 17–19.

and the circumstances of many Ulster Protestants reinforce each other, we should appreciate why such a transformation in the Free Church is unlikely.

7

Tradition and Charisma

Types of Leadership

The notion of charisma is often invoked to explain Ian Paisley's popularity. Clifford Smyth, for example, talks of 'the charismatic leadership qualities of the Rev. Ian Paisley'.[1] Unfortunately the term is generally used so loosely as to mean little more than that Paisley is a good orator or that he has considerable personal charm. Both of these things are undoubtedly true but, as will be demonstrated, they are secondary considerations. Furthermore, charisma has been claimed for such an array of leaders as to make worthwhile comparison almost impossible. What, after all, do Hitler, Richard Nixon, Ian Paisley, the present Pope, Sun Myung Moon, and Moses David (the leader of the Children of God) have in common?[2] In this chapter I want to clarify various types of authority and leadership in order to show that while Paisley is marginally charismatic, his main source of authority lies in a tradition.

Most social science discussions of authority begin with Max Weber's definitions of three types: charismatic, traditional, and rational–legal.[3] Although the third type is the most common in modern industrial societies, it is least important for understanding Paisley and can be defined briefly as authority based on claims to efficiency, increased procedural rationality and rule-following. It is the sort of authority which is invoked when someone says, 'I

[1] Clifford Smyth, 'The Ulster Democratic Unionist Party: a case study in religious and political convergence', Ph.D. thesis (The Queen's University of Belfast, 1984), p. 274.

[2] The curious claim that Richard Nixon and Spiro Agnew were charismatic leaders was made in Michael A. Toth, 'Toward a theory of the routinization of charisma', *Rocky Mountain Social Science Journal*, 9 (1972), pp. 93–8; and *The Theory of the Two Charismas* (Washington, DC: University Press of America, 1981).

[3] Max Weber, *The Theory of Social and Economic Organization* (London: Collier-Macmillan, 1964), Part III.

know our fathers and grandfathers used to build boats in that manner but my new method is more efficient', or when a bureaucrat justifies a decision by claiming that it results from following the appropriate rules for such cases. Although rational–legal authority is almost ubiquitous in the modern worlds of bureaucracy and industrial production, it is not characteristic of the early years of social, political and religious movements. When it does appear in such formations, it normally does so as part of a process of change which was touched on earlier in the consideration of whether or not the Free Presbyterian Church and the DUP were showing signs of moderation and accommodation to the prevailing culture.

The core of the distinction between charisma and tradition is intuitively obvious enough. The traditional leader justifies his decisions by locating them within the time-honoured traditions of the culture: 'We build boats this way because that is how we have always built boats.' In contrast, the charismatic leader rejects the tradition and claims some new revelation. His platform is justified solely by his claim to divine or supernatural gifts: 'I know we used to build boats that way but the gods have told me that we should use wood instead of wattle.' The archetypal charismatic leader is the Christ of the New Testament who says 'Ye have heard that it was said by them of old time. . . . But I say unto you . . .'. He feels free to challenge the tradition, and does so solely on the basis of his claim to be the Son of God.

The confusions in the identification and understanding of charisma stem from Weber's own lack of consistency in the way in which he defined and illustrated traditional and charismatic styles of leadership but a certain clarity can be achieved if we follow Wallis in distinguishing two elements of leadership: the role being played or the position being held by the leader, and the message which he offers. A leader may occupy some position which is sanctified by the tradition—for example, pope, priest or prophet— and still offer either a traditional or innovative platform to his followers. The point can most easily be made with Wallis's typology[4] and some examples.

---

[4] Roy Wallis and Steve Bruce, *Sociological Theory, Religion and Collective Action* (Belfast: The Queen's University of Belfast, 1986), Ch. 4. This chapter draws heavily on Wallis's work on charisma, and especially on the above source, which contains a more detailed technical discussion of the issues dealt with in the first half of this chapter.

Sanctified by Tradition?

	Role	Platform
1	Yes	Yes
2	Yes	No
3	No	Yes
4	No	No

The first type of leader is the archetypal traditional leader who both holds an office which is sanctified by tradition and promotes that tradition. Most popes would serve as examples. The second type is the unexpected case of someone who uses a traditional office to innovate. A good recent example is King Juan Carlos of Spain who has used the authority of his office as king to prevent right-wing monarchist forces overthrowing Spain's fledgeling democracy. Trained by Franco to maintain the regime which Franco bequeathed to him, Juan Carlos has used a traditional office to promote a major political innovation.

The fourth type of leader—an outsider who innovates—exemplifies charismatic leadership. He is not supported because he occupies any traditional sanctified office or role and he does not present his ideology as the exemplification or continuation of any tradition. Moses David, the founder and leader of the Children of God, a small but none the less interesting new religious movement, is such a leader.

Ian Paisley fits best into the third type. The son of an independent Baptist, trained by the Reformed Presbyterians, Paisley came from the margins of Protestantism in Ulster to proclaim that the main denominations had lost their way and to offer a purified traditional alternative. Similarly in politics, his career has been that of an outsider who proclaimed the untrustworthiness of the supposed guardians of unionism and offered a vehicle for a return to genuine 'Protestant Unionism'.

The nature of Paisley's leadership can best be established if we consider for a moment the reasons why he has been, to my mind inaccurately, described as a charismatic leader. Smyth and Taylor both rightly note that Paisley's followers see him as a 'man of God'. A man who has been a member of the Rasharkin congregation since its foundation, and who was active in Paisley's first Bannside election campaign, said: 'I believe that he has the call of God and God has raised him up for such a time as this'. Given that the 'call' was not mediated through some well-established and conventional procedure such as being accepted for the ministry of a major denomination, there seems some reason for taking Free Presbyterians' belief that he is divinely inspired as evidence of charisma. But to do so misses an important point. How does Bob Wilson know that Paisley is a man of God? Would he persist in such a belief if Paisley announced that God had given him the new revelation that all true Christians should join the ecumenical movement? I think not. Wilson's acceptance of Paisley as a man of God seems to be based on Paisley enunciating doctrines which are sanctified by the traditions in which Wilson was raised. Wilson and others know Paisley to be a man of God because Knox, Calvin, Luther, and Spurgeon were men of God and Paisley says the same things as these people.

The idea that Paisley is charismatic would be more plausible if we could demonstrate that he says things which these previous Protestant leaders did not say: that is, if his platform were innovative. Smyth has suggested a number of ways in which Paisley departs from the Ulster Protestant tradition and I have previously identified some innovations.

According to Smyth, Paisley has made an original contribution to Ulster Protestantism (*a*) by using the American pattern of following evangelistic services with 'altar calls' in which those who feel themselves to be having a conversion experience are encouraged to declare themselves; (*b*) by stressing the need for 'separation from apostasy'; and (*c*) by fusing the politics of Orangeism with the religion of fundamentalism.[5]

Taking the question of the altar call first, it is certainly the case that the main representatives of traditional Presbyterianism would have been unhappy with the techniques of those American fundamentalists who end their meetings with repeated and emotional appeals for members of the audience to declare their desire for salvation by making themselves known. In the first place, they would have objected that repeated appeals to sinners to be 'born again' encourage people to produce their own conversion experience and thus undermine the work of the Holy Spirit. At times

[5] Smyth, op. cit., pp. 234–47.

Calvinists have laid such stress on predestination and the work of the Holy Spirit as to be unhappy about people claiming a conversion experience. In accounts of religious revivals in eighteenth-century Scotland, for example, one finds the quaint habit of referring to all professions as 'claimed' conversions. Secondly, critics have argued that altar calls create an unhealthily emotional atmosphere in which weak-minded people feel forced by social pressure to claim an experience which they have not had. Thirdly, and to place the dispute in its proper theological context, 'high' Calvinists have objected to the practice because to ask people to 'decide for Christ', as Billy Graham does, is to imply that people are saved by their own efforts rather than by the freely given and entirely undeserved grace of God. For these reasons, many conservative Protestants prefer simply to preach the gospel, making God's offer of salvation clear and then leaving it to the Holy Spirit to work on individuals in the audience, unaided by social and psychological pressures.

Paisley's evangelistic preaching style is closer to that of the American fundamentalists than to that of the Scots Calvinists of the last century. He closes his meetings with an 'invitation' to those who wish to be saved to make themselves known by raising their hands and by staying behind for prayer and counselling. However, this is not, as Smyth suggests, the classic American 'holy roller' method, with its ten minutes of repeated, almost hysterical appeals for sinners to come forward. Nor is it universally practised in the Free Church.[6] Some ministers offer very muted 'invitations'— often doing no more than announcing that they will be available for anyone who wishes further help—at the close of their meetings. There is actually nothing in the organization of Paisley's meetings which is essentially anti-Calvinist. It is quite possible for someone who believes that our salvational fate has already been determined by God to see the 'invitation' as a useful way of identifying which members of an audience are coming under 'conviction of sin', and

[6] It is worth spelling out the relevance of this point. The question of the degree of innovation and the appeal of 'Paisleyism' cannot be dealt with simply by examining what Paisley himself does and believes. The vast majority of Free Presbyterians belong to congregations other than that pastored by Paisley. Hence, what 'Paisley as leader' stands for, and what people follow, is often 'Free Presbyterianism' rather than 'Paisleyism'. Or, to be more precise, what people know of 'Paisleyism' is what is filtered to them through ministers other than, and in addition to, Paisley himself.

to see their public declarations as 'signs' of grace rather than as 'causes' of conversion. Furthermore, it is wrong to suppose that Paisley's evangelistic style is something which was alien to Scotland and Ulster until Paisley borrowed it from the Jones family and his other American contacts. Although many Scots were initially opposed to the methods of those American evangelists such as Finney and Moody who visited Britain in the nineteenth century, many of them became convinced of the value of the 'new methods'. Irish Protestants gave Moody a very warm welcome when he preached in Belfast and Dublin in 1874. Nicholson, who had preached in America, was a major influence in the Ulster of the 1920s, and by the time Paisley began his career the evangelistic methods he adopted were commonplace, even among the most conservative Presbyterians.

'Separatism', the belief that one should be both sound in doctrine and free of all association with those who are not sound, does appear to be something which Paisley has introduced to Ulster Protestantism. Free Presbyterians believe that one must both denounce apostasy and ensure that one's own orthodoxy is not called into doubt by one's associations. Separation is, for them, almost 'double separation' in that they must distance themselves not only from error, but also from other organizations which, although themselves orthodox, maintain cordial relationships with unsound denominations. It is undoubtedly the case that the doctrine of separation was first given its clearest development and its most aggressive promotion in the context of disputes in America in the 1920s between 'liberals' and 'fundamentalists'; hence the notion that Paisley was 'importing' separatism to Ulster when he began to advocate it in 1951. Although Paisley has been the most vocal spokesman for separation, this does not represent a major innovation of the sort that we would look for as evidence of charismatic leadership. In the first place, Paisley's father had already followed the example of the great nineteenth-century Baptist preacher, Charles Hadden Spurgeon, by taking a separatist stand in Ballymena. The elders of the Ravenhill Evangelical Mission Church who invited Paisley to become their pastor had also separated from a major denomination. Paisley was not the first separatist in Ulster. In the second place, the appearance of separatism in Ulster was as much a product of indigenous tensions as it was an imitation of an American movement.

The history of Protestantism is littered with the debris of frequent schism. Some group or another has always been arguing that the dominant organization has become corrupt beyond redemption and that the only recourse is the creation of a new purified church. Perhaps the term 'separation' is new: the phenomenon it describes is not. That it became an identifying slogan for a variety of conservative Protestantism in America before it became popular in Ulster is simply explained by the conservative nature of the major Ulster denominations. The Irish Presbyterian Church was not in the vanguard of modernism or ecumenism. Hence the objective circumstances which gave rise to 'fundamentalism' were created later in Ulster than in America. Critics of Paisley are keen to dispute his often claimed identification with Henry Cooke, the leader of the conservatives in the Presbyterian Church in the first half of the nineteenth century.[7] They point out that, although Cooke was conservative, he was never an advocate of separation. This misses the obvious point that he did not *have* to advocate separation because he succeeded in driving the liberals out of his church. He won. Instead of separating himself and his followers from the mainstream, he expelled his opponents.[8] Paisley is only a separatist because he is in a minority. If the beliefs that he represents had remained dominant in the Irish Presbyterian Church, Professor Davey and other 'heretics' would have suffered the same fate as Henry Montgomery and the 'non-subscribers' (so called because they refused to accept Cooke's proposal that subscription to the Westminster Confession of Faith be introduced as a test of ministers' orthodoxy). They would have been expelled. Paisley does not promote separation for its own sake. He does so because he sees it as the only way of protecting and promoting his beliefs while they remain the ideology of a minority. To the very slight extent that separation is an innovation, it is promoted for the purpose of preserving traditional beliefs.

I have a similar view of Smyth's idea that Paisley's wedding of Orangeism to fundamentalism is novel. This only seems novel because what was taken for granted in the last half of the nineteenth century has since become unpopular. Paisley is trying to re-create the close intertwining of conservative unionism and evangelical religion that was displayed by Henry Cooke, who not only moved

[7] P. Marrinan, *Paisley: man of wrath* (Tralee: Anvil Books, 1973), pp. 17–18.
[8] R. F. G. Holmes, *Henry Cooke* (Belfast: Christian Journals Ltd, 1981).

the Church to the right but also encouraged Irish Presbyterians to become involved in the Orange Order, by Canon Thomas Drew, and by 'Roaring' Hugh Hanna. Clearly, if one compares Paisley to secular unionist politicians, then there is something unusual about his combining strongly held and genuinely believed conservative religious beliefs with unionism, but if one compares him to other clerics who were also politically influential, then he ceases to stand out as an innovator.

In an earlier book about conservative Protestantism, I suggested that the pre-millennialism of the Free Church was an important American-influenced innovation.[9] This is a mistake. It is true that the dominant tradition in Scots and Ulster Presbyterianism was post-millennial. Many Calvinists believed in what Iain Murray has called 'the puritan hope': the notion that widespread religious revival would bring in the thousand years of righteousness on the earth which would be enjoyed before, rather than after, the Day of Judgement. However, there were Calvinists who were pre-millennial. Among them one would place the small but interesting group of Reformed Presbyterians who sided with the United Irishmen and the 1798 rebellion in Ireland for the curious reason that they saw the French Revolution as the start of the 'end-times' and wished to hasten the Day of Judgement by promoting anarchy. I had also overlooked Horatio Bonar and Robert Murray Mc-Cheyne, leading nineteenth-century Scots Calvinists who were convinced pre-millennialists. There was always a pre-millennial strain in Calvinist thinking, and the demise of the more optimistic post-millennial view long pre-dated Ian Paisley's Free Presbyterian Church.

Furthermore, the idea that Free Presbyterian eschatology has been borrowed from American fundamentalism rests on the assumption that they are similar. They are as similar as liberalism and socialism. Neither of these political philosophies is fascist but that does not make them the same. To be technical about it, any American fundamentalists are 'pre-tribulation rapturists'.[10] The

---

[9] S. Bruce, *Firm in the Faith: the survival of conservative Protestantism* (Aldershot: Gower, 1984).

[10] A good introductory guide to the various views of the second coming is W. J. Grier, *The Momentous Event: a discussion of Scripture teaching on the second advent* (Edinburgh: Banner of Truth Trust, 1970). The strength of Free Church feeling against the 'pre-tribulation rapture' position is made clear in Alan Cairns's view that its proponents 'dismember the Scriptures in a disastrous fashion'. After ex-

'tribulation' is the period of extremely hard times which will be produced by the rise in power of Antichrist. The traditional view was always that all people, including 'saved' Christians, would have to live through this period before the second coming of Christ. In the late nineteenth century, the idea that the Christians would be lifted up—'raptured'—before the tribulation became popular and is now dominant in American fundamentalist circles. As an aside, it is the fact that he believes in the pre-tribulation rapture which worries people about the presidential aspirations of Pat Robertson, a leading American television preacher. If he and the other Christians are going to be saved the pain of living through the apocalypse, might he not be less hesitant than others about encouraging nuclear war?[11] To return to the main point, the claim that the Free Presbyterian views of the 'end-times' and the second coming were heavily influenced by American thinking can hardly be sustained. Paisley's eschatology has its own British roots and differs considerably from that of American fundamentalism.

By far the most obvious example of doctrinal innovation in the Free Church is its indifference to arguments about the nature of baptism. Some Christians believe that children should be baptized as a sign that they have some special relationship with God (along the lines of the role of circumcision as a sign of the covenant between God and the Children of Israel). Others hold that baptism should be restricted to people who are old and mature enough to be aware of their having experienced a religious conversion. This argument has frequently divided Protestants. As their name suggests, the Baptists owe their identity to the issue. Given the heat previously generated by baptism, it is remarkable that the Free Church has to date avoided any major disputes. It permits both infant and 'believer's baptism'; a compromise which has allowed the Church to recruit disaffected Irish Presbyterians, who practise infant baptism, and disaffected 'adult dipper' Baptists.

Although we can see why the Church should have wanted to remain agnostic about the issue, this does not explain how it has managed to avoid problems. One thing that helps is having

amining the Scripture texts that are offered in support of the idea of a secret pre-tribulation rapture, Cairns concludes: 'there is no real textual proof at all, for if the strongest "proofs" are devoid of proof, what shall we say of the rest?' (A. Cairns, *Dictionary of Theological Terms* (Gilford, Co. Down: Whitefield College of the Bible, 1982), pp. 39 and 119.

[11] Simon Hoggart, 'Born-again Bush Woos God Squad', *Observer* (26 Jan. 1986).

baptisman services, infant and adult, kept separate from the normal Sunday services and clearly announced so that only those who will not be offended by the particular form need attend. But a more important factor is suggested by the large number of Free Presbyterian ministers who have never been asked to baptize either adults or infants. It is not so much that the Church has both forms, as that it has very little of either. Parents who want some sort of religious office to greet new additions to their family can request the 'child dedication' service, which has largely replaced infant baptism. And the Church places such stress on the conversion experience that many of those people who are 'born again' feel no great need for symbolic celebration of their entry into the band of saints. That these alternatives have proved generally acceptable suggests that people have lost interest in the theology of baptism, which is what one would expect from a form of Christianity which lays singular stress on correct belief and has little interest in symbols and liturgical forms. Having said that, one is still driven back to the bitter disputes between old Ulster Baptists and Presbyterians and the question of why interest in such matters has so markedly waned. The answer lies in changes in the wider environment. One has to recall that the Baptist schisms took place in an era when almost everybody took it for granted that there was a God, that the Bible was his word, that miracles did actually happen, and so on. When almost everyone accepts the basic Christian doctrines, protagonists of particular views on subsidiary questions are free to ride their 'hobby horses' without fear that, by so doing, they are undermining the fundamentals of the faith. Free Presbyterianism grew up in an environment in which increasing numbers of people were challenging the fundamentals. As fewer and fewer people take for granted the basic elements of Christianity, it becomes more and more important to sink differences and unite around what are seen as the core doctrines of the faith. Again, what at first sight appears to be an innovation, when placed in the context of changes taking place outside Free Presbyterianism, looks more like a tactical withdrawal. The innovations, slight as they are, are designed to preserve the tradition. On the few occasions on which Free Presbyterians have shifted ground, it has not been because they want to cede territory to the forces of change, but because they have been pushed to narrower and higher and, for that reason, more readily defensible, ground.

To summarize, I am not convinced that there is any great evidence of innovation in either Paisley's religion or, as the previous chapters should have made clear, his politics. To return to the typology of leadership presented on page 201, although Paisley lacked any traditionally sanctified role or office, he built his political and religious movements on highly traditional platforms.

The Independence of Charisma

Wallis has suggested as an acid test for charismatic leadership, the degree to which any particular leader is free from traditional or ideological constraints. The example of Moses David, the founder of the Children of God, should make the point. On a number of occasions David has radically changed direction. At one time his followers were instructed to live communally. Then they were instructed to return to the conventional world and live in nuclear families. At one time they were supposed to pursue asceticism; at another the women followers were instructed to offer sexual favours to strangers, initially as practical demonstration of God's love and later as a means of fund-raising. People were promoted to leadership positions and then abruptly cast aside. Every major change of direction was a test of the loyalty of the followers and allowed David to distinguish between those who followed him and those who followed a particular set of beliefs which were independent of his person.[12]

Moses David passes Wallis's charisma test, which is that:

Charismatic authority . . . can only be accorded to leaders who are not only seen to possess charismatic endowments, but whose legitimacy to command, rebuke, praise or prescribe for others, arising from these endowments, is relatively unconstrained by instrumental, ideological, rational–legal or traditional considerations.[13]

Paisley does not pass this test. He is entirely constrained by ideological and traditional considerations. Or so we might suppose. The problem, of course, is that we can never really be sure until he seriously tests the loyalty of his followers by promoting a major deviation from the traditional line and we then see whether or not

[12] Roy Wallis, 'Charisma, Commitment and Control in a New Religious Movement', Ch. 3 in R. Wallis (ed.), *Millennialism and Charisma* (Belfast: The Queen's University of Belfast, 1982).

[13] Wallis and Bruce, op. cit., p. 107.

he is followed. Although a conclusive judgement cannot be made, reasonable inference is possible. The Free Presbyterian Church is so identifiably traditional that only those who wish a return to the evangelicalism of the last century (moderated by some minor innovations such as freedom over the baptism issue and a more lively style of hymn singing) would join it. One simply cannot imagine the majority of Free Presbyterians remaining loyal to the Church if some major change of direction—such as a desire to join the ecumenical movement—were announced by Paisley.

In the political realm we have two events which strongly suggest that support for Paisley and the DUP is conditional on both remaining conventionally unionist.

The first was something of a media creation, but it none the less makes the point. In 1971 Paisley was quoted as having told an RTE interviewer that the principal objection to a united Ireland was the Republic's theocratic constitution and that if it were changed 'you would have an entirely different set of circumstances'.[14] This and other moderate remarks were welcomed by republicans and made much of by Brian Faulkner, the beleaguered Prime Minister, who seized upon the rare opportunity to present himself as more unionist than Paisley. According to Smyth, Paisley's followers met the reported statements with 'incredulity'.[15] Paisley immediately denied that he had in any way moderated his position. The text of the interview makes it clear that his words had been taken out of context. He followed his 'bombshell' about 'an entirely different set of circumstances' by adding, 'But, let's be realists. The constitution is not scrapped. We have heard a lot of talk about minor clauses which to me are only fruits and not the root, and it would have to be the doing away with the root.' And he went on to make it clear that the root was the general influence of the Catholic Church, rather than any specific constitutional provisions, which offended Protestants.

However, it is not what Paisley intended, but the response of his followers, which is of interest. Although the incident was used by his political opponents to promote the old chestnut that he was really only interested in personal power and was prepared to

---

[14] RTE News, *This Week* (28 Nov. 1971). The reaction to Paisley's comments is described in David Boulton, *The UVF, 1966–73* (Dublin: Torc Books, 1973), pp. 147–9.

[15] Smyth, op. cit., p. 46.

compromise with the Republic in return for lucrative office, the response was genuine enough. It was made clear in that minor episode that Paisley was followed only so long as he continued to represent conservative unionism. Any signs of departure from that narrow ground called his leadership into question. This hardly seems the stuff of charisma.

The second minor deviation concerned William Beattie. In 1975 Beattie led the DUP delegation to the talks with Vanguard and the SDLP over the future of devolved government. It was here that Craig made his politically fatal suggestions about 'voluntary co-alition' with the constitutional nationalists. Although Beattie has always insisted that he did not support the proposals, there were many in the DUP who felt that he had not been sufficiently outspoken in his denunciation of them. In February 1976, he was replaced as party chairman by William McCrea and observers concluded that his (as it turned out, temporary) fall from grace was punishment for not asserting the traditional unionist position more clearly.[16] This reaction to Beattie's supposed straying from the straight and narrow confirms the impression made by the reaction to Paisley's 'constitution' interview. Only so long as they remained within the tradition would Paisley and his lieutenants be supported.

A Sense of History

The above presentation was designed to put the argument that Paisley is a charismatic leader at its most convincing. In fact, the grounds for seeing Paisley's authority as deriving from a tradition are even stronger than has so far been suggested. In the first place, the role which Paisley has played is neither unknown nor of low status in the Protestant tradition. Although the leaders of the Irish Presbyterian Church ridiculed his credentials, Paisley could, and did, point to similarities between his beliefs and actions and those of great Protestant leaders. Although he had never been expelled from a major denomination, he could still present his own position *vis-à-vis* Irish Presbyterianism as being similar to that of Wesley and Anglicanism, or Spurgeon and the British Baptists. When he wanted a biblical model, Paisley could compare himself with the

[16] D. McKittrick, 'Beattie Ousted as DUP Chairman', *Irish Times* (10 Feb. 1976), p. 7.

Israelite prophets calling the people back to the ways of righteousness.

Paisley has also been able to legitimate his political activities by invoking previous unionist leaders. Shortly before his second imprisonment for blocking civil rights marchers in Armagh in 1969, Paisley defended his policy of defying bans on marches by pointing to someone who had done it before:

You will remember that great figure Johnston of Ballykilbeg. We would need another Johnston alive tonight, wouldn't we? The Orangemen carry him on their banner. The government talks about him at the Twelfth of July because it suits their purpose and policy. What did he do? They said 'You will not march' and he marched! And they put him into prison and when he came out the people put him into parliament and he became a great Ulster leader. I want to say, friends, we are prepared to march too. And if they put us into prison, we will just have to go to prison.[17]

In retrospect, his words could hardly have been more prophetic. He marched and was put into prison, and, like Johnston, was elected to Parliament and became a great Ulster leader; a consequence which suggests that many unionists came to accept Paisley's own view of himself as an heir to Johnston.

Paisley has consistently shown a good appreciation of the value of traditional symbols. When the *Clyde Valley*, the old UVF gunrunning ship, was brought back to Northern Ireland, Paisley was at the welcoming rally in Larne Harbour. The O'Neill government was not represented.[18] When the December 1980 meeting of British and Irish Prime Ministers provoked unionist fears of the sort of settlement which was achieved five years later, Paisley organized a series of protest meetings.

These rallies, to be addressed by the three Democratic Unionist MPs, will commence in Omagh on Friday night and will continue across the Province until Saturday 18th March when they will culminate in a massive demonstration at Carson's Monument at Stormont. Eleven rallying points have been chosen to coincide with the fact that in advance of Covenant Day in 1912 Lord Carson held eleven consecutive rallies across the Province.[19]

[17] Ian R. K. Paisley, *This Is My Life* (Belfast: Martyrs Memorial Publications, 1980).

[18] The rusty *Clyde Valley* was brought back to Larne Harbour on 23 November 1968 to a reception organized by Paisley's Ulster Protestant Volunteers but not enough money was raised to restore her, and she was broken up

[19] DUP press statement, 9 Feb. 1981, reprinted in S. Wilson, *The Carson Trail* (Belfast: Crown Publications, 1982), p. 29.

There can be no clearer example of Paisley's self-conscious appreciation of traditional symbolism than the 'Carson trail', as the campaign was called. Other unionist politicians would simply arrange a series of meetings. Only Ian Paisley would have the self-confidence, and the sensitivity to the resonances of history, to model his meetings on those held by Carson and hence, by implication, to present himself as the legitimate heir to Carson. When he addresses an audience with a rhetorical question such as 'We would need another Johnston tonight, wouldn't we?', he and they know that they have one: Ian Paisley.

To summarize, I am not suggesting that Paisley is *inadvertently* a traditional leader in that he just happens to believe in the values of nineteenth-century Ulster evangelicalism and Ulster unionism. He is quite self-consciously traditional in that he has modelled himself on previous Ulster Protestant leaders. He began his twin careers as an outsider, deprived of formal credentials by the dominant religious and political institutions. He has managed to move to the centre of the political stage by successfully promoting his claims to represent traditional unionism. At the same time, he has built a reputation as a traditional evangelical preacher. To describe him as 'charismatic' is either to use charismatic in a very loose way or to be mistaken. Paisley's ideology, actions, and 'presentation of self' are all profoundly traditional and hence, we can suppose, so is his appeal. Although he has never seriously tested the loyalty of his supporters by departing in any significant way from the traditions, we can guess, from the reactions to the occasions on which such departures have been suspected, that he would be deserted if he tried to move outside the traditions of Ulster unionism and evangelicalism.

The Parochial Style

Paisley not only says very traditional things; he says them in traditional ways. Where other politicians such as Terence O'Neill cultivated a modern cosmopolitan style of campaigning (for example, by televised address to the people), Paisley has always been more at home on the pavements and streets, marching at the head of 'kick the Pope' bands, or playing 'party tunes' through a loudspeaker tied to the top of a car. His use of old-fashioned means of opinion-formation was rather forced upon him by his lack of access to alternative methods for contacting potential supporters. At one point, the main evening newspaper, the *Belfast Telegraph*, refused to take his advertisements. But it also suits both his personality and his ideology. He is the common man, the man of the people, and he is perfectly at home knocking on doors and shaking hands with well-wishers. And both his religious and his political ideologies give him reason to prefer the views of ordinary people over those of the élites. Élites, even Protestant élites, have too often proved untrustworthy. In Protestant religious philosophy, it is the ordinary people who preserve the simple religious truths which élites pervert and complicate so as to enhance their own positions. Underlying Paisley's preference for the parochial over the cosmopolitan is the suspicion that those who stress good manners, dignity, and decorum do so at the expense of content and belief. Paisley has always been willing to break the social norms of civility in pursuit of what he sees as a higher calling.

For example, at the Oxford Union debate in November 1967, he took out a communion wafer and mocked the Roman Catholic view that the biscuit was actually the sinews, flesh, and blood of Christ. Catholics were revolted. Middle-class Protestants were offended. Polite and respectable culture insists that one should not mock the deeply held beliefs of others, even if privately one finds them laughable. Paisley sees this as a lack of real commitment to one's own religion. False beliefs do not deserve respect because they enslave. At least one person who is now active in the Free Church and the DUP was initially attracted by the televised debate.

The degree to which Paisley's apparently boorish behaviour is deliberate is clear from the following discussion between him and Peter France:

FRANCE. You seem also, do you not, to go out of your way to antagonize. I mean, remember the well-known debate in Oxford when you produced the wafer. Now that was intended, wasn't it, to be shocking.

PAISLEY. That was intended to bring people to the reality of the central truth that the Roman Catholic says the Mass, uh, you see, a lot of people said to me 'I never really knew that before, but when you held up that wafer, and you said "This is the God that they worship, and they bow down before it, and they're going to get so many days out of Purgatory for the worshipping of it as it's elevated, and it's a sacrifice for the living and the dead".' The fact that I had that wafer in my hand brought home the fact of it.

FRANCE. You didn't do that in order to be educational. It wasn't an educational gesture. It was a shocking gesture, wasn't it? Let's be honest about this . . .

PAISLEY. Oh, no, it was educational, but it was educational in a way in which the ordinary individual could grasp it.

FRANCE. But you were in the Oxford Union. They weren't ordinary individuals. They were educated human beings, surely. Weren't they?

PAISLEY. Oh, no. I wasn't talking to the Oxford Union. I had lost the debate before I started. I was talking to the televised audience. I was talking to the people beyond the Oxford Union. I was talking to the wider audience who were going to see that and understand something about Romanism that they never understood before. But let me say that the prophets were shocking. I mean, Elijah was shocking. So was Amos. So was the Lord Jesus Christ. I mean, the Lord Jesus Christ took the religious leaders of his day, and, in Matthew 23, he makes the most terrible judgement. He didn't say 'You are beautiful liars'. He said 'You're a generation of vipers'. He didn't say 'You're wonderful sepulchres'. He said 'You're old whited sepulchres'.[20]

Where other evangelicals have preferred to ignore apostasy or write polite letters of complaint, Paisley and his followers have been consistently willing to engage in the sort of public protest which many people find insulting and embarrassing. They have disrupted ecumenical services and been arrested for their pains. In 1970, twelve Free Presbyterian ministers were arrested for an anti-popery protest outside Buckingham Palace. William McCrea, one of the twelve, was back in court six months later for interrupting a Catholic mass in the Anglican Canterbury Cathedral. When the Pope visited Britain in 1982, Free Presbyterian ministers and student ministers led the protests. In fact, they were almost alone. Pastor Jack Glass of Glasgow and two or three other independent evangelical ministers were at the demonstrations, but, without the Free Church, the attendance would have been embarrassingly thin.[21]

[20] BBC Television, 'Paisley: child of wrath . . . man of God?', first shown on BBC 1, 25 Apr. 1985. The BBC, of course, has no responsibility for the interpretation which I place on the material which was used in the making of that film.

[21] Not only were the Free Presbyterians important in swelling the numbers. They also took the lead in mobilizing opinion in the year before the papal visit. Gordon Ferguson, later minister of Kilkeel Free Presbyterian Church, worked for a year as full-time secretary to the British Council of Protestant Churches, organizing anti-popery meetings around the country.

Tactics which others reject as loutish are seen as acceptable by Paisley, not because he has no sense of decorum or good manners, but because he regards these virtues as being of considerably less importance than the injunction to promote the gospel vigorously. Civility is important but it is secondary to the promotion of the true gospel and the doing of God's will. There would, of course, be no need for such protests if the major churches and the country as a whole had remained orthodox in their Protestantism. It is only because the culture has become secular, and the Roman Catholic Church is now treated as a 'permitted variant' of Christianity, that Free Presbyterians feel obliged to heckle ecumenical services or to parade outside with their placards. If the world were recreated in the image which Paisley desires, he would no longer need to use 'street corner boy' methods because the major guardians of Protestantism would not be inviting Catholic priests to celebrate mass in Protestant cathedrals.

In politics, Paisley's refusal to present his aims and aspirations in a measured and 'statesman-like' fashion has earned him the opprobrium of the educated middle classes, but it has won him a reputation for being a man who speaks his mind and does not mince words. As he put it himself at an Orange rally:

I have not come here to beat about the bush. I never do, and please God, I never shall. You will not require a dictionary to understand what I am speaking about before I finish. The time has come for straight-dealing and straight-preaching. This is no time for a velvet tongue.[22]

And, of course, the precarious position of Ulster Protestants has meant that, for the committed loyalist, no time is the right time for a velvet tongue. Similarly, Paisley sees the whole of his religious career as a time in which the fundamentals of the faith were being bargained away by 'velvet tongues' who did not have the courage to come right out and admit that they no longer believed most of the Westminster Confession. Instead, by careful choice of words to describe their beliefs, they disguised from their congregations the extent to which they had abandoned traditional dogmas. In such circumstances, Paisley felt a duty to expose the heresy and apostasy of his day.

[22] Ian R. K. Paisley, *Protestants Remember!* (Belfast: Puritan Printing Co., 1965), pp. 1–2.

Interestingly, Paisley has generalized his own success into a theory about Ulster people:

All Ulster people speak strong. I mean, an Ulsterman calls what we say a spade, a spade. That is the Ulster way and, I mean, that's done on the republican side and the Roman Catholic side. It's done on the unionist side. That is the language, the trademark, the hallmark of an Ulsterman. He's blunt. He's straight. He doesn't diplomatically tell you you're a liar. He just looks you in the eyeball and says 'You're a liar'.[23]

Implied in this stereotype is a contrasting notion of what the English are like. For obvious reasons, Northern nationalists do not like the English. Ulster Protestants are hardly more sympathetic. They certainly do not feel any great sense of kinship with them. A recent survey asked people if they thought various other groups were like themselves. Eighty-two per cent of Ulster Protestants thought themselves similar to the Scots. Sixty-two per cent thought themselves like the Southern Irish and only forty-three per cent thought they were like the English.[24] Ulster evangelicals may be wary of the English because of their obvious lack of religiosity. Ulster unionists expect (with good cause) that the English will betray them. There is also an element of class conflict involved in a dislike of 'the English'. The Ulster upper classes have traditionally looked to London and the English aristocracy for their values and culture. They are educated at English public schools and universities and speak with English accents. The *Protestant Telegraph* often accompanied its attacks on O'Neill with some snide remark about his accent.[25] While the Ulsterman is direct to the point of bluntness, the Englishman (and hence the Ulster aristocrat) is evasive. His evasions hide treachery.

If one understands such stereotypes, Paisley's style becomes comprehensible. The point can be made with the example of his behaviour at the European Parliament.

In 1973, Paisley had been at the centre of a fracas in the newly created Assembly and was taken out of the chamber by the police. His translation to the more exalted forum of the European Parliament did nothing to blunt his protesting fervour and he managed to disrupt the opening formal session. As soon as Madame Weiss

[23] BBC Television, op. cit.
[24] Edward Moxon-Browne, *Nation, Class and Creed in Northern Ireland* (Aldershot: Gower, 1983), Ch. 1.
[25] *Protestant Telegraph* (2 Feb. 1969).

called the Parliament to order, Paisley rose and asked for an assurance that in future the Union Jack would be flown the correct way up and not, as it was outside the building, in the 'distress' position. According to the BBC's correspondent, W. D. Flackes, Paisley's intervention brought 'gasps of astonishment' from Euro MPs.[26] Paisley interrupted again when Madame Weiss made a passing reference to De Valera in her speech. John Hume, the SDLP leader, signally failed to understand which audience Paisley was speaking to when he remarked that 'it is tragic that so many people in Northern Ireland are so represented' and added, 'He will not achieve anything for Northern Ireland at European level'.[27] The next day Paisley made his third interruption. This time he barracked the Republic of Ireland's Premier Jack Lynch over the Republic's failure to extradite terrorists to Northern Ireland to stand trial. The French Gaullist leader Jacques Chirac called for Paisley to be banned. A Fine Gael spokesman called his interruption 'an undignified outburst' and 'an ugly display of bad manners'. When asked how he reacted, John Taylor, the Official Unionist MEP, said that he agreed with the comments on extradition but 'disagreed entirely' with Paisley's tactics.[28]

Short interviews conducted in Belfast city centre by a *Newsletter* journalist produced the expected range of responses. One shopper thought 'he will put people's backs up at the Parliament and they may not listen to our views afterwards. He is starting off badly.' Another thought him right to 'have a go at Eire for harbouring criminals'.[29] However, there was an interesting spontaneous display of support when, on his return from Strasburg, Paisley had to pass through a crowd of some 600 Ulster people who had been delayed in Heathrow while waiting for the Belfast shuttle. When he appeared, a section of the crowd broke into applause and people congratulated him on 'sticking up for Ulster'.

Being polite is an admired social quality. So is loyalty to a set of principles. When Paisley and his supporters view their own protests, they see circumstances or the actions of others forcing them into a position where principle and civility clash; they cannot campaign for their principles and continue to be polite. When they

[26] BBC Radio Ulster news (17 July 1979).
[27] *Irish News* (18 July 1979).
[28] Ibid., and *Newsletter* (19 July 1979).
[29] *Newsletter* (20 July 1979).

contrast themselves with conservative Irish Presbyterian ministers, or unionist politicians who do not appear sufficiently aggressive in defence of unionism, they interpret the stress on good manners as evidence of a lack of genuine commitment to principle. For the true believer, embarrassing oneself or others is small price for defending the faith. Furthermore, a hostile reaction is often interpreted by the believer as proof that he is promoting the gospel truth. After all, Christ did say, 'Blessed are ye, when men shall hate you, and when they shall separate you from their company, and shall reproach you . . .' Thus public protests in a style which many people find offensive are good in their own right because they are God's will. They are also good because they prove that the believer puts God's will above the judgements of men. Finally, they have the minor unintended consequence of reassuring the believer that he is on the side of the angels.

It is clear that many Ulster Protestants share Paisley's analysis of the correct relationship between civility and principle. Whether or not John Hume was right when he said that Paisley's interruptions would make him ineffective in Europe, he missed the point that Paisley was playing to the Ulster unionist voters, just as he was playing to Ulster evangelicals in the Oxford debate. And the part he was playing was that of the blunt Ulsterman who meant what he said and who, in marked contrast to the leaders of the Unionist Party or the main Protestant churches, would never abandon parochial interests and identify in favour of cosmopolitanism.

8

Secularization and Ideology

This chapter is intended to do two related things: to describe some of the apparently more exotic Free Presbyterian beliefs and to throw some light on the question of why such beliefs should appeal to certain people rather than to others. Do Free Presbyterians have something in common, other than their Free Presbyterianism, which helps to explain why they were attracted to the Free Church?

The assumption which informs this discussion is that, while social scientists have nothing to say about the truth or falsity of particular religious ideologies, sociological analysis can tell us something about the *plausibility* of certain types of beliefs. That is, leaving aside the question of whether any particular belief is correct, we can offer general observations about social circumstances which go some way towards explaining the likelihood of certain beliefs remaining or becoming widely accepted.[1] It must, however, be stressed that this sort of analysis can offer no assistance to people who wish to decide what they ought to believe. The position of the sociologist is quite different from that of those modern theologians who use sociological analyses of plausibility to argue that the Christian faith should be changed in this or that way in order to make it more acceptable. For us, plausibility, like popularity, is a neutral concept which neither confirms nor denies the truth claims of any particular ideology.

The Distinctive Elements of Free Presbyterian Ideology

Free Presbyterianism is a subspecies of conservative evangelicalism. Its adherents share with other evangelicals the belief that the Bible is the divinely inspired word of God, that Christ was the Son of God, born of a virgin, whose death was the 'once,

[1] This sociology of knowledge approach is derived from Berger's phenomenological sociology. See Peter L. Berger and Thomas Luckmann, *The Social Construction of Reality* (Harmondsworth, Middx.: Penguin, 1973).

complete and never to be repeated sacrifice' which atoned for our sins. They believe that neither good works nor correctly performed ritual will save a sinner from hell-fire, but that being 'born again' will. One cannot choose to be born again. According to the Calvinist wing of evangelicalism to which Free Presbyterianism belongs, conversion is produced by the working of the Holy Spirit and it is a freely given and entirely undeserved gift of God's sovereign grace.

One could go on detailing specific beliefs and many have already been mentioned. I am interested here in the points where Free Presbyterians most obviously differ from other conservative Protestants: their continued commitment to most of the seventeenth-century Westminster Confession of Faith and the vigour of their anti-Catholicism. The two things are related. Although liberal Protestants have abandoned almost all of the Westminster Confession, they find that document's description of the Pope as the Antichrist particularly embarrassing. Given that remaining 'separate' from liberal apostasy is such an important part of Free Presbyterianism, and that Roman Catholicism is seen as the most complete exemplification of apostasy, anti-Catholicism offers a convenient area for the exploration of the more distinctive beliefs of Free Presbyterianism.

Mystery, Babylon the Great

And there came one of the seven angels which had the seven vials, and talked with me, saying unto me, Come hither; I will shew unto you the judgement of the great whore that sitteth upon many waters: With whom the kings of the earth have committed fornication, and the inhabitants of the earth have been made drunk with the wine of her fornication. So he carried me away in the spirit into the wilderness; and I saw a woman sit upon a scarlet coloured beast, full of names of blasphemy, having seven heads and ten horns. And the woman was arrayed in purple and scarlet colour and decked with gold and precious stones and pearls, having a golden cup in her hands full of abominations and filthiness of her fornication: And upon her forehead was the name written, Mystery, Babylon the Great, the Mother of Harlots and abominations of the earth. And I saw the woman drunken with the blood of the saints, and with the blood of the martyrs of Jesus.

All Free Presbyterians read chapter 17 of the book of Revelation, of which the above is part, as a description of the Roman Catholic

Church. If one is going to suppose that this revelation refers to an actual person or organization, then Rome seems like a reasonable candidate, especially given other references to sitting astride seven hills. Many people who wish to find a naturalistic interpretation for this and other references to the 'Mother of Harlots' suppose that it was a veiled denunciation of the Roman Empire, written in allegory to safeguard the author from the wrath of the occupying Romans. Free Presbyterians, however, prefer the more traditional view that this and other passages refer to the evil system of the Roman Catholic Church. In their eyes Rome goes beyond simply offering false teaching; the Catholic Church is actively evil in that it has a history of both persecuting 'true' Christians and suppressing the democracy which Protestants regard as something which was created by their faith (and as the political system which offers the conditions of freedom which are necessary if they are to maintain and promote their faith).

There is no problem in finding evidence of Roman Catholic persecution of Protestants in the seventeenth and eighteenth centuries. These were times when few people thought there was anything wrong with using violence to enforce religious conformity.[2] More recent examples can be found in Franco's oppression of Protestant missionaries in Phalangist Spain. As I have already mentioned, Free Presbyterians suppose that the Roman Catholic Church is quietly supportive of the IRA and INLA, the statements of the Irish Catholic hierarchy to the contrary notwithstanding.

But an absence of evidence of evil Roman Catholic intent poses no problem for anti-Catholicism because one can always posit a secret conspiracy. If there is little modern evidence that the Jesuits, who are seen as the 'storm-troops' of the Vatican, are actively engaged in conspiring to subvert Protestantism and democracy, then one simply supposes that they have become more subtle and devious. At first sight clinging on to theories for which there is little obvious evidence by invoking a conspiracy may seem like

[2] In the interests of accuracy, it is worth noting that even those early Protestants who are nowadays cited as apostles of religious freedom were happy to see state violence used to suppress heresies. The Covenanters, for example, accepted the general principle of the civil magistrate 'extirpating' 'false worships'; they merely disagreed with the actual application of the principle to themselves. For an example of Free Presbyterian reminders of the earlier evils of Catholicism, see I. R. K. Paisley, *The Massacre of St Bartholomew* (Belfast: Martyrs Memorial Productions, 1972).

evidence of the irrationality of Free Presbyterians, but if it is irrationality, it is an irrationality which is common to most belief
systems which claim to have found the key to interpreting the
world. Free Presbyterians believe that there is a God and that all
that occurs in the world happens, ultimately, at his behest. The
Bible is the word of God and contains his plans for the world.
Suppose one finds in the Bible the prophecy that Rome will grow
in power and, as the end of the world approaches, will actively
persecute the saints. If there is a temporary shortage of evidence
that Rome is actually doing this, then one can conclude that the
word of God is fallible (in which case he is not much of a God),
that one's interpretation is mistaken, or that Rome is engaged in
secret conspiracy. There is nothing unusual about hunting around
for some subsidiary hypothesis which saves a theory by showing
that what looked at first sight like refuting evidence is actually no
such thing. Even natural scientists, supposedly the exemplars of
the most rigorous reasoning and testing methods, are reluctant to
give up a good theory just because there is little evidence for it.[3]
Most of us find ways of sustaining our beliefs by finding subsidiary
explanations for the lack of evidence and the simplest way of maintaining faith in the idea that one understands what is really going
on in a particular setting is to suppose that 'true' reality is to be
found under the surface, to which access is gained by possession
of the correct key. The Roman Catholic Church may seem to act
like one denomination among others but those people who know
the truth about history and who have the correct interpretation
of the Scriptures can penetrate this miasma and see the global
conspiracy. Marxists reason in precisely the same manner. They
believe that they correctly understood the underlying dynamic of
history. When Marx's prophecies fail to be supported by actual
events, they find subsidiary explanations which allow them to believe that things are 'really' going as planned. Despite the fact that
the working class shows no sign of developing class-consciousness,
the dedicated Marxist does not conclude that Marx was actually
wrong. Instead he argues that there 'really' is a working class in
the sense the theory requires but that it has not yet been permitted

---

[3] On natural scientists' tendency to see refutation as mere anomaly, and the
problems which this causes for the Popperian falsificationist view of the development of scientific knowledge, see Steven Yearley, *Science and Sociological
Practice* (Milton Keynes: Open University Press, 1984), pp. 39–44.

by the ruling class (the Marxist equivalent of Rome) to develop a 'correct' awareness of its destiny.

The only point in mentioning the cases of natural scientists who buttress collapsing theories, and Marxists who insist that class, as defined by Marx, really is an important variable, is to make clear the commonplace nature of what Free Presbyterians do with the notion of a secret conspiracy. If it is irrational, then it is a form of irrationality practised by many of us much of the time. But a full understanding of the rationality of Free Presbyterianism requires recognition of another point. The natural scientist who fails to change his theories to accord with the weight of the evidence would be judged by most people to be failing to apply systematically the same standards of judgement to evidence he likes and to evidence he does not like. His sin is inconsistency. The determined anti-Catholic who invokes a conspiracy theory to fill the gap left by a possible lack of convincing evidence is not being inconsistent, because the original belief that Catholicism is evil is taken to be supported by supernatural authority. The conservative Protestant knows that Rome is 'Mystery, Babylon the Great' because the Bible says so, and the Bible is a more impressive source of authority than the observations of journalists, politicians, and even one's own senses.

Free Presbyterians differ from most other conservative Protestants in the strength of their anti-Catholicism, which leads them to attribute more power and influence to Rome than would other Protestants. For the Free Presbyterian, Rome is not only totally evil but also extremely effective. Where others might see a large and cumbersome bureaucracy having trouble keeping control over its own functionaries in, for example, Latin America, the dedicated anti-Romanist sees a well-organized and never-deflected attempt to promote Rome's aims. There are no mistakes, nor errors, only subtle attempts to lull the rest of the world into complacency.

This faith in the efficacy of Rome leads Free Presbyterians to attribute most things they do not like to the influence of Rome. They do not see the ecumenical movement as a genuine, if misguided, attempt to create a Christian movement which is sufficiently united to be able to stand against secularization. They do not believe that ecumenical Protestants have promoted 'reconciliation' for their own reasons. Instead, the ecumenical movement is seen as 'Rome-inspired and Rome-led'. Free Presbyterians are so firmly convinced of the hidden hand of Rome that they will argue that someone like Michael Ramsay was not 'really' an Anglican archbishop seeking better relations with the Roman Catholic Church; he was actually a Roman bishop, having secretly been ordained by the Pope.[4]

Similarly, Rome is thought to be behind such diverse threats to Protestantism and democracy as fascism and communism. In addition to conflating contemporary enemies, Free Presbyterians discover unity in ancient enemies of the true religion and argue that Rome is actually Babylon. After all, the verses of Revelation quoted above tell us that the Mother of Harlots had 'Mystery, Babylon the Great' written on her forehead. Hislop's *The Two Babylons*, which is on sale in Free Presbyterian bookshops, lists hundreds of similarities between Babylonian worship and the practices, beliefs, and symbols of Roman Catholicism.[5] Thus Rome is seen, not just as being like Babylon in that both religions are wrong, but as actually being the continuation of Babylon, which explains why Romanism is wrong.

In his pamphlet on the Jesuits, Paisley argues that the Order is not even Christian. Although the Jesuits claim that their sign— IHS—stands for 'Jesus Hominum Salvator (the Latin 'J' being written as 'I'), Paisley believes that it actually stands for 'Isis, Horub, Seb': the pagan Egyptian trinity of the Mother, Child, and Father of the Gods. 'IHS pay the semblance of a tribute to Christianity, but they are in reality the substance of devil-worship. The cloven hoof is upon them.'[6] Thus Rome is not, as liberal Protestants would avow, a permitted variant of Christianity. It is not Christian at all and never has been.

For the present, all that need be said about the foundations of

---

[4] *Revivalist* (Jan. 1970), p. 1.

[5] Alexander Hislop, *The Two Babylons or the Papal Worship Proved to be the Worship of Nimrod and his Wife* (New Jersey: Loizeaux Brothers 1980; originally published 1916). Sceptics who find such work fanciful might note that a number of anthropologists of religion, Mircea Eliade for example, have argued in academically respectable publications that one should expect continuities in even apparently very different religious belief and symbol systems because the human experiences which give rise to such systems are essentially similar. Of course, Free Presbyterians (and most traditional religious believers) would reject Eliade because they wish to assert that there is a fundamental break between their own religion and all others. While they might accept the existence of continuities between other religions (which are human products) they would insist that their own is true and is divinely inspired.

[6] I. R. K. Paisley, *The Jesuits: their start, sign, system, secrecy and strategy* (Belfast: Puritan Printing Co., n.d.), p. 6.

Free Presbyterian views of the Roman Catholic Church is that they are not new. Hislop's *The Two Babylons* was first published in 1916 and, although some of the specifics might have been contested, the basic drift would have been acceptable to very many Protestants since the Reformation. Such views were certainly common among eighteenth- and nineteenth-century Presbyterians and John Wesley identified the Roman Catholic Church with the Mother of Harlots.[7] The problem, then, is not to explain why Free Presbyterians believe such things. Correctly put, it is to explain why they continue to believe what other Protestants have given up. I will return to this shortly.

Free Presbyterian Eschatology

Another area in which Free Presbyterians differ from other conservative Protestants has already been briefly touched on in the last chapter: the study of 'the end-times' or, to give it its technical name, eschatology. Eschatology is a profoundly difficult subject and, unlike some denominations which were created specifically to embody a particular eschatological theory, the Free Presbyterian Church has always been careful to avoid making any one particular theory a 'fundamental' of the faith. In his *Dictionary of Theological Terms*, Alan Cairns asks 'each believer to hold his views in humility and with due love and regard for the equally sincerely held views of differing brethren'.[8] Nevertheless, there is considerable agreement about certain points which I will introduce in the context of Ian Paisley's views on the European Community.

In the 1984 EEC election campaign, Paisley made it clear that he was fundamentally opposed to British membership. One objection was shared by both the British political left and right, namely that membership would entail a loss of sovereignty. The distinctive Christian moral standards of Ulster were already threatened by the unrepresentative and undemocratic rule of Westminster. To subordinate Britain to the European Community with its Court of Human Rights and law-making powers would further reduce the ability of Ulster people to control their own future.

---

[7] A range of authorities for the identification are given in Ronald Cooke, *Paisley and Mystery Babylon the Great* (Hollidaysburg, Pennsylvania: Manna Press, 1985).

[8] Alan Cairns, *Dictionary of Theological Terms* (Gilford, Co. Down: Whitefield College of the Bible, 1982), p. 92.

There had already been a case in point. In deference to Ulster conservatism, the Westminster legislation which had legalized consenting adult male homosexuality had not been extended to cover the province. The European Court of Human Rights had judged Britain to be in violation of basic freedoms by permitting this exception. The government bowed to the Court and passed an Order in Council extending the law to Northern Ireland.

But Paisley had another reason for opposing continued membership:

The countries of the EEC are overwhelmingly Roman Catholic . . . Apart from Denmark (which has a population of only five million) Britain is the only really Protestant country in the EEC with about 10% of its 56 million population being Roman Catholic. When Spain and Portugal join the Roman Catholic percentages will be overwhelming.[9]

The treaty which established the EEC—the aptly named 'Treaty of Rome'—was drafted by Adenauer, Monnet, and Schumann: three Catholics. The Roman Catholic Church has diplomatic representation at the EEC and Pope John Paul II has expressed a desire for European unity. Thus the general threat to sovereignty was compounded by it also being a Catholic threat.

These considerations were offered by Paisley to the electorate in his election literature. In a series of sermons in Martyrs' Memorial, he presented a complementary analysis which examined the place of the EEC in Bible prophecies about the end of the world.

Those Christians who believe that there will be a literal Second Coming of Christ, a Day of Judgement, and a thousand years of righteous rule on earth may still disagree about the order in which these things will occur. The more arcane details of disagreement need not concern us. One school of thought expects the judgement to come before the thousand years of righteousness and is sensibly called 'pre-millennialist'. Others expect the millennium, seen as a period of unprecedented success for the church, to be followed by the day of judgement; hence the title 'post-millennialist'. A third view, amillennialism, denies the reality of the millennium as it is depicted in the other two schools and a large proportion even of conservative Protestants have no firm views about this. Almost all Free Presbyterians are pre-millennial which, as I suggested in the last chapter, is something of a departure from the dominant

[9] I. R. K. Paisley, *The EEC and the Vatican* (Belfast: DUP, 1984).

Presbyterian position of the last century, although it is not unprecedented and is part of the general disappearance of post-millennialism.[10] What is important for understanding Free Presbyterians is the role which Roman Catholicism is supposed to play in the approach to the end-times. Elements of Revelation and the books of Daniel and Isaiah are taken to prophesy the rise of an 'Antichrist' who will not only dominate the Church but who will also be a major political force in the 'tribulation': the period shortly before the Second Coming when the Jews and the Christians will be persecuted for not worshipping the Antichrist. There is some difficulty with the figure of Antichrist who can variously be seen as an individual or a system. When someone like Paisley calls the Pope the Antichrist, he is applying that designation to 'all popes' and not to the current holder of the office. It is the 'system' of the papacy which usurps the place of Christ in the church. Some pre-millennialists expect two Antichrists: one in the church and one in politics. Others see just one, with two spheres of influence, but whichever view is taken, Rome and the papacy is still taken to be the driving force: an identification which is defended by arguing that there is no world-wide organization other than the Roman Catholic Church which has the power, influence, and reach to be the sort of comprehensive anti-Christian force suggested in prophecy. Interestingly, Catholics themselves have at times fuelled Protestant fears by making grandiose claims for authority over all peoples and all spheres of life. For example, in the 1930s, Monsignor Ronald Knox addressed meetings in Edinburgh on the subject 'Wanted: a world leader! Why not the Pope?'

Most contemporary Protestants dismiss these eschatological speculations as misplaced fantasies and many of those who trouble themselves with the interpretation of the relevant Scripture passages explain them as covert references to the original Roman Empire. Free Presbyterians need not necessarily deny such naturalistic interpretations. One minister suggested that Bible prophecies have the peculiar quality of being able to refer to more than one event in more than one era so that any particular prophecy could be a veiled reference to something in the writer's time, his future but our past, and our future. Thus the Whore of John's Revelations could be the original Roman Empire, the present

---

[10] Horation Bonar, the great Free Church of Scotland preacher, for example, was pre-millennial.

Roman Catholic Church, and the future world Church created by the return of the ecumenical Protestants to Rome.

The details of Paisley's series of sermons on 'The Common Market Prophetically Considered' are not important. The basic theme is that the EEC is part of the growth of the Antichrist and is in the political sphere what the Roman Church is in the religious. Its main purpose is to assist Romanism in its campaign for world domination. It is thus something to be opposed and something to interpret as evidence of the gradual approach of the end-times. It is also further confirmation of the general prophetic scenario.

I would make the same point about Free Presbyterian eschatology as I did about the identification of Rome with 'Mystery, Babylon the Great'. While the particular applications of prophecy to contemporary world events are obviously novel, the general scheme of interpretation is not new. But it is also not popular. Although it would be shared by many American fundamentalists (who would add their own details), it would not be widely accepted by most British evangelicals. Yet it once was. And even when these particular stories were not orthodox, the background assumptions which make them 'reasonable' certainly were. After all, however strange such beliefs may now appear, they are perfectly reasonable if one assumes an all-powerful God and a very powerful Devil and assumes that the world evolves as a result of struggles between good and evil. Provided one accepts the supernatural, there is nothing particularly implausible about these beliefs. This suggests that any serious analysis of why they remain popular among one group of people long after they have been abandoned elsewhere may usefully begin by considering the very general question of the decline of belief in the supernatural.

However, before embarking on a general explanation of secularization, I will briefly describe and eliminate a popular explanation of why Free Presbyterians believe the sorts of things described above. Many commentators imply, even if they do not openly state, that Free Presbyterians are not only mistaken in their actual beliefs but also flawed in their reasoning processes. Sometimes this is overt, as in the case of Boulton talking of the 'weak and wanting minds' who are attracted to Paisleyism.[11] Often, it is suggested by the introduction of words to describe Free Presbyterian thought which the author would not normally use to

[11] David Boulton, *The UVF, 1966–73* (Dublin: Torc Books, 1973), p. 31.

describe his own beliefs. Gallagher uses the term 'mentality' to describe Free Presbyterian thought.[12] Smyth talks of a 'mind set'.[13] In both cases there is the implication that people who hold unpopular beliefs do so because they do not reason as efficiently or as critically as the rest of the population. That is, odd beliefs are explained by defects in reasoning or, in the tradition of social science derived from Adorno and Rokeach,[14] by defects in the personality of the believer.

I do not want to become involved in a philosophical argument about the nature of rationality or about the relationship between personality and belief. Neither of these problems is crucial to an understanding of Free Presbyterianism. For personality explanations to be vital or even important, it would have to be the case: (*a*) that these unpopular beliefs were rather randomly distributed across a population; (*b*) that they were acquired late in life, after something which could sensibly be investigated as a 'personality' had been created; (*c*) that people who had been raised by their parents in particular ways developed personalities which were identifiably different from the 'normal' personality; and (*d*) that people with a certain sort of personality—'authoritarian' people, for example—were more likely than others to accept 'extremist' beliefs. If these conditions were met, then we would have reason to concern ourselves with personality. As it is, there is no need to delve in the deep and badly charted waters of the psyche and its rationality because it is clearly the case that most Free Presbyterians were raised to believe the things they believe, or other things quite similar to them. To put it bluntly, Free Presbyterians have acquired their beliefs in much the same way as the rest of us acquired ours: by accepting what our parents and others who were important to us in early life taught us. This still leaves those who shifted a long way in their world-views to become Free Presbyterians (a not very large group) and the question of why some people continued to hold such beliefs when others who were

[12] Tom Gallagher, 'Religion, Reaction and Revolt in Northern Ireland: the impact of Paisleyism in Ulster', *Journal of Church and State*, 23 (1981), p. 427.

[13] Clifford Smyth, 'The Ulster Democratic Unionist Party: a case study in religious and political convergence', Ph.D. thesis (The Queen's University of Belfast, 1984), pp. 247 and 263.

[14] For a critical discussion of this work, see Steve Bruce, *Firm in the Faith: the survival of conservative Protestantism* (Aldershot: Gower, 1984), pp. 197-202.

similarly raised abandoned their conservative Protestant beliefs. Although complete answers are never possible—sociology deals with the general and the typical rather than with the particular and the individual—fairly convincing explanations which concentrate on the social location of specific ideas can be constructed. To do this, I must first offer a brief sketch of the causes of secularization.

The Sociology of Secularization

We can mean many things by the 'decline of religion'. We could, for example, refer to the gradual narrowing of the functions of religious organizations as the secular state assumes tasks previously performed by churches. We could examine the actual decline of church membership and attendance. However, both of these are themselves related to the general decline in religious belief[15] and I will begin by considering those features of modern industrial society which may have reduced the plausibility of belief in the supernatural.

A central feature of the development of modern societies is 'differentiation'.[16] An increased division of labour causes societies to become fragmented into class and status groups and at the same time the once relatively homogeneous culture becomes subdivided as different social groups develop the dominant religious tradition in directions best suited to their needs and interests. Increased social differentiation thus produces cultural pluralism as what was once a dominant religious establishment (the position of which will

[15] There are sociologists who would argue that neither the loss of functions of religious organizations to the state nor a decline in church membership are necessarily evidence of a decline in belief in religious world-views. Although many factors come between these things, I do not accept the anti-secularization argument that declining participation in organized religion cannot be taken as a decline in belief in the supernatural. Although it is the case that very many non-church members claim some sort of religious experience, when probed on what they have in mind when they make such claims, their answers range from a vague sense that there is more to life than meets the eye, to stories of surviving car crashes which might have been expected to be fatal. See David Hay and Ann Morisy, 'Secular Society/ Religious Meanings: a contemporary paradox' (Nottingham University/ Manchester College, Oxford Religious Experience Research Project, 1980). This sort of non-specific rejection of a completely atheistic world-view is a very long way from shared belief in a series of specific beliefs about God and the supernatural.

[16] In addition to the works cited below, the major sources of my account of secularization are Bryan R. Wilson, *Religion in Secular Society: a sociological comment* (London: C. A. Watts, 1966); and *Contemporary Transformation of Religion* (London: Oxford University Press, 1976).

often have been recognized by it being a legally established state church) is fragmented into a variety of competing religious world-views. In the cases of Scotland, England, and Wales a legally established church was maintained but only with the removal of its powers to suppress competing religions and to raise money by something like general taxation.[17]

One consequence of the fragmentation of the religious culture is choice. To use Berger's pompous but accurate expression, plural-ism 'universalises heresy'.[18] Fate is replaced by choice. People in traditional societies could hardly be said to have selected their religion. Most people born in the non-Muslim areas of nineteenth-century India did not choose to be Hindu. They were simply born into a Hindu world. There are extremely few places in the modern western world where any particular religion has the taken-for-granted quality of an unchallenged monopoly. Even in countries such as the Republic of Ireland where the vast majority of the population are active supporters of one church, the believers know that other religions exist because they read about them and see them on the same television programmes that most people in Britain and America watch. It may still be 'natural' to be a Catholic in that one would have to go out of one's way to become anything else, but even the rural Irish Catholic cannot be unaware that there are large proportions of the world's population that are not Catholic. The consequence of pluralism is that:

Subjectively, the man in the street tends to be uncertain about religious matters. Objectively, the man in the street is confronted with a wide variety of religions and other reality-defining agencies that compete for his allegiance or at least attention, and none of which is in a position to coerce him into allegiance.[19]

Having to choose removes, even from those who choose to believe, the certainty that was enjoyed by members of traditional cultures dominated by a religious monopoly.

The consequence of pluralism for the democratic state is re-

[17] For a detailed discussion of the links between Protestantism, schism and the rise of religious tolerance, see Steve Bruce, 'A House Divided: Protestant schism and the rise of religious tolerance', *Sociological Analysis*, 47 (1) (1986).

[18] Peter L. Berger, *The Heretical Imperative: contemporary possibilities of religious affirmation* (London: Collins, 1979), Ch. 1.

[19] Peter L. Berger, *The Social Reality of Religion* (Harmondsworth, Middx.: Penguin, 1973), p. 131.

ligious neutrality. When a democratic society possesses a number of competing religious organizations, the institutions of the state cannot favour one over another. The Church of England may be called the state church of England but it enjoys no tax advantages over the 'dissenting' denominations. American tax law offers charitable tax deductible status to all religions and makes no serious effort to separate the good from the bad. The importance of the state's neutrality was recently recognized by Jerry Falwell, a Baptist fundamentalist and leader of the Moral Majority in America, when he supported the Unification Church (the 'Moonies') in protesting against the prison sentence given to Sun Myung Moon for supposed tax evasion. Falwell joined other conservative Protestant church leaders in arguing that the speedy prosecution of Moon for offences far less serious than those commonly committed by businessmen amounted to government harassment and an encroachment on religious freedom. When even leaders of competing religions advocate toleration, religious pluralism forces the state to be even-handed and, if it maintains any religion at all, it is of a lowest common denominator kind.[20]

Having argued that pluralism forces choice and choice undermines the plausibility of all the choices, we can go further in demonstrating why the general choice of 'religious belief' is difficult to make in modern societies.

The notion of differentiation can be used, not only to describe the fragmentation of the population but also to characterize the fragmentation of life into a number of discrete spheres, each with its values. The first such autonomous sphere is the economy. An important part of the process of industrialization is the separation of work from the home. Work becomes thoroughly secularized; production and exchange become governed by rational considerations of efficiency and productivity rather than religious, sentimental or traditional attachments.[21] No oil company could operate if it insisted on shutting down its wells on the sabbath. Even if it could, it would be put out of business by the first competitor which refused to temper rational calculations of costs and profits.

In order to maximize efficiency, personal preferences and idiosyncrasies must be subordinated to role performance. The

[20] Robert Bellah, 'Civil Religion in America', *Daedalus*, 96 (1) (1967), pp. 1–21.
[21] Peter L. Berger, op. cit., n. 19 above, pp. 133–5.

coordination of large numbers of people in complex patterns of interaction—the shoppers in a busy city centre, for example—requires that movement and action be made as predictable as possible. Hence ropes to form people into queues, doors divided into 'in' and 'out', and shop assistants who mechanically perform the same operations with each customers' goods, money, and change, irrespective of the person of the customer. Of course some people rebel against the confines of their roles and attempt to rewrite the scripts for the drama of their lives. Others simply distance themselves by going through the motions of acting out their public roles while investing as little as possible of their own emotions in the performance. None the less, the world of work is increasingly the world of 'mechanical' role performance.

The obviously superior efficiency of rational and mechanical methods of processing has led to their transfer from the production of goods to the processing of people. The bureaucracy is simply the factory system applied to people rather than inert matter. Civil servants, for example, are expected to treat all people as 'cases'. Only those properties (such as 'single mother' and 'with two children') which are deemed relevant to the task in hand by the rules of the organization are supposed to be considered.[22] 'Nice-looking' and 'pleasant personality' are notions which the Department of Health clerk may operate with outside working hours or in mental fantasy, but to bring them into the job of 'clerk' is to act in a discriminatory way and, if discovered, might result in punishment. To move from these specific examples to the 'social system' as a whole is to gloss over a number of important considerations but the consequences of the spread of rationality from the economic sphere can be summarized as the replacement of ethical by technical concerns:

A modern social system is increasingly conceived as operating without virtues; it becomes a neutral, detached, objective, rational co-ordination of role performances. The system induces those who actually man the roles—that is, human beings—to behave as if they had neither virtues nor vices. The pressure is towards the neutralization of human personality so that roles might be performed with ever greater calculability.[23]

[22] For an entertaining analysis of the various ways in which people attempt to survive the tedium of the 'everyday life world' of a modern bureaucratic industrial society, see Stanley Cohen and Laurie Taylor, *Escape Attempts: the theory and practice of resistance to everyday life* (London: Allen Lane/Penguin Books, 1976).

[23] Bryan R. Wilson, *Religion in Sociological Perspective* (Oxford: Oxford University Press, 1982), p. 48.

The problem with rationality, of course, is that it is concerned with method. If a car manufacturer wishes to increase his productivity, it is rational to replace one method of wheel fitting by a faster one, provided the faster method does not produce more substandard products. But rationality cannot tell us whether or not it is good to want to increase productivity. Thus Wilson concludes that an important feature of modern industrial societies is the disappearance of 'ends'. The Shorter Catechism, the document constructed by the seventeenth-century Protestant divines as an aid to general religious instruction, begins 'what is the chief end of man?'. The answer given—'Man's chief end is to glorify God and to enjoy him for ever'—is far less important than the fact that the question was asked at all. The obsession of modern societies with increased efficiency and procedural rationality has made it almost impossible for us to consider 'the end of man'.

This is the most abstract and comprehensive part of my explanation for secularization: the dominant values of the world of work—procedural rationalities—have permeated so much of our activity and thought processes that a fundamental element of religion—a concern with purpose—is far less common in our culture than it is in those of most pre-industrial societies. We can also offer more specific observations about the consequences of what Berger *et al.* call 'technological consciousness'.[24] By this they mean a cluster of fundamental assumptions about the nature of the world and our place in it which, even though we may often be unaware of them, are part and parcel of modern work. A good example of an element of technological consciousness is 'componentiality'. We assume that any radiator for a 1976 Viva will fit any 1976 Viva. We suppose that complex objects can be subdivided into a range of components, all of which can be readily replaced by a substitute. Nothing is sacred. No particular bond between two components has any greater value or merit than that between one of those components and a replacement. Another element is 'reproducibility'. Modern technological work takes it for granted that complex creative acts can be subdivided into simple acts which can be repeated over and over. It also assumes that the same act will always produce the same results, and that the same act done by two quite different people will produce the same results. The fitting

[24] Peter L. Berger, Birgitte Berger and Hansfried Kellner, *The Homeless Mind: modernization and consciousness* (Harmondsworth, Middx.: Penguin, 1974).

of the wheels to a Viva may be performed by a fascist one day and a communist the next but, provided they both perform the actions in the right way, the Viva will be the same.

Although it would take more space than is available here to trace all the links between technological consciousness and secularization, the basic point should be clear. Technology takes for granted certain assumptions about the world, time and ourselves. These assumptions are basically antithetical to any kind of expressive activity and they gradually erode genuine belief in the supernatural. To offer a simple example, imagine a highly religious culture in which people genuinely expect miracles and where the intervention of the gods in the day-to-day affairs of men is taken to be commonplace. Such people could not successfully operate a world which had train timetables. They would not be able to confidently expect that, human error and mechanical failure permitting, the 10.10 to Bangor would leave at 10.10 today, as it did yesterday and as it will tomorrow. The arrival of technology and its attendant rationality brings patterns of thought and action which gradually erode the expectation of miracles. The Victorians persisted in announcing their train times 'God willing', but by then 'DV' was little more than a pious token of a faith which had disappeared. Few Victorians expected that God would be 'unwilling' to permit the 10.10 to leave.

Industrialization thus creates a general 'consciousness' which subtly undermines religion. This is more important in the explanation of secularization than the more often mentioned clash between religion and science. The odd intellectual may have had his or her faith called into doubt by some particular scientific production—Darwin's theory of evolution, for example—but to suggest that people gave up religious explanations because competing scientific ones were better fails to show why people accepted that science was a superior source of knowledge. Berger *et al*'s technological consciousness' thesis suggests a partial answer. Science appeared more convincing because it was in harmony with the values and procedures of the world of production. Another part of the explanation is that it was easy, for those already slightly distanced from religious presuppositions, to believe that technology worked better than religion. Prayer may save one's cattle from ringworm but chemicals are more reliable. The religious farmer may begin by combining prayer and chemicals and gradually reduce the range of things which he 'takes to the Lord in prayer' as technical solutions are found. Technical advances gradually remove areas of uncertainty and unpredictability and, by so doing, shrink the regions of life for which religion is still thought to offer the best explanations and remedies.

Far more could be said about the impact of pluralism and technology but I have done enough to show that members of modern industrial societies are in the historically novel position of having to choose a faith from a range of competing alternatives (one of which is 'no religion') and having to make this choice in an environment which is fundamentally corrosive of religion. One solution to the predicament is to rewrite religion so as to remove as far as possible the supernatural elements and in various ways this is what 'liberal' Protestantism did.[25]

This is an 'all other things being equal' story and all other things are not. While we can assume that secularization is characteristic of modern industrial societies, we must also expect that there may be reasons why particular cultures remain traditionally religious. Religious world-views are most easily abandoned where they do least; that is, where they have the fewest consequences for important areas of social action. As was made clear in the first chapter, the fact that Ulster was settled at a time when most people were committed adherents of religious world-views, when religious identity was 'attended to' in many areas of personal social interaction and was an important criterion of qualification for civil and political rights, meant that religious identity became imbedded in political and economic conflict. In the age of nationalisms, religion acquired additional resonances.

We would thus expect that societies which were ethnically or politically divided and where religion played a part in those divisions would remain more traditionally religious. Ulster readily fulfils such an expectation. Although church membership figures are not, on their own, an infallible index of religiosity, it must be significant that, according to the most recent reliable figures, something like eighty per cent of the Ulster population claims church membership while the comparable figure for England is only thirteen per cent.[26] However, not all people in Ulster are

[25] Peter L. Berger, 'A Sociological View of the Secularization of Theology', ch. 14 in his *Facing up to Modernity* (Harmondsworth, Middx.: Penguin, 1979).

[26] Peter Brierley, *UK Christian Handbook; 1985/86 Edition* (London: MARC Europe/Bible Society/Evangelical Alliance, 1984).

equally traditional in their religiosity. If we accept the characterization of Free Presbyterianism as a more conservative form
of Protestantism than that offered by most branches of the Irish
Presbyterian Church or the Church of Ireland, then our explanation of secularization should allow us to identify what sorts
of people are attracted to the religion of Ian Paisley. Speaking
generally of western societies, Berger said:

The impact of secularization has tended to be stronger on men than on
women, on people in the middle age range than on the very young and
old, in the cities than in the country, on classes directly connected with
modern industrial production (particularly the working class) than on
those of more traditional occupations (such as artisans or small shopkeepers). . . . Church related religiosity is strongest . . . on the margins of
modern industrial society both in terms of marginal class (such as rem-
nants of the old petty bourgeoisies) and marginal individuals (such as
those eliminated from the work process).[27]

Although this summary of the differential impact of secularization
was originally written with America in mind, it fits well with what
is known about Free Presbyterians. Information about the occupations of Free Presbyterians and other denominations can be
extracted from the 1981 Northern Ireland census and some of this
material is presented below in the form of comparisons between
Free Presbyterians and Irish Presbyterians. Table 1 shows the
relative proportions of men from both groups in various kinds of
occupations.

Differences between the two denominations can be seen both in
the sort of work they do and in their status. Free Presbyterians are
far less well represented in groups 1 and 2: the high status jobs
which require higher educational qualifications. Although proportionately slightly more of them are ordinary managers (group
5), far fewer of them are found among the top managers. Especially
important for Peter Berger's predictions are groups 4, 11, 12, and
13. Free Presbyterians are under-represented among pro-
fessionally qualified engineers, an occupational group at the heart
of modern industrial work. Groups 11, 12 and 13 deserve special
attention. They all represent manufacturing or assembling jobs of
various kinds. The totals for the three groups are almost identical
for both denominations: 27.6 per cent of the Free Presbyterians

[27] Peter L. Berger, op. cit., n. 19 above, p. 114.

TABLE 1: *Presbyterian Male Occupations Compared*

		Free (%)	Irish (%)
1	Professionals/top managers	1.5	4.5
2	Doctors/teachers etc.	2.9	5.2
3	Writers/artists/sports	0.3	0.4
4	Professional engineers	2.0	4.4
5	Managers	19.5	18.3
6	Clerks	4.6	7.3
7	Salesmen	3.9	4.6
8	Policemen/soldiers etc.	6.6	6.6
9	Cooks/cleaners/other services	2.6	2.2
10	Farmers/fishermen	4.1	2.3
11	Agri-industrial workers	12.1	8.6
12	Metal and electrical workers	14.6	16.2
13	Painters/assemblers	0.9	2.2
14	Building workers	6.7	4.2
15	Transport workers	12.1	8.4
16	Unclassifiable others	5.8	4.7

and 27.0 per cent of Irish Presbyterians. But almost half of the Free Presbyterians are concentrated in types of processing work which are connected with agriculture: food processing, leather work, and timber processing.

The same point emerges even more clearly from Table 2, the analysis of the industries in which people are employed.

Free Presbyterians are over-represented in agriculture and other rural occupations such as the sorts of manufacturing which appear in industry type 5, and under-represented in the sort of engineering and industrial work most commonly found in the city. They are also noticeably under-represented in the group 9 and 10 industries, which either require higher education or are concentrated in the greater Belfast area.

One of the social classes specifically mentioned by Peter Berger as marginal to modern industrial society is the old petty bourgeoisie; a class which is easier to recognize intuitively than to

TABLE 2: *Industries of Presbyterian Males Compared*

		Free (%)	Irish (%)
1	Agriculture/forestry/fishing	16.5	11.4
2	Energy/water supply	2.4	3.0
3	Mineral extraction	4.2	3.8
4	Metal engineering	8.0	10.6
5	Other manufacture (e.g. textiles)	13.5	11.6
6	Construction	14.3	10.1
7	Distribution/hotel/catering	14.4	14.7
8	Transport/communication	4.1	5.4
9	Banking/finance/insurance	2.7	5.6
10	Medicine/education/public admin.	17.8	22.7

delimit accurately. Although the census data was not constructed to consider this sort of detailed social class analysis, the occupational material has been dissected in a way which does cast some light on this question. The majority of male Free and Irish Presbyterians are paid employees. 18.7 per cent of Free Presbyterians and 13.1 per cent of Irish Presbyterians are 'self-employed without employees'. But when one considers the 'self-employed with employees' category, one finds the positions reversed. 5.5 per cent of Irish Presbyterian self-employed men hire the labour of other people; only 4.9 per cent of Free Presbyterians do so. This suggests that more Free Presbyterians are businessmen in what the Victorians called 'a small way'. Many of them are farmers and the rest are small shopkeepers or small service industry businessmen. The census data also separates managers into those who run 'large' and 'small' enterprises and the figures show that while Irish and Free Presbyterians are quite similar in the percentages who are managers of small businesses, 5.5 per cent of

Irish Presbyterians manage large enterprises while only 1.8 per cent of Free Presbyterians hold similar positions. The final point which emerges clearly from the census occupation data is that while the total proportions of each denomination who work for other people are similar, the Irish Presbyterians have an advantage over the Free Presbyterians in 'professional' work: 3.8 per cent of Irish but only 2.5 per cent of Free Presbyterians are described as 'professional employees'.

The reason for this imbalance is clear from the evidence on educational qualifications presented in Table 3.[28] The census asked for details of any post-school qualifications. The first and most obvious observation is that the population of Northern Ireland is generally very poorly qualified, but there are some interesting differences between the denominations. The following are the percentages of various denominational groups with no post-school educational attainment.

TABLE 3: *Proportion of 18 + Population Unqualified*

	Male (%)	Female (%)
Free Presbyterian	97.46	95.73
Roman Catholic	93.12	90.72
Church of Ireland	92.35	93.15
Irish Presbyterian	90.83	91.65
All	91.68	91.63

Free Presbyterians are considerably less well qualified than Irish Presbyterians or members of the Church of Ireland. They are less well qualified even than Roman Catholics, which may go some way towards explaining Free Presbyterian hostility to the claim that

[28] The data on Irish Presbyterians was published in the Department of Health and Social Services/Registrar General Northern Ireland, 1984, *The Northern Ireland Census 1981: religion report* (Belfast: Her Majesty's Stationery Office). In the published report Free Presbyterian data is buried in a general 'other denominations' group. The census office very kindly made available the Free Presbyterian data.

Roman Catholics have been the victims of discrimination. Free Presbyterian women share with Roman Catholic women the characteristic of being better qualified than the respective men. Interestingly, they have achieved this without the usual involvement in teaching: 3.0 per cent of Catholic women, 2.64 per cent of Presbyterian women, and 1.98 per cent of Church of Ireland women had teaching qualifications. In stark contrast, only 0.09 per cent of female Free Presbyterians were qualified teachers.

These statistical descriptions are easy enough to present. What is less easy to identify is the explanation of these patterns. My first point in explaining the general lack of formal post-school qualifications among Free Presbyterians would be the importance of farming.

One way of trying to identify the social location of Free Presbyterianism is to calculate the 'receptivity' to Free Presbyterianism of different areas of the province by working out what percentage of the total Protestant population in each of the local government districts was Free Presbyterian at the time of the 1981 census. One can also calculate the degree to which each area is 'rural' or 'urban' and see how 'receptivity to Free Presbyterianism' and 'rurality' are related. A detailed description of this analysis can be found in the appendix, but the statistical evidence suggests that there is a strong connection between rurality and Free Presbyterianism. It thus bears out the impression gained from conversations with ministers and elders that many Free Presbyterian congregations are disproportionately reliant on the farming community. This is even true for cases such as Lisburn and Omagh where the church is situated in an urban area: a good part of the congregation is drawn from the surrounding farm lands. The eldest sons of farmers do not need formal qualifications and there are undoubtedly many young men in Free Presbyterian congregations who could go to university or college but who do not because their future careers are already determined. The low attainment rate for female Free Presbyterians probably reflects the generally conservative attitude of Free Presbyterians to the place of women in the home.

Education, Intelligence, and Culture

It might at first sight appear that the census data on post-school qualifications offers support for the idea that attachment to Free

Presbyterianism can be explained by ignorance. There is, after all, plenty of survey research which shows that the more higher education one consumes, the more likely one is to be liberal rather than conservative in one's religion.[29] Such data has often been used by critics of conservative Protestantism, especially liberal theologians, as grounds for dismissing conservative positions as the beliefs of ill-educated people who do not know any better. An example of this attitude was Austin Fulton's dismissal of those 'unqualified' conservatives who accused Professor Davey of heresy.[30]

I would caution against any such argument. It would be a mistake to assume that the consequences of time spent in higher education were necessarily also the consequences of improved reasoning or increased intelligence. It could well be that four years of a liberal arts education makes students more liberal in their religion, not because they become more intelligent and hence better able to reason their way out of conservatism, but because they are taught specifically liberal beliefs and values, and immersed in a pluralistic culture which offers them alternatives to their previous beliefs. Similarly it seems sensible to suppose that conservatives remain conservative, not because they are too stupid to appreciate the superiority of modern liberal and rational culture, but because they have been less exposed to what, for brevity, I will call modernizing influences. And children of rural conservatives, once fully socialized into their traditional religious belief systems, are relatively 'immune' to secularizing influences. The increasing proportion of Free Presbyterian children who are now going into higher education can take 'preventive' measures such as living at home while studying or frequently returning home at weekends. By continuing to mix with other conservative evangelicals, and by

[29] G. E. Lenski, 'Social Correlates of Religious Interest', *American Sociological Review*, 18 (5) (1953), pp. 533–44; E. L. Long, *The Religious Beliefs of American Scientists* (Philadelphia: Westminster, 1964); Rodney Stark and Charles Glock, *American Piety: the nature of religious commitment* (Berkeley and Los Angeles, CA: University of California Press, 1968). My view that isolation and social organization can counterbalance the influence of education and prevent the shift towards liberalism among the better educated is given support by T. R. Ford, 'Status, Residence and Fundamentalist Religious Beliefs in the Southern Appalachians', *Social Forces*, 39 (1) (1960), pp. 41–9.

[30] J. Austin Fulton, *J. Ernest Davey* (Belfast: The Presbyterian Church in Ireland, 1970), p. 33.

maintaining their contact with their youth fellowship activities, they can minimize the impact of the culture which threatens to undermine their beliefs. These are important points because we should not fall into the trap of supposing that beliefs and values spread like diseases so that any contact is enough to produce cultural change. Although certain cultural innovations have considerable appeal, either because they are supported by powerful and authoritative social groups or because they are simply so all-pervading, there is still a voluntary element in social change. Thus although the explanation of secularization was presented at the level of social forces and social groups, we must always allow that particular individuals, families, and groups will be able to maintain their traditional beliefs, provided they perceive the 'threat' and organize themselves to resist it.

The Land and the Threat

So far I have argued that the conservatism of those people who became Free Presbyterians can be explained as part of a general understanding of why traditional supernaturalist religion survives better among social groups who are in some way or another remote from modern industrial production and the rational, pluralistic culture which accompanies it. In this sense Free Presbyterians are similar to other isolated groups such as the southern highlanders of the Appalachian mountains in America. But to return to the theme of 'additional' reasons for remaining conservative in religion, Ulster Protestants differ from Appalachian highlanders in that they are parties to a civil conflict in which religious identity plays a major part. Being possessed of a strongly religious world-view, many Ulster Protestants explain a great deal of what happens to them in religious terms. Thus they see the conflict in Ireland as a religious conflict. It does not need the Irish National Liberation Army (an extreme republican group which split from the IRA) to shoot down Protestant 'civilians' at worship in a Darkley, Armagh, gospel hall for Protestants to see republicanism as a threat to their very existence (although every such act helps to reinforce that conclusion). The conservative evangelical Protestants' view of the world is already so strongly informed by religious considerations that any threat is interpreted as confirmation of the truth of their religious beliefs and the falsity and evil of the religion of their Catholic opponents. Their culture and their present circumstances are thus mutually reinforcing.

An additional observation can be made about farmers. In the last chapter more will be said about social identity but it is important to recognize that small farmers as a social group have a particular sense of belonging to the places they farm. City dwellers, especially the highly mobile middle class, have separate homes and jobs, both of which they expect to change a number of times in their careers. Houses can be bought and sold for economic advantage. There is little sentimental attachment to any particular location among those people who change jobs frequently and who have little reason to expect their children either to live in the same house or to inherit their jobs. Small farmers develop a strong sentimental attachment to the land which is both home and source of income. Where, like the children of Israel, farmers suppose that God gave them the land and let them prosper because they served him faithfully, people link their religion, sense of place, and ethnic identity into a strong attachment to the past. Thus one would expect Ulster farmers to be more conservative than city dwellers, not only because they are more sheltered from modernizing forces, but also because their economic and social locations predispose them against 'moving', either literally or ideologically.

The way in which ideology and circumstance interact can be seen in Protestant reactions to the republican murder campaign in the border areas. A strong sense of loyalty to Ulster meant that most Protestant families in rural border areas had some connection with the security forces, in particular the old B Specials and their replacement, the Ulster Defence Regiment. For the last decade, the IRA and INLA have systematically murdered border Protestants and justified this campaign by claiming that connections with the security forces made them 'legitimate' targets. On the many occasions when the victims have been the eldest sons of farming families, Protestant families have sold up and moved. More often than not, the land has been sold to a Catholic family. The Protestants feel themselves being driven out of the land they have farmed for generations, sometimes centuries. For those who stay, and for those who hear such stories and take them to heart, the result is a deepening animosity against republicanism, and for those with strong religious convictions, a deepening of the sense of being involved in a titanic struggle of good and evil.

Before leaving this discussion of the social background of Free Presbyterians, it is worth making a number of qualifying points. Firstly, the account of the relationship between 'distance from modern industrial society' and conservatism in religion should apply to all conservative Protestants and not just those who joined the Free Presbyterian Church. Unfortunately, we do not have any good survey material which would allow us to compare the beliefs of different class and regional groups within denominations. However, my sense is that rural sections of the major denominations are more conservative than their urban counterparts. Although my only evidence for this comes from conversations with ministers and anecdotes about the strength of the Orange Order in particular areas, the case of David Armstrong's problems in Limavady (and the offer, which he did not accept, of a church in Bangor) would seem to support the notion that rural dwellers are generally more conservative than other Protestants. It should be borne in mind that while I have been contrasting Free Presbyterians with other Protestants as if there were a clear cut division between them, it is actually more realistic to think of a continuum, an axis, with conservatism at one end and liberalism at the other and to see Free Presbyterianism as being simply one, albeit the most vociferous, representative of the conservative end of the spectrum.

A second qualification is that none of the above is intended to replace the explanation of support for the Church which is given by Free Presbyterians, which is that they were saved 'by grace through faith alone' and that, having been saved, they concluded that the Free Presbyterian Church offered the most biblical vehicle for the expression of their faith. This account has no implications of the truth or falsity of the Free Presbyterian view, unless they wish to insist that God's saving grace can only appear erratically. Provided they are prepared to recognize that certain social characteristics do make populations more or less 'receptive to the word of God', there need be no conflict between the believers' and the sociologist's accounts.

Finally, it is worth pointing out that what we do not know about why some rather than other people became Free Presbyterians far exceeds what is known. Most of what we believe about the world is accepted from our parents but not all children of conservative evangelical parents remain in the faith. Although we might expect that those who leave home and move to London or some other major cosmopolitan centre are most likely to abandon the 'old paths', some do not and some of those who do, return to the straight and narrow in later life. While more detailed studies of religious conversion can offer useful suggestions as to what factors are involved in decisions to abandon or acquire particular religious world-views, such evidence is not available for Free Presbyterians.[31]

However, such qualifications do not invalidate the general observations. Although we would like to know far more, what is known clearly suggests that certain social groups are more likely than others to have been receptive to Free Presbyterianism. To return to the theme of the first part of this chapter, I have tried to establish first of all that the conservative evangelical beliefs of the Free Presbyterians, even the more exotic beliefs not shared by other evangelical groups, are not innovations taken up because they justify a dislike for Roman Catholics which has its 'real' roots in political competition. Such beliefs were very widely held 150 years ago. They have now all but disappeared from the 'centres' of modern industrial societies and are now only found on the margins. Thus far, Free Presbyterians are similar to marginal populations in most industrial societies.

If there is a connection between political interests and sustained anti-Catholicism, it is not that the former has suddenly or recently produced the latter, but that the latter made the former inevitable. Religious conflict, combined with differences in language, ethnic identity, and economic circumstances created basic divisions in

---

[31] The problem with macro-sociological analyses of religious change, be it recruitment or defection, is that even the most sophisticated combinations of variables run into the explanatory problem that the population bearing the characteristics which, for example, are correlated with joining the Moonies, is considerably larger than that which joins. To go further in trying to understand why the reactions of members of a particular group vary as they do, we must become interested in the micro-sociology of personal relationships and social networks. References to many of the best recent conversion/defection/recruitment studies can be found in the following: James T. Richardson, 'The Active vs. Passive Convert: paradigm conflict in conversion/recruitment research', *Journal for the Scientific Study of Religion*, 24 (2) (1985), pp. 119–236; David A. Snow and Cynthia L. Phillips, 1980, 'The Lofland-Stark Conversion Model: a critical reassessment', *Social Problems*, 27 (4), pp. 430–47; David G. Bromley and Anson D. Shupe, ' "Just a Few Years Seem Like a Lifetime": a role theory approach to participation in religious movements', *Research in Social Movements, Conflicts and Change*, 2 (1979), pp. 159–78.

the people who populated Ireland. Such divisions meant that the formulation of political interests would deepen and reinforce the religious divisions. The point will be pursued in the next chapter but the general principle must be that religious and political interests are mutually reinforcing. Those people with the most conservative religious world-views and the social positions most conducive to conservative unionist politics were thus the people most likely to be attracted to Paisley's Free Presbyterianism.

A subsidiary purpose of this chapter was to show that an examination of the social background of Free Presbyterians tells us more about what sorts of people were drawn to the Free Church than does concentration on 'irrationality' or the 'personalities' of the believers. Although it seems plausible to suppose that different types of people will be attracted to different types of religion, we actually know nothing at all about the personalities of Free Presbyterians and most of the commentators who refer to 'mind sets' and 'mentalities' are telling us more about themselves than about Free Presbyterians. Rather than engage in what, no matter how interesting, is no more than unsupported speculation, I have concentrated on what is known about the social location and background of Free Presbyterians. The things which they have in common seem to be related to modernity. The people most likely to become Free Presbyterians are those least likely to have been thoroughly exposed to the values and assumptions of modern industrial production and the rational pluralistic culture which it brings with it.

9

Religion and Protestant Identity

The Northern Ireland conflict is a religious conflict. Economic and social differences are also crucial, but it was the fact that the competing populations in Ireland adhered and still adhere to competing religious traditions which has given the conflict its enduring and intractable quality. This is the only conclusion that makes sense of Ian Paisley's career. This concluding chapter is concerned with Paisley's general appeal and it will argue that his political success can only be understood if one appreciates the central role which evangelical religion plays in Ulster unionism.[1]

What needs explaining can be simply stated: why have even those 'Protestants' who do not share Paisley's religious beliefs been prepared to support him rather than other unionist political leaders? Were Paisley a liberal Protestant minister, this might be more readily understandable. One could suppose that 'secular' Protestants would be able to ignore his religion and support him simply because he had the correct political postures. However, Paisley is not just someone who earns his living as a clergyman. He is a man driven by religious convictions which many Protestants regard as extreme. Far from playing down his role as cleric, he has often made it abundantly clear that he is in politics because of his religious beliefs. He has never disguised the fact that he is a unionist because he is a religiously conservative Protestant. One recent example should make this clear. In the weeks before the Westminster by-elections which the unionist MPs had organized as a referendum on the Anglo-Irish accord, the Democratic Unionist Party was committed to promoting a united front with other unionist groups. Yet only three days before the crucial poll, more than

[1] I am grateful to Roy Wallis and David Taylor for their permission to draw heavily for the detail and theme of this chapter on Roy Wallis, Steve Bruce, and David Taylor, *No Surrender!: Paisley and the politics of ethnic identity in Northern Ireland* (Belfast: The Queen's University of Belfast, 1986).

fifty Free Presbyterians disrupted an ecumenical service in the Church of Ireland's St Anne's Cathedral in Belfast. The Belgian Cardinal Leon-Joseph Suenens had been invited to take part in a service to celebrate the 'Week of Prayer and Christian Unity'. Three times the Cardinal's words were drowned out and as each group of Free Presbyterians was ejected from the cathedral, they were cheered by a crowd of some 200 supporters outside. The Dean later said: 'These were the sort of bully boy tactics we have come to associate with Paisley. I think Paisley will lose hundreds of votes over this.'[2]

That the demonstration had Paisley's blessing is clear from the fact that William Beattie and Paisley's daughter Rhonda were involved. The next day he described himself as being pleased with the protest. Perhaps it did lose the unionist alliance some votes as more moderate unionists refused to vote for the three DUP candidates; perhaps not. It does not matter. The important point is that, even though it might have caused ill-feeling among Church of Ireland unionists, Paisley did not hesitate to make the protest. Protesting against Rome and ecumenism was more important than unionist unity. For Paisley religion comes before politics.

How then has he managed to win the political support of a constituency which at almost a quarter of a million voters is considerably larger than the evangelical milieu?

Many outsiders explain Paisley's popularity by seeing it as proof of the basic irrationality of Irish politics. The notion of 'tribalism' is sometimes invoked to suggest a political culture which has failed to develop out of an age of clan warfare and blood feuds. This may be good poetry but it is no basis for sensible analysis. Ulster is not the highlands of Scotland in the eighteenth century; it is a province of a major industrial democracy and it has a considerable—albeit now slightly decayed—industrial base, excellent schools, and a considerable proportion of its population have participated in higher education.

A slightly more sophisticated version of this approach argues that Ulster is the home of two 'nations'.[3] There is some merit in this, but it misses an important lack of symmetry between Cath-

[2] *Newsletter* (22 Jan. 1986).

[3] For a discussion and critique of the two nations thesis, see J. H. Whyte, 'Interpretations of the Northern Ireland Problem: an appraisal', *Economic and Social Review*, 9 (4) (1978), pp. 257–82.

olics and Protestants. There is no doubt that most Catholics in Ulster see themselves as part of an Irish nation. It was their failure to be located in the nation-state created in the South which explains why very many Catholics refused to give their whole-hearted support to the Northern Ireland state. But it is not clear that Ulster Protestants constitute a nation. In the first place, they see themselves as British. 'British rights for British citizens' was a slogan carried on banners by the young loyalists on their New Year 1986 march from Londonderry to Belfast to protest against the Anglo-Irish accord. But the loyalty to Britain has always been conditional. George Graham, a DUP Assemblyman, expressed this clearly when he said:

My loyalty is to the British Throne being Protestant. I have no loyalty to any Westminster government. I have no loyalty to a government which prorogued a democratically elected government, destroyed our security forces and left us prey to the IRA. Nor have I loyalty to a British government going over the heads of our people, conniving and double-dealing behind our backs with a foreign government.[4]

When Ulster Protestants do want to be British, the Britain they want to be part of seems to be a country which ceased to exist a century ago. The present-day British mainland offends Ulster Protestants' religious and ethical sensibilities. On moral issues such as the legalization of abortion and homosexuality, Ulster's Protestant leaders were firmly opposed to Westminster policy. In deference to Ulster conservatism, the British government refrained from applying the liberalizing legislation, which had been passed by Westminster, to Northern Ireland. Consenting adult male homosexuality was only legalized in Ulster when the European Court of Human Rights ruled that such an exemption was unacceptable.

The lack of religiosity in mainland Britain also offends. A woman who had been a councillor in Bangor and a staunch Paisley supporter from the early 1960s explained what it was that she found admirable about Ulster when she moved here (from England) in the 1940s. She mentioned 'the keeping of the sabbath' as one of the things which had 'made Ulster such a great wee country' and

---

[4] *Protestant Telegraph* (6 Feb. 1976). There is a parallel religio-political position which justifies limited commitment to the state. Paisley argues for the 'covenanting' view of what is involved in rendering unto Caesar. He believes that one only has a binding obligation to support the state so long as the state acts in a godly manner.

she used the term 'republican Sunday' to describe what was threatening to become the norm in Ulster. If, in the 1940s, she was struck by the difference between the Lord's day in England and Ulster, she could hardly feel at home in the England of the 1980s where only thirteen per cent of the population claim any kind of church membership.[5]

It is not only on moral and religious matters that Ulster Protestants seem closer to Victorian Britons than to their twentieth-century descendants. Anyone who reads quantities of Orange and loyalist publications cannot help but be struck by the datedness of the image of Britain there presented. Ulster loyalists want to be part of that British Empire whose world domination was displayed in school wall-maps with huge areas of red. They sing more than one verse of the national anthem and mean it. They are the most fervent admirers of the British monarchy. Their Britain is the one which accepted the Ulster Volunteers into the First World War British Army, whose King said 'Your prompt patriotic answer to the nation's call to arms will never be forgotten',[6] and which solemnly appreciated the sacrifice of most of the Ulster Division in the Battle of the Somme. Ulster Protestants are British in the way in which Kipling was British. A more telling comparison: they are British in the way in which the Anglo-Indians and other marginal groups are British. Their zeal in claiming to be British is both a mark of the uncertainty which they feel about their identity and a response to the obvious unwillingness of many British people to accord them that identity.

Ulster loyalist views of Britain are anachronistic in that they refer to something which has all but disappeared. They are also selective in their focus. George Graham's separation of the British Crown from the British government is important because it allows him to retain a commitment to being British while every action of the Westminster government seems to threaten his position. Ulster Protestants quite rightly suspect British politicians of all parties of being willing to undermine Protestant self-determination in return for better relations with the government of the Irish Republic. If they previously had any doubts on this score, any number of

[5] Peter Brierley, *UK Christian Handbook* (London: MARC Europe/Evangelical Alliance/Bible Society, 1984), pp. 107–9.

[6] Quoted in Hugh Radcliffe, 'The Faithful and the Brave', in H. Radcliffe and M. Smyth (eds.), *The Twelfth: in God we trust* (Belfast: Grand Orange Lodge of Belfast, 1971).

actions since the introduction of direct rule in 1972 should have convinced them. Perhaps the most galling was Harold Wilson's dismissive description of Ulster people as 'spongers' on British democracy in his televised speech during the 1974 UWC strike.[7] The Labour and Liberal parties are ideologically committed to a united Ireland and, although there are a few Conservative MPs who remember that they are members of the 'Conservative and Unionist' Party, Tory governments have hardly been any more sympathetic to the Ulster unionist cause.

The logical conclusion of a commitment to being British would have been for Ulster Protestants to react to the proroguing of Stormont by advocating complete integration with the British mainland. Yet this has hardly been a popular position. For a short time in the early 1970s, Paisley supported it, but when it became clear that the British government would not welcome closer integration, and that the return of some sort of devolved government was likely, Paisley moved back to a more orthodox unionist position: provincial self-determination within Britain. Nowadays, apart from a few socialists, only Enoch Powell and a small section of the Official Unionist Party openly advocate integration.

Although few unionists have been prepared to speculate about the possibility in public, it is clear from private reactions to the recent Anglo-Irish accord that, as a last alternative, they would prefer independence to incorporation in a united Ireland. While Ulster Protestants regard themselves as 'British', this identity is very firmly subordinated to their identity as Ulster Protestants. To recap, the problem with the 'two nations' view of the Northern Ireland conflict is that it is difficult to see Ulster Protestants as a 'nation'.

An alternative to the 'two nations' theory, favoured by some Marxist commentators, explains the conflict by pointing to economic advantage. In one formulation, loyalists' unwillingness to join a united Ireland is seen as a result of their desire to maintain economic advantages over Catholics. Alternatively, it can be explained as a consequence of ruling-class manipulation. Either working-class Protestants have real advantages over Catholics or

[7] Robert Fisk, *The Point of No Return: the strike which broke the British in Ulster* (London: Andre Deutsch, 1975), pp. 196–203.

they have been duped into thinking they enjoy such advantages.[8] No one would deny that the uneven economic development of Ireland has enhanced a sense of difference between North and South. And given the considerable amount of evidence, no one would deny that the operation of the Northern Ireland state during its fifty years of existence involved considerable discrimination in those areas—housing, local employment, education, welfare spending, and policing—which it controlled. We can sensibly assume that such discrimination increased Protestant commitment to the state. It also reinforced the alienation of Catholics who had begun by being reluctant to pledge themselves to active participation in the institutions of the North. The economic and political advantages enjoyed by the Protestant working class *were* an element in their refusal to form 'class alliances' with working-class Catholics. But it is hard to see this as an adequate explanation for the continuation of sectarian conflict, especially in recent years when the relative advantages of being a Protestant have diminished. Direct rule, as even its critics concede, has led to the introduction of universalistic criteria in such matters as housing allocation, welfare benefit distribution, and Civil Service employment.[9] Furthermore, the economic recession has forced more

[8] Both versions of the Marxist account are deployed in Michael Farrell, *Northern Ireland; the Orange state* (London: Pluto Press, 1980). A good critique of the Marxist approach can be found in John Hickey, *Religion and the Northern Ireland Problem* (Dublin: Gill and Macmillan, 1984), pp. 49–56.

[9] Of course, the formal introduction of universalistic criteria does not guarantee the end of discrimination or disadvantage. The power of the state to prevent people 'favouring their own' is clearly limited in its own organizations and all but non-existent in private organizations. Furthermore, universalistic criteria may still favour Protestants over Catholics. If Protestants do better at school, hiring strictly by the possession of appropriate credentials, will have the effect of maintaining Protestant advantage, even though it is not what we normally think of as discrimination. However, the only alternative is 'affirmative action', which has often proved unsuccessful in America and which involves the massive expansion of the powers of the state. Ironically, it is often the same people who criticize the expansion of state control and the lack of state will to remove disadvantage. They fail to see that, unless it is supported by a powerful state apparatus, affirmative action is self-defeating. For example, a company which resents having to promote members of ethnic minorities in proportion to their presence in the company, rather than according to the company's judgement of their abilities, will simply reduce the number of ethnic minority people hired in the first place. Then the state has to step up its control and insist on quota hiring. Marxist analysts tend to see no irony here because they assume that the initial discrimination was a consequence of élite or state manipulation. As it was artificially produced, the state intervention required to remove it is taken to be minimal. If, on the other hand, one assumes that Protestants and Catholics discriminate in favour of their own people because they

members of both communities into dependence on welfare. This, of course, is not to argue that both populations share an 'equality of misery', but it is the case that there is an increasing equalization of misery.[10]

But there is another and more important objection to an economic advantage explanation for sectarian division. What guides people's actions is not the situation in which they find themselves but their *perception* of their circumstances. It is considerably easier to show that the objective position of Protestants *vis-à-vis* Catholics was one of advantage than it is to show that Protestants appreciated this and incorporated it into their political attitudes. Although some Protestants felt that they were better off than Catholics (a situation which they justified in terms of rewards for loyalty to the state), many did not believe themselves to be privileged. Take the matter of housing. We can now see that much of the housing development of the 1960s (especially of the density of such schemes as the Divis flats) replaced old slums by new, and often far worse, slums. But at the time, many working-class Protestants saw new housing in West Belfast as an undeserved bonus given to Catholics when Protestant housing was every bit as bad.

It is also the case that, in many matters of public policy, Protestants felt themselves to be the disadvantaged party. Although this may at first sight suggest that Ulster Protestants had only the most tenuous grasp of reality, there is an important theoretical point here which is worth elaborating. Catholics created their own educational and welfare institutions because the church insisted on

want to, then state action, beyond the formal introduction of universalistic criteria, will have to be supported by massive coercion; that is, by the very expansion of the authoritarian state which Marxists find so unpleasant. For an example of the Marxist argument, see Bill Rolston, 'Reformism and Sectarianism; the state after civil rights', Ch. 9 in John Darby (ed.), *Northern Ireland: the background to the conflict* (Belfast: Appletree Press, 1983).

[10] The extent to which Protestants continue to enjoy advantages over Catholics and the direction of recent trends are matters of considerable disagreement. Bob Rowthorn has recently argued (*Fortnight* (16 Dec. 1985), pp. 4–5) that, relative to the position of Protestants, Catholic unemployment is getting worse rather than better. However, this case is built on rather poor statistical analysis. See Roy Wallis and Richard Bland, forthcoming, 'What is the Truth about Religion and Changing Patterns of Unemployment in Northern Ireland?: a research note', *British Journal of Sociology*. For general information on equal opportunity, see the various chapters of R. J. Cormack and R. D. Osborne (eds.), *Religion, Education and Employment: aspects of equal opportunity in Northern Ireland* (Belfast: Appletree Press, 1983) and Cormack and Osborne, 'Inequality of Misery', *New Society* (22 Nov. 1985), pp. 328–9.

it and because they feared that, as a minority, they would be excluded from the institutions of the state. The creation of two parallel systems permitted Protestants to feel that they too were the victims of discrimination. An example will illustrate the point. As an institution maintained by private donations, the Catholic Mater Hospital felt free to display Catholic symbols and to encourage Catholic religious practices in its wards. Although there is no evidence that the Mater ever turned away Protestant patients or treated them any less well than Catholics, it remained a *Catholic* hospital. In contrast, the Royal Victoria and City hospitals were state-funded and state-run institutions and as such were obliged to serve the whole population. Thus they had to appear to be religiously neutral and, by the 1960s, a more strict notion of neutrality was being operated. In a trivial but symbolically important case, a gospel group was barred from the Royal Victoria Hospital. Paisley's letter to the *Belfast Telegraph* clearly articulates Protestant resentment:

The time has surely come when a stand must be taken for the rights of the Protestant majority of our city.

For well over 30 years the Sunshine Singers have been doing the valuable work of bringing the Gospel to the patients of the Royal Victoria Hospital. Now the wishes of the Protestant majority are to be sacrificed at the whim of certain Roman Catholic patients and medical staff, and the Sunshine Singers are to be barred from the wards.

That it is the work of the Roman Catholic community cannot be gainsaid.

The Mater hospital is forever crying out for Government help. Are the Management prepared to forgo their religious ceremonies in the wards because of their few Protestant patients of which they are always boasting? I think not.

The Royal Victoria Hospital was built by Protestant money, but Protestant rights are sacrificed on the altar of appeasement.[11]

Had there been a third party to the conflict—a substantial liberal atheistic population—one could have had a balanced system consisting of a neutral and secular state and two voluntary sectors:

Protestant and Catholic.[12] Instead one had a Catholic voluntary

[11] *Revivalist* (Mar. 1963), p. 9.

[12] This is the case in Holland, which is often and mistakenly presented as a model for Northern Ireland. For a comparative analysis of conservative Protestant politics, see Roy Wallis and Steve Bruce, *Sociological Theory, Religion and Collective Action* (Belfast: The Queen's University of Belfast, 1986), Ch. 9.

sector and a state sector which was neither convincingly neutral nor sufficiently Protestant to prevent many Protestants feeling that the Catholics were being given two bites of the cherry while they were being offered less than one. At the same time, the Catholics drew no satisfaction from this, seeing their own position as one of paying for the public sector through their taxes while also financially supporting their own voluntary institutions.

In understanding reactions, it is not the real extent of discrimination nor who was favoured by particular examples of it, but rather shared perceptions, which are important, and, far from feeling privileged, many Protestants felt that they were being given neither the advantages they deserved nor even fair play.

The other Marxist notion—that sectarianism was maintained by ruling-class manipulation—also has fundamental flaws, the most obvious being that the religious divisions between the two populations could only have been manipulated if they existed in the first place. The Belfast bourgeoisie did not create the Reformation, the Counter-Reformation, or the Inquisition. They did not even invent Victorian evangelicalism. By 'playing the Orange card', the ruling classes may have at times taken advantage of existing religious differences to heighten religious antagonisms but they did not invent them. Furthermore, such antagonisms could be heightened, quite independently of the actions of the upper classes, by other things such as periodic escalations of nationalist or republican violence. One simply cannot, as some Marxist analysts wish, make the religious differences go away by showing that they paralleled other divisions.[13] As Conor Cruise O'Brien somewhere put it, if religion in Northern Ireland is a red herring, it is a herring the size of a whale.

Ethnic Conflict

The first step towards understanding the political behaviour of the Protestants of Northern Ireland is to see them as an 'ethnic

[13] Paul Bew, Peter Gibbon, and Henry Patterson, *The State in Northern Ireland, 1921-72* (Manchester: Manchester University Press, 1979), refers in its final chapter to the need to recognize that the purpose of the capitalist state is to hinder the unity of the dominated classes, and to *dissolve* 'the primacy of the problem of Protestants and Catholics as generic subjects (p. 212). Which, being translated, means that the conflict is not really about religion and ethnic identity but about class. This is something Marxists know, because their theory tells them so.

group'.[14] They see themselves as the outcome of shared historical experiences and as the embodiment of a culture of a distinctive kind, with its shared traditions, values, beliefs, life-style, and symbols. They expect the bearers of this culture to be granted certain rights and privileges. In particular, they feel that they have a right to see their values and cultural symbols displayed in the operations of the state; the Union Jack flying on government buildings and 'On Her Majesty's Service' printed on official envelopes, for example. As an aside, it is worth adding that they see their values as beneficial, even for those who do not share their religion. While they would deny fundamental rights to 'rebels', they have always argued for equality of opportunity irrespective of religion. That the reality often fell far short of this does not alter the fact that Protestants saw the dominance of their culture as having universal social benefits.

The conflict in Northern Ireland involves a nation on the one hand and an ethnic group on the other. That the loyalists form an ethnic group and not a nation has important consequences. Let us take first the Catholic situation. For Northern Catholics, national identity has become so secure and taken for granted that it can be separated from its religious base. Although for a long time the Catholic Church was almost the sole carrier of Irish identity, the rise of the home rule movement in the last century and the creation of the Free State (later, the Republic) has given Irish nationalism such a strong base that it can 'dispense' with Catholicism. This can clearly be seen in those parts of the republican movement which have gone so far as to adopt positions actively hostile to the Church and its hierarchy. The position of loyalists is quite different.

Although overt commitment to religion (measured, for example, in church attendance rates) may be weaker among Protestants than Catholics, loyalism depends on its religious base. As will be argued, beyond evangelical Protestantism, no secure identity is available.

I have already suggested that an identity as 'British' is fundamentally threatened by British actions and attitudes. Ulster Protestants are well aware that the British public is largely indifferent to their efforts to preserve themselves and entirely un-

---

[14] Weber speaks of 'ethnic honour': the sense 'of the excellence of one's own customs and the inferiority of alien ones'. Ethnic honour is a form of status honour which is open to all members 'of the subjectively believed community of descent'. Max Weber, *Economy and Society* (New York: Bedminster Press, 1968).

comprehending of their history, attitudes, and culture. What alternatives are available? The paramilitary UDA has recently pursued another line which combines elements of socialism with a strategy for independence. As if aware of the need to ground an identity in a shared history, the UDA has promoted the attempts of some local historians to argue that the Ulster Protestants are the true heirs to ancient Ulster, having left Ireland to settle Scotland and later returned.[15] By sponsoring such publications, the UDA hopes to convince its potential supporters and foreign backers that Ulster Protestants are not 'Johnny-come-lately' colonizers but the original occupants of the north-east of Ireland.

It is impossible to gauge the impact of this historical reconstruction. However, we can take the election performances of UDA candidates as an index of the popularity of the UDA's political platform and we must conclude that Ulster Protestants have not been impressed. To give a recent example, in 1982, John McMichael, the deputy leader of the UDA, stood in the South Belfast by-election. He won 1.3 per cent of the vote. There are a number of subsidiary reasons for the failure of the paramilitaries to translate the grass-roots support they enjoyed in the early 1970s into a political platform and these have already been discussed in chapter 4. The political interventions were *ad hoc* affairs which were never supported by all sections of the paramilitaries at the same time. They were poorly led by people who performed badly as spokesmen. The candidates were also hampered by their close associations with unsavoury acts of violence. But behind all of these problems lies the basic unpopularity of socialism. In the first place, socialism is unpopular with religious Protestants because it is atheistic. But it is also unpopular with 'secular' Protestants. Socialist rhetoric plays a major part in the republican movement and any shift to the left among the Protestant paramilitaries reduces what separates loyalists from their Catholic counterparts. The more the UDA commits itself to socialism, the more it undermines precisely what is distinctive about Ulster Protestants. The less they differ from Catholics, the fewer reasons they have for resisting a united Ireland. Furthermore, socialism is tainted by the fact that the vast majority of socialists outside Ulster generally favour the republican cause.

[15] Ian Adamson, *The Identity of Ulster; the land, the language and the people* (Belfast: the author, 1982).

Ulster Protestant identity has also been threatened by the other major move away from evangelical Protestantism: the liberal unionism of Captain Terence O'Neill. In his period as Prime Minister, O'Neill formed tentative links with the Dublin government and engaged in such conciliatory gestures as the opening of a Roman Catholic school. Irrespective of the extent to which O'Neillism represented a genuine departure from previous unionist positions, O'Neill and his close supporters saw themselves as breaking with politics based on intransigence and a 'zero-sum' game. O'Neill sought to move Ulster towards the political culture of other western European countries: a culture based on democratic and rationalistic principles in which the management of the economy would take precedence over sectarian identity.

For O'Neill and his supporters, nothing much would have been lost had he succeeded in transforming Northern Ireland. The O'Neillites were cosmopolitan, drawing their values more from London and international circles than from provincial Ulster. Very firmly middle-class, they could see the advantages in abandoning traditional discriminatory practices: greater international respectability and a greater ability to attract multinational capital. When Brian Faulkner saw his political career ended and accepted a peerage, he remained in Northern Ireland. It hardly seems accidental that, on his elevation to the House of Lords, O'Neill moved to England. Recently, a Stormont MP who resigned his seat at the same time as O'Neill, Richard Ferguson QC, moved to London to practise at the English Bar. Largely Anglicized, their local identity thoroughly eroded, the supporters of O'Neill could happily embrace liberal unionism because they had nothing to lose. They overlooked those for whom their local identity was virtually all they had. In the long run, O'Neillism threatened to remove those parts of the Protestant identity which justified Ulster's refusal to become part of a united Ireland. In the short run, it meant abandoning claims to cultural superiority and related status privileges.

As has already been stressed, such privileges undoubtedly included some material advantages but what was most important was the sense of inherent superiority; the symbolic benefits of *seeing themselves as better*, even if they were little better off. And such benefits were obviously most important to the poorest Protestants: those who were little better off than their Catholic counterparts.

This is in contrast to what one would expect from the Marxist 'economic advantage' thesis. In that model, the poorest Protestants should have the weakest attachment to unionism because they gained least under it. Both O'Neillite cosmopolitanism and UDA socialism threatened the only claim Protestants had to a distinctive identity and thus to both cultural dominance in their own territory and a future apart from a united Ireland. Although both political philosophies could be defended as making small compromises in order to save Northern Ireland from a worse fate, the 'small' compromises, as the Paisleyites recognized, would be fatal to the organism because they undermined its *raison d'être*.

A similar analysis could be offered for participation in the ecumenical movement. It is no coincidence that O'Neillism and ecumenism drew support from the same social groups. The people who could most readily participate in the ecumenical movement were those whose reference group was the world Christian community. They were religious cosmopolites who took their values from Lausanne, Geneva, and New York, rather than from the streets of Belfast and the 'dreary spires of Fermanagh and Tyrone'. Although they defended their 'modernizing' of Protestantism as essential for the continued survival of any Christianity in a hostile secular environment, they were proposing fundamental changes in the traditional faith. Such changes may have seemed necessary to the university-educated, mobile, middle classes who wished to preserve something of their Protestantism while accommodating to the pluralistic culture in which they moved. Not only were such changes unnecessary for those social groups described in detail in the previous chapter but they would have removed the satisfaction that rural evangelical Protestants derived from their certainty of possessing the right religion: the faith which guaranteed salvation. In return for what?

Although alternative identities were presented to Ulster Protestants, it was unlikely that they would have broad appeal. Socialism, although it sometimes attracted support as a means of criticizing the indifference of unionist élites to the lot of working-class Protestants, has never sunk deep roots for the loyalist community, even among those skilled working-class trade unionists who worked in the Belfast engineering industries. At its most popular, the Northern Ireland Labour Party won only four seats at Stormont. The appeal of the cosmopolitan identity of the liberal and ecumenical middle classes was limited to an educated section of the bourgeoisie with extensive contacts outside the province, and two things limited the size of this population. In the first place, the recession with its limiting influence on social and geographical mobility has ensured that this section is not expanding. In the second place, it is a self-limiting population because it exports its members. It is not just public figures such as Terence O'Neill, Richard Ferguson, and David Armstrong who have moved to England. Many of the children of the educated middle classes use their good A level performances as means of entry to English or Scottish universities.[16] They do not return after graduation. Their very cosmopolitanism limits their impact in the province because they react to their failure to stamp their values on the local political and social culture by migrating to the 'centre' of their value system: mainland Britain.

The Rise of Paisley

In times of relative security, Ulster Protestants have been willing to experiment with deviations from their historical identity, either in the direction of socialism or in a liberal unionist direction. Any major challenge to their position produces a return to the only identity that makes sense of their history and that justifies their separation from the South: evangelical Protestantism.

Every major political change since 1963 has undermined the position of Ulster Protestants and increased their fear that future developments will mean their submersion in a Catholic united Ireland. They saw first O'Neill and then the Westminster government trying to court Catholic and nationalist support by removing those things which most offended them (the B Specials, for example) and which were, therefore, most precious to Protestants.

Ian Paisley's political success follows from this background. He represents the core of unionism. Even before O'Neill came to power, Paisley was constantly warning against élite untrustworthiness. He has remained consistently opposed to the

---

[16] According to Osborne, Cormack, Reid, and Williamson (in Cormack and Osborne, 1983, op. cit., n. 10 above), 'In the early 1960's just over 80 per cent of students remained in Northern Ireland, while during the 1970's this gradually declined to around 65 per cent at the end of the decade', (p. 193). Of a sample of the Protestants who went to study on the British mainland, 67.1% had not returned to Northern Ireland seven years later.

adoption of the language and style of British mainland politics and has continually presented his analyses and aspirations in the rhetoric of evangelicalism.

Clearly not all of Paisley's political supporters are evangelical Protestants but a large proportion of those who might usefully be called 'secular' Protestants are not far removed from an evangelical religious commitment. The parents of many of them will have been 'Bible-believing' Christians and many will have been raised in churches and Sunday schools. Many of the working-class urban Protestant men who do not attend church still display a considerable knowledge of religious ideology and retain enough of a commitment to a Protestant faith to encourage their wives and children to attend church. Thus, while Paisley addresses them in a language which they no longer speak themselves, he talks in terms which many have heard before, both often enough, and in such circumstances, as to instil a strong respect. The Grand Master of the Orange Order, the Revd Martin Smyth MP, may have been overstating the case when he once said that Shankill Road Protestants were Bible-lovers even if they were not Bible-readers, but he was not far from the mark.

This is the explanation for the point I made when analysing the proportion of DUP candidates who were Free Presbyterians or members of other small evangelical denominations. I do not believe that the party leadership discriminates in favour of co-religionists. If it does not, then the candidates must reflect the wishes of the members. Anyway, if it were the case that the leaders of the DUP foist 'saved' Christians on a membership who would rather select people more representative of DUP voters, surely the disillusioned members would vote with their feet? Given that the Party's sabbatarian and temperance platforms have proved far less of a liability than one might expect, it is reasonable to suppose that many of the non-evangelicals who support the DUP find something appealing about evangelicalism. Why else would DUP candidates list their church activities on their election literature? Some commentators find this surprising but we can draw an analogy with the British Conservative Party. Its elected representatives do not share the same characteristics as either the rank-and-file members or the voters. They are disproportionately members of the aristocracy, the business élites, or the professions. People vote for them, not because they are like the voters, but because they are what the voters like. They are 'virtuosi': members of an élite which carries the values which the mass of their supporters admire, even if they cannot live out those values themselves. Although ordinary DUP members or voters are not evangelical Protestants, they recognize that evangelicalism is at the heart of what it means to be a Protestant. Although the people who actually live out that faith may occasionally be infuriating in their self-righteousness, and although they may sometimes appear as 'spoil-sports', they are still to be admired and supported.

The analogy with the British Conservative Party allows us to clear up one remaining objection to this explanation. It could be argued that the aristocrats and business millionaires of the Tory Party are supported, not because many voters admire them and their values, but because they have the *power* to mislead and, as a final resort, coerce the people into supporting them. It is possible to reject this line of reasoning with Conor Cruise O'Brien's whale. Of course, the ruling class has enormous power to influence how people think. However, if they are successful in persuading people to see the world through ideas and beliefs which serve the interests of the ruling class, then it still makes sense to talk in terms of ordinary people 'wishing' to see such values advanced. It is not the social scientist's job to tell people what they ought to believe. Even if we can clearly identify the source of particular beliefs, and show that they promote the interests of a minority, this does not alter the social reality that ordinary people actually accept such beliefs.

In the case of evangelicalism in Ulster unionism, the idea that ordinary loyalists have been coerced or hoodwinked by powerful élites into a 'false consciousness' which causes them to misunderstand their own best interests is ridiculous. Ordinary loyalists did not have to vote for Paisley's evangelical Protestant brand of unionism; others have always been on offer. Within the DUP, branches did not have to select evangelicals; other candidates were available. Members of the Orange Order did not have to maintain a rhetorical commitment to religious symbolism; the Bible could have been left behind on the Orange Hall table. That Paisley's brand of unionism has proved popular with such a large section of the Ulster Protestant population defies any explanation other than the obvious one: evangelicalism provides the core beliefs, values, and symbols of what it means to be a Protestant. Unionism is about avoiding becoming a subordinate minority in a Catholic state.

Avoiding becoming a Catholic means remaining a Protestant. In times of stability and prosperity, the religious basis of the Protestant identity can be forgotten. Any serious challenge to the Protestant identity presents only two genuinely viable alternatives: abandonment of, or recommitment to, traditional Protestantism. I have already suggested the limits on the appeal of the first response. Those who choose the other road, even if their recommitment does not extend to religious conversion, will be attracted to a form of unionism which makes clear its evangelical foundations.

The Zero-Sum Game

A front-page headline in a 1957 *Revivalist* said: 'Concession to Roman Catholicism spells curtailment to Protestantism.' This single sentence neatly encapsulates conservative Protestant views of the relationship between Catholics and Protestants in Ireland. Ulster Protestants do not see their future as a choice between remaining citizens of the Ulster province of Britain or becoming equal participants with Roman Catholics in a secular democratic Republic of Ireland. They see the future as a choice between the preservation of Ulster and their subordination in a Roman Catholic theocracy. That was the choice in 1912, and it is the choice today. It is this view of the world which Ian Paisley absorbed in Ballymena in the 1930s and which he has vigorously promoted since beginning his career in Belfast in 1946. For a long period he was attended to by only a small handful of evangelicals who respected his preaching powers, and a coterie of working-class unionist mavericks. He is now attended to by a very large proportion of the Protestant population of Northern Ireland.

Paisley's rise can be seen in one of two contrasting ways. His own view is that the actions of, first, the civil rights marchers, and later the IRA, proved that his analysis of the Protestant position in Ireland was correct. Liberals had believed that minor reforms to the state would increase Catholic commitment. Paisley argued that the rebels would never be content with anything less than a united Ireland. When Paisley's prophecies were apparently confirmed by the IRA's campaign of violence, and then by the electoral successes of Sinn Fein, many Protestants became convinced that 'the Big Man' was right all along.

The critics of Paisley argue that he himself created the present position in which anything which pleases Catholics must be seen as a loss to Protestants, and vice versa. They believe that there was a point when Catholic aspirations could have been met within the framework of Northern Ireland had the Protestants been willing to extend equal rights to Catholics and not insisted on continuing their discriminatory practices.

To see the Ulster civil rights movement as parallel to the black civil rights campaigns in America misses the crucial difference between Ulster and America. American blacks were always assimilationist because they had nowhere else to go. There was never a time when any more than a handful of eccentrics advocated the establishment of a separate black nation-state. The issue in America was, and still is, the relationship between two populations *within* a nation-state. Concessions to blacks, while they did amount to debits from poor whites, were not major threats to the continued existence of the state. Some of the concessions—those relating specifically to economic status—need have involved no loss at all to whites if they were granted in a buoyant economy. Everybody could get happy at the same time.

The Ulster situation has always been quite different. Perhaps some parts of the civil rights movement were genuinely, rather than tactically, assimilationist. Presumably the small number of liberal unionists who became involved believed that to be the case. However, the speed with which many of its leaders shifted to more traditional nationalist and republican positions suggests that a large part of the movement was always ultimately interested in dismantling Northern Ireland. As Arthur makes clear, People's Democracy drew considerable support from traditional republicans.[17] In addition, members of that strand of the IRA which became the 'Official' IRA and, later, the Workers Party were involved in the early days of the civil rights campaign.[18] This does not rule out the posibility that some civil rights activists began as assimilationists and then abandoned their commitment to an Ulster solution when they saw the Unionist government alternating reformism with repression. But the tentative and tenuous nature of their commitment to an Ulster solution should not be overlooked

[17] Paul Arthur, *The People's Democracy, 1968–73* (Belfast: Blackstaff Press, 1974), p. 112.

[18] Sunday Times Insight Team, *Ulster* (Harmondsworth, Middx.: Penguin, 1972), p. 47.

in the rush to lay the blame for Ulster's present problems on Ian Paisley.

Paisley led Protestant opposition to the civil rights movement in the sense that he galvanized loyalist opposition. He did not create that opposition. It would be a wild exaggeration of his power to suppose that he turned an assimilationist movement into a separatist one.

There has always been a liberal wing of unionism which blames Paisley for the proroguing of Stormont and which supposes that his real ambition throughout has been to lead an independent Ulster. My response to this view is the same as my response to the claim that Paisley and his Ulster Protestant Volunteers prevented the peaceful evolution of Northern Ireland into a genuine democracy. Although Paisley's leadership certainly played a part in exposing the contradictions in liberal unionism, he did not bring down Stormont. Stormont collapsed because successive Stormont and Westminster governments have mistakenly assumed that a moderate 'centre' could be created in Northern Ireland.

The correct judgement must be that Paisley has risen to political prominence because he has steadfastly expressed most clearly the core of unionist ideology and the heart of what it means to be a Protestant.

In religion, he challenged the liberal and ecumenical tendencies in the major denominations and attracted the support of many of those Protestants who wished to maintain their traditional conservative religion. However, his success in this should not be exaggerated. He failed to win over many others who accepted a great deal of his criticisms of the ecumenical movement but who, for a variety of reasons (such as their dislike for his domineering style or his too-public merging of religion and politics), preferred to remain within their denominations and fight against the 'Romeward' trend there. But many even among those who rejected his personal leadership none the less accepted his analysis and acted on it. But again, Paisley did not create conservative evangelicalism, just as he did not invent the identification of Roman Catholicism with the 'Antichrist' and 'Mystery, Babylon the Great'. All he did was to defend such beliefs vocally in a climate in which they were becoming less and less popular. That he could be so publicly identified with an unpopular religious philosophy and still win the political support of half of Ulster's unionist voters brings me back to ethnic identity.

The Scots Presbyterians settled in the north-east of Ireland at a time when most people's world-views were heavily influenced by religious beliefs. Hence religious affiliation became a central part of ethnic identity. Social, economic, and political competition ensured that the identities of native Irish, Anglo-Irish, and Scots Irish would only be eroded to the extent that the last two groups gradually merged, leaving a simple division between the Irish and the tenuously British: Catholic and Protestant. Partition, by creating a 'Green' state and an 'Orange' state, reinforced this division. Although elements of the Catholic and Protestant populations in Northern Ireland have abandoned some or all of their ethnic identities, the recent 'Troubles' have pushed the bulk of both populations back into their traditional positions. Ian Paisley has achieved his prominence by offering the most explicit and articulate representation of evangelical Protestant unionism.

What has correctly been understood by both republicans and loyalists, but overlooked by analysts and successive Westminster governments, is that there is no Northern Ireland 'problem'. The word 'problem' suggests that there is a 'solution': some outcome which will please almost everybody more than it displeases almost everybody. Conflict is a more accurate term for Protestant/Catholic relationships in Northern Ireland. Conflicts have outcomes, not solutions. Somebody wins and somebody loses.

Nationalists think that the Protestants will lose. Most analysts think that the Protestants will lose. A respected Oxford constitutional lawyer is so convinced that the Protestants will lose that she has argued that they should accept their fate and strike the best bargain while bargains can still be struck.[19] Sometimes it even seems as if the Protestants think that they will lose. In these perilous times, as these excerpts from a recent sermon show, Paisley returns to the faith of the fathers.[20]

. . . I was reading . . . the seventh chapter of the prophecy of Micah. In this chapter I realised that there was a description here of the sad and terrible plight into which our land has fallen. In verse two we read 'The

[19] Clare Palley, 'When an Iron Hand can Beckon a Federal Union', *Guardian* (20 Jan. 1986).

[20] 'A Prime Text for the Prime Minister', preached in Martyrs Memorial, evening service (15 Dec. 1985).

good man is perished out of the earth, and there is none upright among men. They all lie in wait for blood'. . . . As we read on we are told that they do evil with both hands earnestly. There is a dedication today in the doing of evil. There is a revival of evil. There is a resurgence, a renaissance of evil, and it seems that the whole world has become polluted with a confrontation against the truth, righteousness and godliness of God's law, of God's standards and of God's commandments. . . .

Then this old prophet asks 'What will I do?'. All the props on which I have leaned, the foundations on which I ought to rely, the confidences I ought to have, the supports on which I ought to rest, they are all swept away. On whom will I rely? Where shall I find a sanctuary, a refuge for my soul? He turns and draws his conclusion in verse 7. 'Therefore will I look unto the Lord'. He lifts up his eyes away from the turmoil, away from the deceit, away from the lying, away from all the programme of confusion, and he lifts up unto the Lord.

That is what we need to do in this day. If ever there was a day that God's people needed to look up and put their confidence in the Lord, it is now.

Paisley goes on to consider the lesson of the Children of Israel in Egypt. A mighty power oppressed the Lord's people but he delivered them from out of bondage. The mighty Pharaoh chased after them with his army. Moses asked for deliverance and the God of Heaven parted the waves. The Children of Israel passed to the other side. The chariots of Egypt were dashed.

In the tenth verse of the chapter—'Then she that is mine enemy shall see it, and shame shall cover her which said unto me, Where is the Lord thy God? mine eyes shall behold her: now she shall be trodden down as the mire of the streets'—Paisley sees God's judgement on Margaret Thatcher:

The Protestantism of Ulster is an embarrassment to her. The old way of thinking that the Bible is true, that men need to be changed by the power of that Holy Word, that there is a separation demanded between God's people and those that live for the devil and sin, she does not like. So she takes Ulster and puts Ulster in a marriage bond with the Republic in order to destroy the identity of the Ulster Protestant people. . . . I have news for the Prime Minister. God is in Heaven. You may have no respect, Mrs Thatcher, for praying people. You might laugh at their religion, laugh at their Bible, and laugh at the Day of God but 'He that sitteth in the heavens shall laugh at you, the Lord shall have you in derision'. . . .

God has a people in this province. There are more born-again people in Ulster to the square mile than anywhere else in the world. This little province has had the peculiar preservation of divine Providence. You only have to read the history of Ulster to see that time after time when it seemed humanly impossible to extricate Ulster from seeming disaster, that God intervened. Why? God has a purpose for this province, and this plant of Protestantism sown here in the north-eastern part of this island. The enemy has tried to root it out, but it still grows today, and I believe, like a grain of mustard seed, its future is going to be mightier yet. God Who made her mighty will make her mightier yet in His Divine will.

MAP
and
APPENDIX

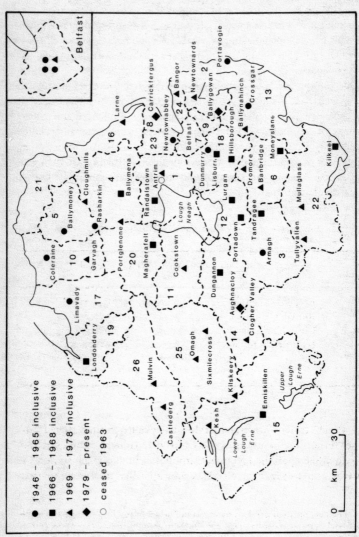

Free Presbyterian Congregations: Date of Foundation

District Council Areas

Numbers on the map refer to the following district council areas:

1 Antrim
2 Ards
3 Armagh
4 Ballymena
5 Ballymoney
6 Banbridge
7 Belfast
8 Carrickfergus
9 Castlereagh
10 Coleraine
11 Cookstown
12 Craigavon
13 Down
14 Dungannon
15 Fermanagh
16 Larne
17 Limavady
18 Lisburn
19 Londonderry
20 Magherafelt
21 Moyle
22 Newry and Mourne
23 Newtownabbey
24 North Down
25 Omagh
26 Strabane

APPENDIX

A STATISTICAL ANALYSIS OF CHURCH AND PARTY

Free Presbyterian Congregations

The following is a list of Free Presbyterian congregations in Northern Ireland by date of formation.

		County
1946	Ravenhill, Belfast	Antrim
1951	Crossgar	Down
	Cabra (later Ballymoney)	Antrim
	Rasharkin	Antrim
1952	Mount Merrion, Belfast	Antrim
1953	Whiteabbey (later Newtownabbey)	Antrim
1954	Ballyhalbert (later Portavogie)	Down
1957	Coleraine	Londonderry
	Dunmurry	Antrim
1959	Antrim (ceased 1963)	Antrim
1964	Sandown Road, Belfast	Antrim
	Limavady	Londonderry
1965	Armagh	Armagh
1966	Ballymena (founded 1931)	Antrim
	Moneyslane	Down
	Hillsborough	Down
	Lisbellaw, Enniskillen	Fermanagh
	Tandragee	Armagh
	Lurgan	Armagh
	Londonderry	Londonderry
	Portadown	Armagh
	Dungannon	Tyrone
	Kilkeel	Down
1968	Lisburn	Antrim
	Magherafelt	Londonderry
	Randalstown	Antrim
1969	Omagh	Tyrone
	Larne	Antrim
	Cloughmills	Antrim

		County
1970	Clogher Valley	Tyrone
	Castlederg	Tyrone
	Banbridge	Down
1971	Newtownards	Down
	Mullaglass, Newry	Armagh
	Garvagh	Londonderry
1972	John Knox Memorial, Belfast	Antrim
1973	Cookstown	Tyrone
	Portglenone	Antrim
1974	Kilskeery	Tyrone
	Antrim	Antrim
1975	Dromore	Down
	Sixmilecross	Tyrone
1976	Bangor	Down
	Mulvin	Tyrone
	Kesh	Fermanagh
	Tullyvallen	Armagh
1978	Ballynahinch	Down
1979	Ballygowan	Down
	Carrickfergus	Antrim
1982	Aughnacloy	Tyrone

Establishing the foundation date of a congregation is not simple. There are a number of points in time which could reasonably be taken as the 'start' of the work in any particular area: the missions which created the first real interest, the first afternoon services, the first regular Sunday morning and evening services, the formal acceptance of the new congregation by the Presbytery, or the calling of the first full-time minister. As my interest was to chart the spread of interest in the Free Presbyterian Church I have usually dated each congregation from its first regular services. The basic pattern of the spread of the Church is clear from the county locations. The Church initially recruited from the 'Bible belt' of Antrim and Down, and only later moved into Fermanagh, Tyrone, and Londonderry.

Free Presbyterian Churches Outside Ulster

In the last ten years, the following Free Presbyterian congregations have been founded outside Northern Ireland: in *America* – Greenville, South Carolina; Philadelphia, Pennsylvania; Londonderry, New Hampshire; and Phoenix, Arizona; in *Canada* – Toronto, Ontario; Calgary, Alberta; and Vancouver, British Columbia; in *Australia* – Port Lincoln, South Australia; and Perth, West Australia; in the *Republic of Ireland* – Corragary, County Monaghan; and in *England* – Oulton Broad, East Sussex; and Liverpool.

A Statistical Description of Free Presbyterianism

The first task was to establish just how many Free Presbyterians there were in various parts of Ulster. The 1971 and 1981 censuses present an area by area count but the large number of people who refused to complete the census (not all of whom were Roman Catholics), and the fact that the announced total for Free Presbyterians was smaller than observers expected, suggested that the 1981 figures might be inaccurate. I therefore constructed a rough measure of Free Presbyterian strength by asking ministers for an estimate of the size of their average Sunday morning congregation. This figure was then increased by 20% in order to make it comparable to that produced by the census, which counts every member of a household. According to the 1981 census age breakdown figures, 20% of Free Presbyterians were under the age of 10 and most ministers would not have counted young children, even those who would be present in the body of the congregation during services.

Unfortunately, congregations do not immediately translate into district council areas (DCAs). Although some churches are so firmly in the middle of a council area that all of their congregation live in the district, others draw support from a number of districts. In such cases I have normally discussed the perimeters of his constituency with a minister and divided the congregation between appropriate DCAs. For example, some of Moneyslane were placed in Down while most were presumed to reside in the Banbridge area.

Table 4 shows the total number of Free Presbyterians in each of the twenty-six district council areas in 1971, 1981, and by my 1985 estimate.

Although there may be doubts about the numbers estimated for any particular DCA, the total is quite likely to be accurate. If one assumes even growth between 1971 and 1981, calculates a growth rate for each year of the decade, and then extrapolates a 1985 figure, the estimated total is 10,723 and for 1986, 11,017; only 202 away from the number arrived at by a quite different route. As they appear to be generally reliable, the 1981 census figures, rather than my own estimates, have been used in the computations which follow.

Church Size and Growth

In looking for a possible explanation of why Free Presbyterianism has proved more popular in some places than in others, one possible factor, suggested by the discussion of secularization (see chapter 8), is urbanism. Are there more Free Presbyterians in rural areas? In Table 5, the 26 DCAs are ranked in order of the percentage of the population living in a 'rural' area. The position of each area in a ranking of Free Presbyterian growth

TABLE 4: *Free Presbyterians in District Council Areas*

		1971 census	1981 census	1985 estimate
1	Antrim	160	230	216
2	Ards	203	444	468
3	Armagh	471	710	990
4	Ballymena	430	728	829
5	Ballymoney	351	399	536
6	Banbridge	349	471	666
7	Belfast	1360	785	1194
8	Carrickfergus	55	134	48
9	Castlereagh	429	519	690
10	Coleraine	159	321	456
11	Cookstown	119	223	180
12	Craigavon	562	962	942
13	Down	204	250	318
14	Dungannon	265	399	522
15	Fermanagh	263	291	270
16	Larne	110	180	180
17	Limavady	69	87	72
18	Lisburn	641	723	792
19	Londonderry	128	102	114
20	Magherafelt	157	537	548
21	Moyle	10	7	0
22	Newry and Mourne	278	387	432
23	Newtownabbey	153	166	168
24	North Down	120	177	168
25	Omagh	243	268	376
26	Strabane	60	121	144
TOTAL		7349	9621	11319

between 1971 and 1981, and in a ranking of the proportion of non-Catholics which was Free Presbyterian in 1981, is also displayed.

One elementary method of testing for a relationship between two series of rankings is Spearman's 'coefficient of rank–order correlation'. If five people were ranked in terms of their height and then in terms of their weight, and if there was a perfect match between the two sets of rankings – that is, if the tallest was the heaviest, the second tallest, the second heaviest, and so on – then the value of Spearman's 'r' would be 1.00. Alternatively, if the first on one scale was the last on another (say, height and 'lack of weight') then

Spearman's 'r' would be −1.00. The nearer the score is to zero the less of a relationship there is. In this, as in other calculations which would be distorted by it, the case of Moyle has been discarded because the number of Free Presbyterians is so small that it contaminates the calculation. Spearman's 'r' for rurality and the proportion of the non-Catholic population which is Free Presbyterian is 0.66; sign of a fairly strong relationship.

It seems intuitively sensible to see what the picture looks like if one removes those DCAs where Roman Catholics form more than half the population. The fifteen DCAs in which Protestants are a majority are shown in Table 6.

TABLE 5: *District Council Areas by Rurality*

		Position in growth table	% FP rank
1	Fermanagh	21	11
2	Magherafelt	1	1
3	Ballymoney	19	3
4	Moyle	25	26
5	Dungannon	11	7
6	Cookstown	6	10
7	Armagh	10	2
8	Omagh	22	8
9	Strabane	5	18
10	Limavady	16	20
11	Banbridge	5	5
12	Down	17	12
13	Newry and Mourne	14	6
14	Ballymena	8	9
15	Antrim	13	19
16	Coleraine	4	14
17	Ards	3	16
18	Larne	9	17
19	Craigavon	7	4
20	Londonderry	24	22
21	North Down	12	24
22	Lisburn	20	13
23	Carrickfergus	2	21
24	Castlereagh	18	15
25	Newtownabbey	23	25
26	Belfast	26	23

TABLE 6: *Protestant Majority District Council Areas by Rurality*

		Growth Rank	% FP rank
15	Belfast	15	13
14	Newtownabbey	14	15
13	Castlereagh	11	8
12	Carrickfergus	1	12
11	Lisburn	13	6
10	North Down	8	14
9	Craigavon	5	2
8	Larne	7	10
7	Ards	2	9
6	Coleraine	3	7
5	Antrim	9	11
4	Ballymena	6	4
3	Banbridge	10	3
2	Cookstown	4	5
1	Ballymoney	12	1

The removal of areas in which Catholics are in a straight majority has the effect of slightly strengthening the relationship between rurality and the proportion of the non-Catholic population which is Free Presbyterian. Spearman's 'r' is now 0.69.

Had the figures been available, it would have been fascinating to compare growth rates for different congregations to test, for example, whether smaller or larger congregations grew faster. Unfortunately, not only is there the problem of knowing how to treat the many congregations which have subdivided since 1971 but there is the practical problem that reliable congregational membership figures for 1971 are not available. Hence we can only compare the three sets of figures at the aggregate level of DCAs, which is done in Table 7.

The areas which have seen the greatest Free Presbyterian growth in the decade from 1971 are:

Magherafelt	242%
Carrickfergus	144%
Ards	119%
Coleraine	102%
Strabane	102%

The areas with the worst growth rates are:

Belfast	−42%
Moyle	−30%

TABLE 7: *Free Presbyterian Growth in District Council Areas*

		1971 census	1981 census	Gain	% Gain
1	Antrim	160	230	70	44
2	Ards	203	444	241	119
3	Armagh	471	710	239	51
4	Ballymena	430	728	298	69
5	Ballymoney	351	399	48	14
6	Banbridge	349	471	122	35
7	Belfast	1360	785	−575	−42
8	Carrickfergus	55	134	79	144
9	Castlereagh	429	519	90	21
10	Coleraine	159	321	162	102
11	Cookstown	119	223	104	87
12	Craigavon	562	962	400	71
13	Down	204	250	26	23
14	Dungannon	265	399	134	51
15	Fermanagh	263	291	28	11
16	Larne	110	180	70	64
17	Limavady	69	87	18	26
18	Lisburn	641	723	82	13
19	Londonderry	128	102	−26	−20
20	Magherafelt	157	537	380	242
21	Moyle	10	7	−3	−30
22	Newry and Mourne	278	387	432	39
23	Newtownabbey	153	166	109	9
24	North Down	120	177	57	48
25	Omagh	243	268	25	10
26	Strabane	60	121	61	102
TOTAL		7349	9621	11319	

Londonderry	−20%
Newtownabbey	9%
Omagh	10%
Fermanagh	11%
Ballymoney	14%

Nothing about the nature of these DCAs immediately suggests a single factor which might explain the growth rates. What Belfast, Londonderry, and Moyle have in common is a shrinking Protestant population and it is quite likely that the losses in the case of Belfast are directly related to the growths in Carrickfergus and Ards as people have moved out of the city to the suburbs located in these areas. Londonderry, Omagh, and Fermanagh have in common a high proportion of Catholics but there are relatively more Catholics in Strabane, which has the fifth highest growth rate, and Newry and Mourne (of which 71.4% of the population were non-Protestant in 1981) is fourteenth in the growth rate table; just under half way.

It is equally difficult to see what the areas in which Free Presbyterianism has recently been most successful have in common. Carrickfergus and Ards have both benefited from the migration of people from Belfast, but then so has Newtownabbey, which failed to translate this into increased support for Free Presbyterianism. Nor is it possible to explain the difference between Carrick and Newtownabbey in terms of the 'supply' of Free Presbyterianism (in terms of a church) rather than demand. The Free Presbyterian churches in both areas are either of similar age (if one does not count the Whiteabbey church, founded in 1953, as the 'Newtownabbey' church) or the Newtownabbey presence is much older. Although it had previously been supplied by students, the Carrick congregation only called an ordained minister in 1986.

To what extent is rurality a predictor of growth? The short answer is not at all. The Spearman's 'r' for growth ranking and rurality is only 0.325 and the more subtle way of correlating percentage growth and 'degree of rurality' – regression analysis – produces a completely insigificant result.

We should only expect geographical areas to be related to attitudes and behaviour if all or most of the people in particular areas shared experiences which were not equally well shared with people in other areas. That is, no one supposes that simply living in a particular place has any consequences for what one thinks of the world.

Northern Ireland local district council areas are neither so large nor so different from each other as to give us any great hope that the experiences of people in one area will be much different from those of people in another. Although one can rate DCAs by 'urbanism', the degree of 'rurality' in the lives of people within any one DCA may vary considerably while the degree of 'rurality' will hardly vary between DCAs. Lisburn is a predominantly urban area but it contains farm lands and many members of the Free Presbyterian congregation are farmers. None the less, although rurality is not a good predictor of growth between 1971 and 1981, it is a reasonable predictor of overall receptivity to Free Presbyterianism. It thus confirms the impression given by the data on Free Presbyterian occupations which was presented in chapter 8.

While looking for social characteristics which might explain receptivity to Free Presbyterianism, it seems sensible to consider the overall denominational make-up of an area, although the two most obvious hypotheses run counter to each other. On the basis of the early congregations, we might guess that areas with a higher proportion of Presbyterians would be most receptive.

Equally well, one might guess that 'threat' is an important element and that Protestants in areas with a high proportion of Catholics would be particularly attracted to the FPC. In fact, neither of these guesses is supported by the available evidence, which is displayed in Table 8. The correlation coefficient for the relationship between Free Presbyterianism and 'all non-Roman Catholics' (which is obviously the inverse of 'Roman Catholics') is 0.124; about as meaningless as one can get. The relationship between Free Presbyterians and all Presbyterians is hardly stronger: −0.29.

We should not immediately conclude from this that denominational background is unrelated to Free Presbyterian recruitment; that is, that the Free Presbyterian Church recruited from all denominations in proportion to their strength in the population at large. The problem is that the number of people who became Free Presbyterian is so small in comparison with the other denominations or with 'all non-Catholics' that even if all Free Presbyterians were identical in, for example, having been Irish Presbyterians, this would still not appear as a statistically significant relationship. What one has to do is to examine what is known about the people who became Free Presbyterians and compare that with what is known about the population at large. If, for example, 80% of Free Presbyterians had been Irish Presbyterians, when only 46% of the non-Catholic population in, to take the most sensible baseline, 1951 were, then we would have a statistically significant relationship which would strongly suggest that Free Presbyterianism was more attractive to Irish Presbyterians than to, for example, Methodists. Unfortunately, no information is available on the previous denomination of ordinary Free Presbyterians. However, previous denominations of Free Presbyterian ministers are known.

Free Presbyterian Ministers

Where they are known, the previous denominations of Free Presbyterian ministers and their parents are presented in Table 9. Five people who had regularly attended more than one denomination are entered twice. Given the ages of the ministers, it seems sensible to compare these figures with the 1951 data, although the relative strengths of the Protestant denominations have not changed significantly since then.

Table 10 presents the comparisons and shows two major deviations from the normal Protestant population: a considerable under-representation of Church of Ireland members and a considerable over-representation of 'other Protestants'; in particular, Reformed Presbyterians and Baptists. Although the numbers involved are too small to be definite, the explanation for this seems to be that, where the Free Church recruited from rural areas, it was from those areas where Presbyterianism or Baptism (which for many was a temporary refuge from the modernizing trends in the Irish Presbyterian

TABLE 8: *Percentage of Total 1981 Population (a) Free Presbyterian, (b) Non-Roman Catholic, and (c) Presbyterian*

	(a)	(b)	(c)
Antrim	0.51	66	31.4
Ards	0.77	86	40.7
Armagh	1.44	52	17.4
Ballymena	1.33	79	47.8
Ballymoney	1.74	70	43.4
Banbridge	1.58	67	32.2
Belfast	0.24	62	18.5
Carrickfergus	0.47	91	32.9
Castlereagh	0.84	93	33.2
Coleraine	0.68	75	33.4
Cookstown	0.76	49	16.2
Craigavon	1.32	55	12.0
Down	0.47	42	16.9
Dungannon	0.88	48	13.6
Fermanagh	0.56	43	3.3
Larne	0.61	73	39.7
Limavady	0.32	50	21.0
Lisburn	0.85	78	23.6
Londonderry	0.11	28	11.6
Magherafelt	1.50	45	17.9
Moyle	0.05	45	20.9
Newry and Mourne	0.49	25	11.4
Newtownabbey	0.23	88	33.9
North Down	0.27	91	33.3
Omagh	0.58	34	14.7
Strabane	0.33	41	18.6

Church), rather than Episcopalianism, were strong. This also reflects the class composition of the Church of Ireland which, more than the other denominations, recruited from the landed gentry and the agricultural labourer. The Free Church recruited small farmers.

The analysis of rurality presented in chapter 8 can be strengthened with an examination of the occupations of the parents of Free Presbyterian ministers. As Table 11 shows, there is a clear over-representation of farmers. Tentative support for Berger's 'technological consciousness' explanation of secularization can be drawn from the large number of the skilled manual workers who were in non-industrial work and/or who lived

TABLE 9: *Previous Denominations of Free Presbyterian Clergy and Parents*

	FP Clergy		Parents
Irish Presbyterian	24	46%	64%
Church of Ireland	7	13%	14%
Baptist	5	10%	5%
Reformed Presbyterian	5	10%	9%
Methodist	3	6%	5%
Faith Mission	3	6%	–
Independent Evangelical	2	4%	2%
Elim Pentecostal	1	1%	2%
Pres. Church of S. America	1	1%	–
Salvation Army	1	1%	–
TOTAL	52		

TABLE 10: *Previous Denominations of Free Presbyterian Clergy and Non-Catholic Population, 1951*

	FP Clergy	N-CP
Irish Presbyterian	46%	46%
Church of Ireland	13%	39%
Methodist	6%	7%
Other Protestant	33%	7%

somewhere other than the greater Belfast area. Of the ten skilled manual workers, four lived in Belfast and they were a painter, an electrician, a baker, and a wood turner. The other six were a stonemason, an electrician, two machinists, a painter, and a gardener. Equally interesting is the detail hidden in the 'white collar category'. Not one Free Presbyterian clergyman had a father in a management position in non-agricultural industry. Of the seven, there were two full-time Christian workers, a grocer, a salesman, two civil servants, and the manager of a creamery. In brief, the detail of the occupations of the parents of core Free Presbyterians followed similar lines to the very broad picture presented in chapter 8; Free Presbyterians were recruited from occupational groups marginal to technological production.

DUP Election Results

This section details the performance of the Protestant Unionist and

TABLE 11: *Occupations of Free Presbyterian Clergy Parents*

Farmers	15	34%
White Collar	7	16%
Self-employed (non-farming)	3	7%
Skilled Manual	10	23%
Unskilled Manual	8	18%
Security Forces	1	2%
TOTAL	44	

Democratic Unionist Parties. In order to simplify the citation of sources, a complete list of sources is given at the end of this section and identified by letters. The report of each election is followed by letters which identify the main sources. Where no published source is given, the material has been collected from contemporary newspaper accounts.

The first elections in which Ian Paisley supported 'Protestant Unionist' candidates were in 1958 when the Revd John Wylie contested and won a seat as a 'Protestant Unionist' on the Ballymoney Borough council. Albert Duff, a Unionist Belfast city councillor stood as a Protestant Unionist in the Stormont general election for the Iveagh constituency and made little impression. However, he held his Belfast city council seat and was joined by a second Protestant Unionist: Charles McCullough. Protestant Unionists contested Belfast council elections in 1961, 1964, and 1967. Although personnel changed, representation remained constant at two seats (both in the St George's ward which included the staunchly loyalist Sandy Row), with Mrs Paisley replacing Duff in 1967 (source: (*a*)).

Major Elections

1. February 1969 Stormont general election. This election was the first contested by Paisley and was a direct challenge to the policies of O'Neill. Results were as follows (source (*e*)):

		PUP % vote	OUP % vote
Belfast Bloomfield	W. Spence	24	61
Belfast Victoria	R. Bunting	17	63
Bannside	Ian Paisley	24	29
N. Antrim	J. Wylie	26	74
S. Antrim	W. Beattie	33	67
Iveagh	C. Poots	39	61

2. April 1970 Stormont by-elections. These were caused by the resignation of Terence O'Neill and Richard Ferguson. The Protestant Unionist Party won both (source: (e)).

		PUP % vote	OUP % vote
Bannside	Ian Paisley	44	37
S. Antrim	W. Beattie	35	40

3. June 1970 Westminster general election. The Protestant Unionist Party contested two seats (source: (e)).

		PUP % vote	OUP % vote
N. Antrim	Ian Paisley	41	36
N. Belfast	W. Beattie	19	49

4. May 1973 local district council elections. The election was conducted on a 'single transferable vote' system of proportional representation and was the first contested by the Democratic Unionist Party. However, it is almost impossible to evaluate DUP performance because the decision to enter was made very late and almost half the candidates did not provide an accurate description of their allegiance. 'DUP' people were to be found standing as 'Democratic Unionist', 'Loyalist', 'United Loyalist Coalition', and 'Independent'. Similar confusion reigned among members of the Unionist Party who were divided between liberals and conservatives. Anyone wishing to unpick the threads can find details in sources (k) and (l).

5. June 1973 Assembly elections. This and elections (6) to (9) can only be taken as tangential indicators of DUP support because the DUP contested seats as part of an alliance with other conservative unionist groupings. DUP results were as follows:

Elected at stage 1

W. Beattie	S. Antrim
Ian Paisley	N. Antrim

Also Elected

J. McQuade	Belfast North
C. Poots	North Down
T. E. Burns	Belfast South
E. Paisley	Belfast East
D. Hutchinson	Armagh

Nine other candidates failed to be elected. With eight out of seventeen wins, the DUP did as well as the 'anti-power-sharing' Unionists who had twelve of twenty-three candidates elected and better than Craig's Vanguard Unionist Progressive Party which had only seven out of twenty-five elected. It is noticeable that those candidates with loyalist paramilitary connections did not poll as well as might have been expected and an examination of vote transfers suggests that such votes as they did receive were personal votes which transferred to DUP candidates rather than to other related paramilitary candidates (sources: (*j*) and (*m*)).

6. February 1974 Westminster general election. The DUP fought as part of the United Ulster Unionist Coalition with the right wing of the Unionist Party and the Vanguard Unionist Party. Paisley took 63.6 % of the vote in North Antrim. Johnny McQuade came a close second to Gerry Fitt of the SDLP in West Belfast with 36.3% of the vote to Fitt's 40.8% (source: (*c*)).

7. October 1974 Westminster general election. This was a re-run of the February election with choices being made simpler by Brian Faulkner's liberal unionists standing, not as Unionists, but as members of the newly formed Unionist Party of Northern Ireland. The DUP ran the same two candidates as in February. Paisley increased his poll to 71.2%. McQuade again came second to Fitt with 36.1% to Fitt's 48.4% (source: (*d*)).

8. May 1975 Constitutional Convention election. The convention was intended to be a forum which would produce an acceptable structure for the government of Northern Ireland to fill the vacuum left by the collapse in 1974 of the power-sharing executive. Again the anti-power-sharing unionists fought the election as a coalition.

	Seats	Votes	
		No.	%
OUP (UUUC)	19	169,797	25.8
DUP (UUUC)	12	97,073	14.8
VUP (UUUC)	14	83,507	12.7
Other Loyalists	2	10,140	1.5
SDLP	17	156,049	23.7
Alliance	8	64,657	9.8
UPNI	5	50,891	7.7
Republican Clubs	0	14,515	2.2
NI Labour	1	9,102	1.4
Independents	0	2,052	0.2
Communist	0	378	0.1

Ian McAllister attempted to correlate party votes at the Convention and Assembly elections with a variety of social variables. Little information about divisions within the loyalist electorate emerges from such analysis, although there is enough of a correlation between Vanguard vote and urbanization and households without cars to suggest that the VUP, rather than Paisley's DUP, was most loyally supported by urban working-class loyalists. As one would expect if one concentrated on denomination rather than class, the best (although weak) predictor of DUP vote in both elections was the proportion of Presbyterians in any constituency (source: (*m*)).

9. May 1977 local district council elections. The collapse of the unionist coalition meant that this was the first election since 1973 in which the DUP tested its popularity against other unionist groupings. It fielded 108 candidates (as compared to the 270 of the OUP). The results of the major parties were as follows (source: (*g*)).

	Seats	% Votes
OUP	178	29.6
SDLP	113	20.6
Alliance	70	14.4
DUP	74	12.7

10. May 1979 Westminster general election. The DUP fielded four candidates and won three seats; two by very narrow margins:

		% DUP	% OUP
N. Antrim	Ian Paisley	52.7	23.9
E. Belfast	P. Robinson	31.2	31.0
N. Belfast	J. McQuade	27.2	24.9
Armagh	D. Calvert	8.5	47.9

11. June 1979 European Parliament election. For the first direct election to the European Community the whole of Northern Ireland was treated as a single constituency with three seats. As in local government, Assembly, and Convention elections, the system used was an STV PR vote. The first preference vote results were as follows (source: (*f*)):

	No.	% Votes
Ian Paisley (DUP)	170,688	29.8
J. Hume (SDLP)	140,622	24.6
J. Taylor (OUP)	68,185	11.9
H. West (OUP)	56,984	9.9
O. Napier (Alliance)	39,026	6.8
J. Kilfedder (Ulster Unionist)	38,198	6.7
B. Devlin-McAliskey (Ind.)	33,969	5.9
Six others	24,567	4.2

12. May 1982 local district council elections. In this election the DUP polled more votes than the OUP but gained fewer seats.

	Seats	No.	% Votes
DUP	142	176,816	26.6
OUP	151	176,342	26.5
SDLP	104	116,487	17.5
Alliance	38	59,219	8.9

The DUP had increased its total of council seats by sixty-eight from seventy-four and, more importantly, became the outright majority in Ballymena and the single largest party in seven other councils: Belfast, Ards, Carrickfergus, Castlereagh, Lisburn, Ballymoney, and Larne (source: (*h*)).

13. March 1982 Westminster by-election. The murder of OUP MP for South Belfast Revd Robert Bradford created a by-election in which one conservative Irish Presbyterian minister, Martin Smyth, soundly defeated a conservative Free Presbyterian minister, William McCrea. It seems likely that the middle-class voters of South Belfast were unimpressed by Paisley's 'Third Force' which had been launched on Ulster hillsides in December of the previous year. The result was as follows:

	No.	% Votes
Martin Smyth (OUP)	17,123	39.8
David Cook (Alliance)	11,726	27.2

	No.	% Votes
William McCrea (DUP)	9,818	22.3
Alistair McDonnell (SDLP)	3,839	8.9
John McMichael (UDLP)	576	1.4

14. October 1982 Assembly election. In 1982 James Prior created a second 'assembly'; this one designed to begin with limited powers to scrutinize legislation, and to increase in its authority as it demonstrated that it had popular cross-community support. The SDLP and Sinn Fein fought the election with the promise to abstain if elected. The results were as follows:

	Seats		Votes	
	No.	%	No.	%
OUP	26	33.3	188,277	29.7
DUP	21	26.9	145,528	23.0
SDLP	14	18.0	118,891	18.8
Alliance	10	12.8	58,851	9.3
Sinn Fein	5	6.4	64,191	10.1
Others	2	2.6	57,382	9.1

In terms of competition between the unionist parties, the DUP share of the vote had dropped slightly from the 1981 local council elections: from 26.6% to 23.0%, while the OUP vote had risen from 26.5% in 1981 to 29.7%. On the anti-unionist side, the most important change was the appearance of Sinn Fein in its new 'ballot box and the armalite' mode (source: (*i*)).

15. June 1983 Westminster general election. The DUP fielded its largest ever number of candidates for Westminster: fourteen for the increased number of seventeen seats. The party did not contest Fermanagh and South Tyrone and Newry/Armagh, in both cases allowing the OUP to win seats with the nationalist majority divided between the SDLP and Sinn Fein.

	Seats	No.	% Votes
OUP	11	259,952	34.0
DUP	3	152,749	20.0

	Seats	No.	% Votes
SDLP	I	137,012	13.4
Sinn Fein	I	102,701	13.4
J. Kilfedder	I	22,861	3.0

For comparison it is worth noting that 55,879 OUP votes came from the three constituencies which the DUP did not contest. Removing those brings the OUP percentage down to 26%. Paisley and Robinson held their North Antrim and East Belfast seats. North Belfast, where McQuade had retired, was lost to the OUP but William McCrea won Mid-Ulster. Paisley's personal share of the North Antrim vote was increased slightly to 54.0%. Sinn Fein increased its proportion of the vote on its 1982 performance, while the SDLP vote fell from 18.8% to 13.4%.

16. June 1984 European Parliament election. In this second election to the European Community, the OUP followed the DUP in fielding only one candidate. The three sitting members were all re-elected. Paisley increased his vote and Sinn Fein followed their previous Westminster success by polling well. The fact that Hume's vote also increased suggests that Sinn Fein were supported by people who had previously abstained, rather than by nationalists abandoning the SDLP.

	No.	% Votes
Ian Paisley (DUP)	230,251	33.6
J. Hume (SDLP)	151,399	22.1
J. Taylor (OUP)	147,169	21.5
D. Morrison (Sinn Fein)	91,476	13.3
D. Cook (Alliance)	34,046	5.0
J. Kildfedder	20,092	2.9

17. January 1986 Westminster by-elections. As a protest against the Anglo-Irish accord, the fifteen unionist members resigned their seats. As in the mid-1970s, the unionists nominated the sitting members as joint 'Ulster Says No' candidates. On a lower poll than 1983, the unionists maintained their proportion of the vote but lost the seat of Newry/Armagh, which they had only won by the slimmest of margins in 1983, to Seamus Mallon of the SDLP. Although the unionists were disappointed not to reach the magical figure of half-a-million votes, the result contained an important message

which most commentators ignored. In the three seats held by DUP candidates, OUP supporters were willing to vote for the DUP.

Sources

(*a*) Ian Budge and Cornelius O'Leary, *Belfast: Approach to Crisis – a study of Belfast politics 1613–1970* (London: Macmillan; New York: St. Martins Press, 1973).

(*b*) David Butler and Michael Pinto-Duschinsky, *The British General Election of 1970* (London: Macmillan, 1970).

(*c*) David Butler and Dennis Kavanagh, *The British General Election of February 1974* (London, Macmillan, 1974).

(*d*) David Butler and Dennis Kavanagh, *The British General Election of October 1974* (London, Macmillan, 1975).

(*e*) Sydney Elliott, *Northern Ireland Parliamentary Election Results 1921–72* (Chichester: Political Reference Publications, 1973).

(*f*) Sydney Elliott, *Northern Ireland: the first election to the European Parliament* (Belfast: The Queen's University of Belfast, 1980).

(*g*) Sydney Elliott and F. J. Smith, *Northern Ireland: the district council elections of 1977* (Belfast: The Queen's University of Belfast, 1977).

(*h*) Sydney Elliott and F. J. Smith, *Northern Ireland: the district council elections of 1981* (Belfast: The Queen's University of Belfast, 1981).

(*i*) Sydney Elliott and Rick Wilford, *Northern Ireland: the Assembly elections of 1982* (Glasgow: Centre for the Study of Public Policy, Strathclyde University, 1984).

(*j*) James Knight, *Northern Ireland: the elections of 1973* (London: The Arthur McDougall Fund, 1974).

(*k*) James Knight and Nicholas Baxter-Moore, *Northern Ireland Local Government elections, 30 May 1973* (London: The Arthur McDougall Fund, 1973).

(*l*) R. J. Lawrence, Sydney Elliott, and M. J. Laver, *Northern Ireland General Elections 1973* (London: Cmnd 5851, 1975).

(*m*) Ian McAllister, *The 1975 Northern Ireland Convention Election* (Glasgow: University of Strathclyde Survey Research Centre: Occasional Paper 14, 1975).

The Social Location of Democratic Unionism

In the absence of good large-scale surveys, we know very little about who actively supports the DUP. However, some preliminary observations are possible on the basis of the 1981 census data, which uses the same boundaries as the 1981 local government elections. There is, however, a major weakness in the census data in that many people, most but by no means all of them Roman Catholics, refused to complete the forms. However, statisticians working for the Fair Employment Agency have produced 'adjusted' figures which attempt to compensate for the shortfall (see *Belfast Telegraph* (1 Jan. 1985)). Where appropriate these figures have been used. We can thus compare DUP voting and denominational composition for these areas.

Free Presbyterianism and the DUP

There are a number of different ways of analysing the relationship between Free Presbyterianism and the Democratic Unionist Party. In the first place, it is obvious, from the size of the DUP vote and the number of Free Presbyterians, that most people who vote for the DUP are not Free Presbyterians. The Spearman's 'r' for the relationship between the proportion of Free Presbyterians in local district council areas in 1981, and the proportion of unionists voting DUP in the 1981 local government elections was 0.02: a score which means that there is no discernible connection. This should not surprise us. The numbers of Free Presbyterians are so much smaller than the numbers who vote DUP that, even if all Free Presbyterians turned out and voted DUP, it would not significantly affect the outcome.

There was a stronger but still weak relationship between DUP vote and the proportion of the population who were Roman Catholic ('r' = −0.4). The best predictor of DUP voting turned out to be the proportion of the population who were Presbyterian (which included Free, Reformed, and Evangelical Presbyterians in addition to Irish Presbyterians). This correlation produced a coeffecient of 0.52. This confirms McAllister's observation that 'Presbyterians' were the best (although weak) predictor of DUP vote in the 1973 Assembly and 1975 Convention elections. His analysis produced correlation coefficients of 0.42 for 1973 and 0.30 for 1975.

Rurality and DUP vote

As a matter of interest I also calculated the Spearman's 'r' for 'rurality' and DUP support. It was 0.04; again a result which means there is no significant relationship between them. Again this confirms what we know from interviews. There are at least two clearly separate DUP voting constituencies: rural evangelicals and urban (predominantly working-class) loyalists. This can be seen simply in a listing of the six areas in which the DUP scored its highest percentage of unionist votes:

Rural rank		DUP % of Union vote
3	Ballymoney	62.71
24	Castlereagh	59.29
2	Magherafelt	55.75
22	Lisburn	55.47
13	Ballymena	54.95
9	Strabane	54.74

Thus the best six DUP results were achieved in two of the most rural, two of the most urban, and two mixed areas. When added to the observation that 'religiosity' is itself related to rurality, this explains why no denominational characteristics are good predictors of DUP vote.

DUP Activists

However widely the Party draws its voting support, its activists have always been drawn predominantly from the Free Presbyterian Church. Table 12 presents data on the denominational background of people who have contested various elections as DUP candidates. The list of elected councillors described in lines 3 and 4 was taken from DUP handbooks and may not be complete, although it certainly contains most DUP councillors. The denominations of some activists could not be determined but it is highly unlikely that the 'not known' category contains Free Presbyterians as most of the information came from Free Presbyterian ministers and people who were active in both Church and Party. As the information was usually gathered by asking one person about the denominations of a number of others, it may be that one or two of the identifications are mistaken. However, most informants seemed confident of their knowledge.

TABLE 12: *DUP Activists' Denominations*

		Total	FP	Other Prot.	None	Not Known	%FP
1973	Assembly	17	8	3	2	4	47
1975	Convention	18	14	1	0	3	78
1976	Councillors	31	20	6	1	4	65
1978	Councillors	72	43	13	0	18	60
1982	Assembly	35	27	8	0	0	77
1985	Council Can's	218	125	67	3	23	57

The most obvious conclusion to be drawn is that the DUP recruited its activists predominantly from Free Presbyterian circles.

It is worth considering whether there are major differences between areas. A number of conclusions can be tentatively drawn from the data presented in Table 13. In the first place, there is a strong tendency for the DUP in the more urban areas to draw from a range of denominations. This is more clearly the case if one adds the 1978 data for Carrick and Castlereagh, which have been omitted because the number of councillors whose denomination is not known exceeds those whose is known. However, it is extremely likely that the 'not knowns' were not Free Presbyterian. If one assumed that, the

TABLE 13: *Percentage of Selected DUP Activists Free Presbyterian*

Area	1978 Councils	1985 Candidates
Antrim	33.3	50.0
Ards	100.0	60.0
Armagh	100.0	80.0
Ballymena	58.3	88.0
Ballymoney	66.6	75.0
Banbridge	100.0	86.0
Belfast	71.4	63.0
Carrickfergus	x	11.0
Castlereagh	x	25.0
Coleraine	100.0	45.5
Cookstown	100.0	100.0
Craigavon	100.0	60.0
Down	y	100.0
Dungannon	y	50.0
Fermanagh	y	66.6
Larne	33.3	33.3
Limavady	100.0	50.0
Lisburn	66.6	75.0
Londonderry	100.0	43.0
Magherafelt	66.6	80.0
Moyle	0	0
Newry and Mourne	100.0	75.0
Newtownabbey	25.0	36.4
North Down	0	50.0
Omagh	y	75.0
Strabane	x	33.3

An 'x' signifies a lack of knowledge of the denomination of more than half the councillors. 'y' signifies no DUP councillors in that area.

percentages would be Carrick – 33.3% Free Presbyterian and Castlereagh – 25% Free Presbyterian.

A second point is that the proportion of Free Presbyterians has a tendency to decrease (although it does not fall markedly) in many places as the number of people involved increases. For example, five of the seven Belfast councillors in 1978, but only twelve of nineteen candidates in 1985, were Free Presbyterians. Similarly, all three Ards councillors in 1978 but only six of ten candidates in 1985 were Free Presbyterians. This pattern confirms the impression gained from talking to DUP activists: although the Party was initially heavily Free Presbyterian, in recent years it has expanded its recruiting base as it has expanded.

If they are not Free Presbyterian, what are DUP activists? Table 14 gives an area by area denominational breakdown for the main denominations of the 1985 council candidates. Apart from the high proportion of Free Presbyterians, the other obvious point is the high proportion of 'other evangelicals'. This category contains Salvation Army, Elim Pentecostal, Independent and Free Methodist, and Brethren. In reality, it should be higher because a number of those who are members of 'other Protestant' denominations, a category which includes Methodists, Congregationalists, and Baptists, made it clear from the activities which they listed on their election literature that they are on the evangelical wing of these denominations.

If one considers the more select, and presumably influential, group of constituency party chairmen, the proportion who are Free Presbyterian increases even further. In 1975 when there were twelve imperial constituencies, all twelve chairmen were Free Presbyterians. In 1978, one constituency, West Belfast, did not have a chairman. Of the eleven chairmen, one was a Baptist and the other ten were regular attenders at Free Presbyterian churches.

The senior party officers were, with the short-lived exception of Desmond Boal, all Free Presbyterians until the early 1980s when Peter Robinson began attending a gospel hall and Sammy Wilson, an Elim Pentecostalist, replaced Jim Allister as press officer. However, it is clear from the fact that many full-time employees of the Party are not Free Presbyterians, that the Free Presbyterian character of the Party's activists is not directly as a result of deliberate bias by the leadership.

If it is not leadership bias, then what explains the predominance of Free Presbyterians and other evangelicals? An obvious link is friendship. It is well observed in studies of the diffusion of innovations, be they practical innovations such as new techniques or ideological innovations, that people pass on new information to their friends. Recruitment to many kinds of social, religious, and political movements operates through friendship networks. It seems highly likely, especially in the early days of the DUP, that the first generation of activists recruited their friends, who would most likely be people who were members of the same denomination, or be people

TABLE 14: *1985 Council Candidates' Denominations*

Area	COI	IPC	FPC	Other Prot.	Other Evan.	Not Known
Antrim	0	2	4	1	1	0
Ards	0	0	6	1	3	0
Armagh	0	0	4	0	0	1
Ballymena	0	0	15	0	2	0
Ballymoney	0	2	6	0	0	0
Banbridge	0	0	6	0	1	0
Belfast	0	0	12	2	2	3
Carrickfergus	1	2	1	3	0	2
Castlereagh	1	2	3	3	2	1
Coleraine	1	3	5	1	1	0
Cookstown	0	0	5	0	0	0
Craigavon	0	2	6	1	0	1
Down	0	0	5	0	0	0
Dungannon	0	0	3	1	0	2
Fermanagh	0	0	4	0	2	0
Larne	0	0	3	0	0	6
Limavady	0	2	2	0	0	0
Lisburn	3	0	8	1	0	0
Londonderry	0	1	3	0	0	3
Magherafelt	0	1	4	0	0	0
Moyle	1	2	0	1	0	0
Newry and Mourne	0	0	3	0	0	1
Newtownabbey	0	0	4	3	0	4
North Down	0	1	5	0	3	1
Omagh	1	1	6	0	0	0
Strabane	0	2	2	1	0	1
TOTAL	8	23	125	19	17	26

who shared most of their religious beliefs even though they were members of a different denomination. In urban areas, where such networks are weaker, and as the Party grows, one would expect the importance of primary contacts – friendship networks – to decline.

The other possibility, which is discussed in the text, is that ordinary party members maintain a high regard for evangelicalism, and hence for evangelicals, even when they themselves do not personally hold similar religious beliefs. That is, even non-evangelicals recognize that evangelicalism symbolizes the heart of their unionism, and that political goals are best pursued by evangelicals.

Index

OXFORD

MORE OXFORD PAPERBACKS

Details of a selection of other books follow. A complete list of Oxford Paperbacks, including The World's Classics, Twentieth-Century Classics, OPUS, Past Masters, Oxford Authors, Oxford Shakespeare, and Oxford Paperback Reference, is available in the UK from the General Publicity Department, Oxford University Press (JN), Walton Street, Oxford OX2 6DP.

In the USA, complete lists are available from the Paperbacks Marketing Manager, Oxford University Press, 200 Madison Avenue, New York, NY 10016.

Oxford Paperbacks are available from all good bookshops. In case of difficulty, customers in the UK can order direct from Oxford University Press Bookshop, 116 High Street, Oxford, Freepost, OX1 4BR, enclosing full payment. Please add 10 per cent of published price for postage and packing.

WAR IN EUROPEAN HISTORY

Michael Howard

This book offers a fascinating study of warfare as it has developed in Western Europe from the warring knights of the Dark Ages to the nuclear weapons of the present day, illustrating how war has changed society and how society in turn has shaped the pattern of warfare.

'Wars have often determined the character of society. Society in exchange has determined the character of wars. This is the theme of Michael Howard's stimulating book. It is written with all his usual skill and in its small compass is perhaps the most original book he has written. Though he surveys a thousand years of history, he does so without sinking in a slough of facts and draws a broad outline of developments which will delight the general reader.' A. J. P. Taylor in the *Observer*

'It is, at one and the same time, the plain man's guide to the subject, an essential introduction for serious students, and in its later stages a thought-provoking contribution.' Michael Mallet in the *Sunday Times*

An OPUS book

THATCHERISM AND BRITISH POLITICS
The End of Consensus?

Dennis Kavanagh

Mrs Thatcher has cited the breaking of the post-war political consensus, established with the support of dominant groups in the Conservative and Labour parties, as one of her objectives. In this penetrating study of her style and performance, she emerges both as the midwife of the collapse of consensus and also as its product.

CULTURE AND ANARCHY IN IRELAND
1890–1939

F. S. L. Lyons

*Winner of the Wolfson Literary Prize for History, 1980,
and the Ewart-Biggs Memorial Prize, 1980*

'This book is a balanced attempt to come to honest grips . . .
with the problem of the Irish body politic and with the seeds
of those problems in the more recent past. The author has
isolated various commonly conflicting, overlapping strands in
the Irish mind with a clarity not normally encountered in such
discussions, and . . . his presentation will undoubtedly contribute much to our understanding of our own past and of its
ramifications into the present.' *Irish Independent*

'Dr. Lyons' discussion of Ulster, with regard to both its internal
structures and to its relationship to the rest of the country,
shows the same scholarly broadmindedness and the same lucid-
ity of exposition that mark the book as a whole . . . one can
hardly read it without feeling its relevance to the present day.'
Irish Press

THE STRUGGLE FOR MASTERY IN EUROPE
1848–1918

A. J. P. Taylor

This book describes the relations of the great European powers
when Europe was still the centre of the world. Though primarily diplomatic history, it seeks to bring out the political ideas
and economic forces which shaped day-to-day diplomacy. The
author has gone through the many volumes of diplomatic documents which have been published in the five great European
languages, and the story is based on these original records.
With its vivid language and forceful characterization, the book
is a work of literature as well as a contribution to scientific
history.

'one of the glories of twentieth-century history writing'
Observer

SOCIALISMS

Anthony Wright

'an attractive starting point for anyone who has to teach about socialist politics.' John Dunn in *Times Higher Educational Supplement*

One third of the world's population now lives under a regime which describes itself as socialist. But what precisely is socialism? Marxists claim that they are the only true socialists, but this is hotly denied by Trotskyists, Anarchists, Fabians, Collectivists, Syndicalists, Social Democrats and members of the many other 'socialist' movements.

In this lucid and unitimidating introduction to the subject Anthony Wright argues that the contradictions, rivalries, and antagonisms within socialism arise from the absence of a single socialist tradition. The very word 'socialism' has (as R. H. Tawney put it) 'radiant ambiguities'.

Socialisms develops this theme throughout a wide-ranging analysis of socialist theories and practices, and concludes, provocatively, with a look at the future prospects of contemporary socialisms.

An OPUS book

CAPITALIST DEMOCRACY IN BRITAIN

Ralph Miliband

How has Britain succeeded in avoiding violent political conflict on a wide scale since the suffrage was extended in 1867? Ralph Miliband suggests that the answer lies in a political system that has proved capable of controlling pressure from below by absorbing it. He illustrates his theories with reference to recent political events.

'Miliband's special contribution has made him our foremost Marxist political theorist.' *New Statesman*

HONG KONG IN SEARCH OF A FUTURE

Joseph Y. S. Cheng

During the past few years, the future of Hong Kong has been the subject of heated debate within the Hong Kong community as well as internationally. Widespread discussion and intense speculation have resulted in the voicing of a broad spectrum of opinion.

Hong Kong in Search of a Future records this debate. It contains not only official documents and semi-official statements by the Chinese, British and Hong Kong Governments on Hong Kong's future, but also sets out important opinion polls and a representative sample of the views of major groups and the media. A major focus of the book is the visit to China of Margaret Thatcher in September 1982, and the differences revealed during that visit between the Chinese and British Governments on the question of sovereignty and the 'unequal treatise'. With China refusing to compromise, the British Government may well have begun to prepare for the worst, while the citizens of Hong Kong have grown increasingly uneasy as change appears inevitable.

PSYCHOTHERAPY IN THE THIRD REICH

The Göring Institute

Geoffrey Cocks

At the zenith of Nazi persecution, the profession of psychotherapy achieved an institutional status and capacity for practice unrivalled in Germany before or since. This controversial study of the growth of interest in psychotherapy under the Nazis is essential reading for anyone interested in Nazi Germany or psychotherapy.

'A remarkably interesting book, distinguished by solid research and sound judgement.' *The New York Times*

HEART OF EUROPE
A Short History of Poland
Norman Davies

In this book Norman Davies provides a key to understanding the social and political inheritance of modern Poland. By delving through the historical strata of Poland's past he demonstrates that the present conflict is but the latest round in a series of Russo-Polish struggles stretching back for nearly three centuries.

'Another masterpiece; *Heart of Europe* has sweep, a rare analytical depth and a courageous display of the author's personal convictions. The book begins and ends with Solidarity; the unique labour movement thus serves as a frame for the nation's history.' *New York Times Book Review*

'should never be out of reach of anyone . . . who wishes to keep track of the infinitely complex interplay of forces in Poland today and tomorrow' *Catholic Herald*

'A deep, heartfelt analysis which sets Poland's poignant, but currently stalemate, situation in its historical context.' Linda O'Callaghan, *Sunday Telegraph*

PEOPLE AND PLACES
Richard Cobb

This collection of twenty-two articles and reviews from Professor Cobb's multifarious output over the last ten years includes recollections of old university friends—Jack Gallagher, Arthur Marder, and Christopher Hill—as well as less personal essays on authors and historians such as Pierre Loti and Georges Simenon.

'Richard Cobb has always been a historian of the worm's-eye-view and the grass roots. This collection shows off his virtues admirably . . . A love of his friends and of ordinary people shines through the fun.' Philip Howard, *The Times*

THE RUSSIAN REVOLUTION 1917–1932

Sheila Fitzpatrick

This book is concerned with the Russian Revolution in its widest sense—not only with the events of 1917 and what preceded them, but with the nature of the social transformation brought about by the Bolsheviks after they took power.

Professor Fitzpatrick's account, widely praised on first publication for its clarity and for its historical objectivity, confronts the key questions: what did the dictatorship of the proletariat really mean in practice? And was Lenin's revolution, in the hands of Stalin, accomplished—or betrayed?

'a crisply written, lucid, descriptive analysis from an independent point of view' *British Book News*

'a lucid and indeed instantly classic explanation of the revolutionary spirit in its pre-1917 and Lenin-then-Stalin dominated stages' *Tribune*

An OPUS book

THE WORKSHOP OF THE WORLD

British Economic History 1820–1880

J. D. Chambers

A vivid and authoritative account of Britain's economic life between 1820 and 1880, beginning when the country was in the transitional phase from a primarily agricultural and commercial economy to a modern industrial State. At the end of the period Britain was the world's banker, trader, and collier, and a competitor with other nations whom she herself had materially assisted.

'refreshing and relevant reading. As an introduction it could hardly be bettered' *The Times*

An OPUS book

ROMAN CATHOLICISM IN ENGLAND

from the Elizabethan Settlement to the Second Vatican
Council

Edward Norman

'A brilliantly objective account . . . he has written about English
Catholicism in a manner for which English Catholics can be
grateful and of which he can be proud.' Lord Longford in
Contemporary Review

'Eruditely benign, fair, well-mannered and handling his theological, social and political researches with consummate ease.
Few scholars could take us from half-way through the Reformation to 1962 in fewer than 129 pages of text without
unbalancing history, but that is what the author has done.'
Sunday Telegraph

'full of insights . . . a model of clear and concise historical
writing' *Universe*

'a taut and sensitive history' *Church Times*

An OPUS book

PHILOSOPHERS AND PAMPHLETEERS

Political Theorists of the Enlightenment

Maurice Cranston

The philosophers of the French Enlightenment wrote for a
large public with the aim of promoting political reforms. In
this lively and readable book, Maurice Cranston demonstrates
the richness and variety of their ideas.

Professor Cranston studies Montesquieu's parliamen-
tarianism and Voltaire's royalism as rival ideologies reflecting
competing interests in the *ancien régime*; he analyses Rous-
seau's debts to the republican experience of the city-state of
Geneva, traces the movement from utilitarianism to liberalism
in the thought of Diderot and d'Holbach, and examines Con-
dorcet's endeavour in the first years of the French Revolution
to reconcile democracy with the rule of the wise.

REVOLUTION AND REVOLUTIONARIES

A. J. P. Taylor

Violent political upheavals have occurred as long as there have been political communities. But, in Europe, only since the French Revolution have they sought not merely to change the rulers but to transform the entire social and political system. One of A. J. P. Taylor's themes in this generously illustrated book, is that revolutions and revolutionaries do not always coincide: those who start them often do so unintentionally, while revolutionaries tend to be most active in periods of counter-revolution. He traces the line of development of the revolutionary tradition from 1789 through Chartism, the social and national upheavals of 1848, the 'revolutionaries without a revolution' of the following sixty years—Marx, Engels, Bakunin, and others—to the Bolshevik seizure of power in 1917.

'Based on his 1978 television lectures, a dry, witty, often heterodox glance at some of Europe's political mutterings and upheavals from the French Revolution to Lenin. Amply illustrated.' *Observer*

THE WAY PEOPLE WORK

Job Satisfaction and the Challenge of Change

Christine Howarth

What makes a job satisfying? How can we improve the quality of working life? Does greater job satisfaction mean greater efficiency?

These are some of the many questions which both managers and employees must ask themselves (and each other) if the organizations for which they work are to have any chance of success in today's harsh economic climate. Christine Howarth, who has many years' experience as an independent management consultant, has written this book as a *practical* guide to human relationships in employment.

An OPUS book

WAR AND THE LIBERAL CONSCIENCE

The George Trevelyan Lectures in the University of Cambridge, 1977

Michael Howard

Isn't war rooted in the vested interests of the ruling classes? (But have not democracies proved as bellicose as other states?) Should not political disputes be settled by civilized negotiations? (But what if the adversary is not, by your standards, 'civilized'?) Ought states to steer clear of other states' internal conflict? (Or should they help liberate oppressed peoples?) Which is better, appeasement or a war to end war? Such questions reflect the confusion that still besets liberal-minded men in the face of war despite centuries of trying to discover its causes and secure its abolition.

Michael Howard traces the pattern in attitudes from Erasmus to the Americans after Vietnam, and concludes that peacemaking 'is a task which has to be tackled afresh every day of our lives.'

'so well written that it could be read as a novel—except few novels are so interesting. To take one strand of history and unravel it in this way is not only a service to historians but to the ordinary bus-riding liberal anxious to clarify his own thought'. Jo Grimond in *Books and Bookmen*

THE GREAT WAR AT SEA 1914–1918

Richard Hough

This exciting history of the greatest war ever fought at sea radically reinterprets events, and throws new light on such characters as the Admirals Fisher, Jellicoe, and Beatty, and on the then First Lord of the Admiralty, Winston Churchill.

'an admirable book which everyone interested in the history of the war should read' *Glasgow Herald*

MAFIA BUSINESS

Pino Arlacchi

On 25 April 1982, Pio La Torra, a member of the Italian Parliament responsible for the proposed anti-Mafia laws, was gunned down in Palermo. General Carlo Dalla Chiesa was immediately sent to replace him, but four months later he and his wife were murdered. A week later, anti-Mafia legislation was approved, and in February 1986 the largest ever Mafia trial began in Naples.

These murders and their aftermath result from the emergence of a new Mafia; international entrepreneurs combining large-scale business and banking activity with drug-dealing, political corruption, and widespread violence. Vastly wealthy, they move in fashionable societies all over the world.

'The classic text on *"La Nouva Mafia"* ... Arlacchi's powerful book is a timely reminder of what could happen should the "honoured society" expand its society even further.' *Listener*

THE SIEGE OF DERRY

Patrick Macrory

On 7 December, 1699, the Protestant citizens of Londonderry were anxiously watching from their walls the approach of a regiment of Catholic Soldiers. Rumours were widespread that the soldiers had come to massacre them, yet to deny entry to the King's troops would be high treason.

But who was the rightful King? James II's Lord Deputy ruled in Dublin, but the Protestant cause of William of Orange was gathering support in England. The city fathers were still dithering and the soldiers only sixty yards away, when thirteen apprentice boys siezed the keys of the town and slammed the gates shut. This act of defiance led to the siege of Derry—the siege which Macauley was to call 'the most memorable in the annals of the British Isles'.

'A splendid tale of courage and endurance, with plenty of civilian chutzpah as well as military derring-do ... A sensible and lucid narrative.' *Observer*

THE MILITARIZATION OF
SOUTH AFRICAN POLITICS

Kenneth W. Grundy

Since the 1970s the South African security establishment has carefully positioned itself at the centre of power. Kenneth W. Grundy's book provides many valuable insights into the historical process that has led to the military becoming a dominant force in South Africa, and shows how even greater militarization of society appears inevitable. In its original form, this study provoked the government into an unprecedented press conference to deny the substance of its claims. As Grundy remarks, the suggestion of undue military influence on decision making has 'touched a raw nerve'. Grundy's well-argued and well-documented book, which includes a new postscript on recent developments, allows readers to draw their own sobering conclusions about the future of South Africa.

'Grundy's analysis of the militarization of African society, and in particular of the impact of militarization on the electoral system, the media and the economic structures of the States, is especially original . . . deserves a wide readership.' *Times Literary Supplement*

THE INDUSTRIAL REVOLUTION
1760–1830

T. S. Ashton

The Industrial Revolution has sometimes been regarded as a catastrophe which desecrated the English landscape and brought social oppression and appalling physical hardship to the workers. In this book, however, it is presented as an important and beneficial mark of progress. In spite of destructive wars and a rapid growth of population, the material living standards of most of the British people improved, and the technical innovations not only brought economic rewards but also provoked greater intellectual ingenuity. Lucidly argued and authoritative, this book places the phenomenon of the Industrial Revolution in a stimulating perspective.

An OPUS book